# Congress, the Supreme Court, and Religious Liberty

# Congress, the Supreme Court, and Religious Liberty

## The Case of *City of Boerne v. Flores*

Jerold Waltman

palgrave
macmillan

CONGRESS, THE SUPREME COURT, AND RELIGIOUS LIBERTY



First published in 2013 by PALGRAVE MACMILLAN® in the United States—a division of St. Martin's Press LLC, 175 Fifth Avenue, New York, NY 10010.

Where this book is distributed in the UK, Europe and the rest of the world, this is by Palgrave Macmillan, a division of Macmillan Publishers Limited, registered in England, company number 785998, of Houndmills, Basingstoke, Hampshire RG21 6XS.

Palgrave Macmillan is the global academic imprint of the above companies and has companies and representatives throughout the world.



ISBN: 978-1-137-30063-8

Library of Congress Cataloging-in-Publication Data

Waltman, Jerold L., 1945-
Congress, the Supreme Court, and religious liberty : the case of City of Boerne v. Flores / By Jerold Waltman.
p. cm.
Includes bibliographical references and index.
ISBN 978-1-137-30063-8 (alk. paper)
1. Boerne (Tex.),—Trials, litigation, etc. 2. Flores, Patricio,—Trials, litigation, etc. 3. Freedom of religion—United States. 4. Religion and law—United States. I. Title.

KF228.B613W35 2013
342.7308'52—dc23
2013000409

A catalogue record of the book is available from the British Library.

Design by Scribe Inc.

First edition: June 2013

10 9 8 7 6 5 4 3 2 1

Transferred to Digital Printing in 2013

# Contents

# Acknowledgments

Every writer has many debts to acknowledge. In research that combines interviews and searches through archives with traditional library work, however, those debts multiply.

Many citizens of Boerne have shown a keen civic-minded desire to preserve the segment of their city's history that is the story of the struggle over the fate of St. Peter's Catholic Church. Without their preservation of primary documents and their willingness to share their recollections of the event with me, my book would be far poorer than it is.

My greatest debt is to Bettie Edmonds and her colleague Ede Day of the Boerne Public Library. Bettie and Ede enthusiastically embraced this endeavor from the beginning and were instrumental in helping me complete it. Bettie helped me identify and contact several key figures in the case. As the library's volunteer archivist, she also devoted many hours to accumulating and sorting documents—including many that were made available to us at the last minute when we were nearing completion of the project. In the process, she photocopied mountains of documents for me. Most of all, she offered encouragement during the process and has done her best to help me accurately tell this Boerne story. (Of course, any errors that have crept in are despite her efforts and are my responsibility alone.)

I am also indebted to the staff of the *Boerne Star* who provided easy access to the archives of both the *Star* and the *Hill Country Recorder*. Furthermore, Linda Zartler and the other staff at the city hall in Boerne were generous with their time and expeditious in pulling requested documents from the archives.

A grant from the Institute of Oral History at Baylor University enabled me to conduct several recorded interviews related to the case. I am grateful to the institute's director, Stephen Sloan, and my technical contact, Becky Shulda, for their assistance.

Fr. Tony Cummins, priest at St. Peter's then and now, graciously met me early in the project and showed me around the church. This provided an invaluable "feel" for both the old and the new church. Douglas Laycock, who served as attorney for the archdiocese and is of course a noted scholar of church-state relations, also met with me in the early stages and offered many insights, legal and otherwise. For taking the time to grant me lengthy interviews, I owe an immeasurable thanks to several people in

Boerne who were directly involved in the case: Phillip Bell, Kit Brenner, Patrice Davison, Patrick Heath, Eva Mitchell, Dub Smothers, and Christopher Turk. I am also grateful to Lowell Denton, who served as an attorney for the city, Msgr. Lawrence Stuebben, who was vicar-general for the archdiocese, Patricia Millett, who participated in the case as an attorney for the Department of Justice, and Julianna Sciaraffa, whose parents were actively involved in the affairs of St. Peter's (and who is now herself an attorney) for discussing their involvement with the case with me.

My numerous trips to Boerne were financed in large part by funds from my endowed professorship, the R. W. Morrison Chair in political science. I am thankful for those who generously endowed this chair and to Baylor University for making it available to me.

I probably tried the patience of many librarians at Baylor, but they never showed it. A special thanks go to Rachel Little, the reference librarian at the law school, and her colleague Linda McGennis.

I am also indebted to the staff of the political science department, Jenice Langston and Melanie Pirelo. They fixed many a computer problem and provided all kinds of other assistance.

Matthew Kopel of Palgrave showed confidence in the work from our first contact, and for that I am grateful. Scarlett Neath of Palgrave has guided me superbly through the technical parts of getting the manuscript and other material in proper shape.

# INTRODUCTION

IN 1987, ANNA MARIE DAVISON, A LONGTIME active member of St. Peter Catholic Church in Boerne, Texas, compiled one of those typical, laudatory but still highly informative, local church histories.[1] She discussed in some detail the nineteenth-century founding of the church in a community that was hardly welcoming, inasmuch as the area had been initially settled by freethinking secular German immigrants. She recounted how the parish nevertheless grew, and then how in 1923 it built a beautiful new limestone church, carefully modeled on Mission Concepcion in San Antonio. Much of the work for this edifice, from hauling the stones to the construction site to putting the finishing touches on the interior, was done by the parishioners themselves. Then she brought the story up to date, pointing with pride to the fact that the parish was still growing. Her final sentence was "Who can say what is in store in the future for our parish, St. Peter's?" Little could she have imagined a landmark Supreme Court case emerging from the church a mere decade later, or even less imagined the important role that she would play in the drama surrounding the case.

The late Robert Drinan, one of America's most prominent students of church-state relations, remarked soon after *City of Boerne v. Flores*[2] was handed down that "many years from now, there may be a plaque in a small church on a hill twenty-eight miles northwest of San Antonio telling tourists that this edifice, St. Peter Catholic Church in Boerne, Texas, was the origin of an epic multiyear struggle about religious freedom in the United States. The plaque, reminiscent of the sign outside the courtroom in St. Louis where Dred Scott was tried, will relate the reasons why the *Employment Division, Department of Human Resources of Oregon v. Smith* decision in 1990 prompted Congress to enact the Religious Freedom Restoration Act (RFRA) in 1993 and how the U.S. Supreme Court invalidated RFRA in 1997."[3]

Since 1963, the Supreme Court had employed the "compelling interest" test in free exercise cases.[4] In essence, if the government, state or federal, wished to enforce a generally applicable law against someone who maintained that the measure violated her religious beliefs, it had to demonstrate that it had a compelling interest in doing so. To the shock and dismay of many observers, the *Smith* case of 1990[5] discarded that test and decreed that henceforth any exemptions from such laws would have to be granted by the legislature itself. That decision spawned a great deal of anxiety among both religious leaders and civil rights organizations. They were concerned that government might become overbearing, especially in its treatment of minority religious groups, as they would be unlikely to be able to carry the day in legislative politics. One of the broadest coalitions in modern American politics soon banded together to explore ways to have the compelling interest test reinstated.

Although those concerned were virtually unanimous in seeking this goal, and many in Congress lined up to support them, there was a major strategic question to be faced: how best to go about it? Following numerous discussions, a consensus emerged that a congressional statute requiring the courts to once again adhere to the compelling interest test was the best route. But this presented a technical constitutional question: on what grant of power could Congress base such a statute? In the end, they opted to turn to section 5 of the Fourteenth Amendment, which empowers Congress to enforce the first four sections of the amendment. This was thought to provide adequate authority because section 1 contains the due process clause, which is what the Supreme Court has relied on to make the Bill of Rights, including the free exercise clause, applicable to the states. Although some experts doubted that the Supreme Court would allow Congress to utilize section 5 for this purpose, the weight of congressional opinion was that this was the best path available. On the practical front, as the Religious Freedom Restoration Act (RFRA), as it was called, began to wind its way through Congress, several political roadblocks came up, chiefly regarding whether a carve out should be made for abortion. In the end, though, the obstacles were overcome, and the measure passed in the House unanimously and by a lopsided 97–3 margin in the Senate.

Because previous Supreme Court precedents had made the reach of Congress's power under section 5 cloudy, everyone fully expected that RFRA's constitutionality would be tested sooner or later. What this meant was that while substantively the projected case would be about free exercise, the court's decision would hinge on the justices' stances regarding separation of powers (whether Congress can offer its own views on how the Constitution is to be interpreted or whether that is an exclusive judicial domain) and federalism (how far Congress can go in limiting the discretion of the states).[6]

In the mid-1990s a broad consensus had developed in both the legal and political establishments that the Supreme Court alone possesses the power to interpret the Constitution. Although that was not a view that had been universally endorsed throughout American history, and had only been explicitly claimed by the Supreme Court in 1958, it now had few challengers. During those same years, the Rehnquist Court was in the midst of what has been called a "federalism revolution." Following a key set of decisions in the late New Deal era, the court had generally allowed politics to determine the balance of power between the states and the federal government.[7] In fact, when it did have to take sides the court usually lined up with the federal government. However, beginning in 1991 the court had issued several decisions that checked federal power. Although none of these holdings had directly involved section 5, the drift, especially in hindsight, was unmistakable. Thus, while the *Boerne* decision had enormous implications for free exercise, the streams of jurisprudence that are most relevant for understanding how the case was decided are those of separation of powers and federalism.

Interestingly, and somewhat ironically given the origins of the town of Boerne (it was even named after a left-wing German radical), St. Peter's had come to symbolize the community. Located on the main highway to San Antonio and across from a city park, it was the most photographed structure in town. However, by the late 1980s the parish's growth was outpacing the ability of the church to seat worshipers. When a new priest arrived in 1991, he set up a building committee to examine the church's options. When they recommended demolishing most of the old church and erecting a larger sanctuary, a bitter dispute erupted within the parish. Understandably, many of the longtime members of the church had an emotional connection to the building; others, of course, took the view that the church was more than a building. The archdiocese found itself being pulled in, as the dissenters turned to Catholic authorities and historic preservation organizations outside the area for help. Very soon, too, the controversy spilled out into the community, since many people in Boerne thought of the church as a quasi-public building. Strident debates occurred in several forums, such as the letters to the editor columns of the two local weekly newspapers.

Eventually, the building committee and the priest prevailed, and an architect was engaged to draw up plans for the new building. In December of 1993, the church submitted an application for a building permit. The problem was that, some years before, the city of Boerne had established a historical district, within the boundaries of which any changes to existing structures had to be approved by the Boerne Historic Landmark Commission. The boundary of the district actually passed through St. Peter's, but the most historically significant parts lay within the district. Following several intense and acrimonious public hearings, the commission denied the application for the permit. The church appealed to the city council, but they upheld the landmark commission. Throughout these deliberations, both sides offered various "compromises," all of which were regularly rejected by the other.

Exasperated, the Archdiocese of San Antonio filed a lawsuit against the city in federal district court, alleging among other things that RFRA meant that the city had to meet the compelling interest test for denying the church the right to expand its facilities. In response, the city's attorneys decided to challenge the constitutionality of RFRA. A federal district judge ruled that RFRA was indeed unconstitutional; however, that holding was overturned by the Court of Appeals for the Fifth Circuit. The Supreme Court then agreed to place the case on its docket for the 1996–97 term.

Justice Anthony Kennedy wrote the opinion for a 6–3 majority. As background, he offered up a history of the Fourteenth Amendment's adoption in some detail. In his rendition, the amendment's drafters did not intend for Congress to reach into the affairs of the states except when they acted directly in violation of the prohibitions of section 1. Congress was limited—except under rare conditions, that is—to remedying previous actions of the states. Thus the sweeping preemptive "Thou shalt not" of RFRA was a strike too far. At the same time, he held that by trying to insert its own reading of the free exercise clause into constitutional law, requiring judicial application of the compelling interest test when the courts had deemed that inappropriate, Congress was overstepping separation of powers.

Lawyers and constitutional scholars found much to write about in the decision. It became one of the standard laments in the many strident critiques of the court's federalism decisions. Further, and perhaps more important, it contributed to a renewed discussion of whether the Supreme Court in fact should be the only authoritative interpreter of the Constitution. It is a discussion that has not yet overturned the popular consensus that the court should play that role, but the very fact that prominent constitutional scholars have raised the issue is itself important.

Politically, the decision had two reverberations. First, many states began enacting their own mini-RFRAs. Although they naturally varied somewhat, the intent was the same: to restore the compelling interest test in free exercise cases involving state laws. Second, discussions began anew in Congress about how the decision might be circumvented. Finally a new statute, called the Religious Liberty Protection Act, designed to reinstitute the substance of RFRA but to base it this time mainly on the taxing and spending power and the commerce clause, was cobbled together. However, the coalition that had backed RFRA frayed, largely over the issue of gay rights, and in the end only a scaled-back version covering land use and prisoners could muster the support needed for passage.

Back in Boerne, negotiators for the church and the city council began meeting, and in a relatively short time hammered out a compromise, one ironically nearly identical to a proposal floated much earlier. Important portions of the old church would be saved, most prominently its towers, which face the street, but a new sanctuary would be attached to it. However, when the compromise was presented to the historic commission, they soundly rejected it. That decision, though, was overruled by the city council, an act that led to decidedly strained relations between the people serving on the two bodies. With approval of the city now secured, construction began on the new church. Today, the hybrid building garners mixed reviews. There is as yet no plaque.

In what follows I have tried to accomplish two objectives. The first is to faithfully tell the history and background of the case. It never hurts to be reminded that most Supreme Court cases originate from real human problems. There are people with names, faces, and deep personal concerns connected with the deliberations about constitutional doctrine. This is one of those cases, in particular, where it is impossible to even consider casting it as a tale of heroes versus villains. Two important public goods come into direct conflict here: free exercise and the need for historic preservation. Personally, I found myself being sympathetic to all sides. Given my affinity for old buildings, had I been a member of St. Peter's I would have stood with those who urged that all possible steps be taken to keep the old church intact. However, as an active member of a church (of another denomination) myself, I am deeply committed to the idea that the continued vibrancy of religion in American life depends on churches, synagogues, mosques, and temples being able to order their affairs as they wish, including erecting buildings that meet the religious needs of the people they serve as they see them. At the same time, I think that there is much to be said for cities and towns being able to conserve their architectural history. Public spaces and the sense of history that surrounds them are important features of American life. Even though property is privately owned, there is a public interest in how towns and cities look. There is much to be said, therefore, for historic preservation, and the plain fact is that in many cities churches are an important part of what needs to be preserved. Here, one has only to stand in front of this church after walking or driving through downtown Boerne to appreciate why it was so important to the community's identity. Thus I am of many and conflicted minds about where the right lay in the dispute over keeping, modifying, or demolishing St. Peter's.

The second goal of the book is to place the case within the context of constitutional law. This requires, first of all, a rather lengthy consideration of the development of free exercise jurisprudence. We will need to examine how free exercise was handled before the compelling interest test was forged, the way the test was implemented in the years following its enunciation, and why its jettisoning in the *Smith* decision was so jolting. Here, too, I find myself wavering. Whether or not the compelling interest test is a good idea seems to me a close call. Certainly religious liberty is a central value that needs protection; and certainly it is minority religions that are most in need of protection. However, government needs to be able to implement beneficial legislation, not only for general health and safety, but to accomplish social welfare objectives as well. Thus it may often be necessary for religious people and institutions to have to conform to a given law, even when they disagree with it for perfectly good religious reasons. Forced to choose, I would personally waffle this way: keep the compelling interest test but be rather flexible regarding what constitutes a compelling interest. This was more or less the approach the court took during the years the test was in force, and it seemed to work reasonably well.

More to the point as to the context of this case are the twin issues of the interpretive power of the Supreme Court and federalism. In this area, I have more decided opinions and develop them in the explanation and critique of the court's stance. I concur with the view that the court has assumed far too great a role in our constitutional life and that other political institutions and the people at large have a legitimate role to play in setting forth the meaning of the Constitution. Further, I am sympathetic to the position Sotirios Barber and James Fleming have called "positive constitutionalism."[8] The Constitution was drafted to empower government to carry out the goals enunciated in the preamble; it needs to have as much authority, therefore, to address the problems of the twenty-first century as it had to address those of the eighteenth. Of course, there is a need for limits to be placed on government to ensure that it does not trample on individual rights. But those individual rights should be interpreted in light of the ability of the people to act through democratic institutions to "secure the blessings of liberty." Yet it is important to stress that what occurred here is not the normal case generated when the legislative branch passes a law that allegedly restricts individual rights, with the court then having to decide where the line is between public needs and individual rights. It is instead an unusual instance of Congress trying to force the court to recognize broader rights than it was willing to do.

When we turn from the question of individual rights to issues of inter-institutional relations, particularly federalism, the need for flexibility is paramount. I endorse Justice Stephen Breyer's position[9] that if the American people want to assign certain responsibilities to one level of government or the other, or if they want to order them to work together in some way to attempt to solve this or that problem, then, unless there is some gross violation of the Constitution's provisions, they should be able to do so without the Supreme Court looking over their shoulders. Consequently, I believe the Supreme Court overstepped its bounds on two fronts—separation of powers and federalism—when it decided *Boerne*, and I will elaborate this critique in more detail in the concluding chapter.

However it is seen legally, viewed from the perspective of the exercise of political power, this is a rather odd case. The essence of the narrative beginning with *Smith* is this:

> **Supreme Court:** Even though we have been doing it for 27 years, we no longer want the power to decide when the government has a compelling interest in uniformity of the law that will outweigh claims of religious free exercise. Congress and state legislatures, you decide if an exception to any given law is warranted.
>
> **Congress:** Listen, Supreme Court, we command you to take back the power to decide free exercise cases using the compelling interest test.
>
> **Supreme Court:** Congress, you do not have the power to give us the power to utilize that level of discretion in deciding free exercise cases. And let's be clear, we have the power, and alone have the power, to say that you do not have the power to do so.

Chapter 1 is devoted, first, to sketching out the history of free exercise jurisprudence, which culminated in the *Smith* case, and then to telling the story of RFRA's passage through Congress. In Chapter 2 I trace the early history of St. Peter's, discuss how it became such a landmark to the people of Boerne, and narrate the dispute within both the church and the town about the plan to build a new church. Chapter 3 opens with the church's application for a building permit and the controversy it unleashed. It closes with the filing of the suit by the archdiocese. Because the major constitutional issues now changed from free exercise to separation of powers and federalism, it is necessary to lay out how these matters stood in the Rehnquist Court. This task is taken up in Chapter 4. The following chapter will dissect the decisions of the federal district court and the court of appeals. Then in Chapter 6 I will present a detailed analysis and critique of the court's opinion. Chapter 7 will cover the political reaction to the decision: the passage by many of the states of their own "miniature"

RFRAs and by Congress of the Religious Land Use and Institutionalized Persons Act of 2000. In Chapter 8 I will return to Boerne to review the search for a compromise that would allow the church to expand but still retain the historical façade. We will also look at what has happened to St. Peter's and Boerne in the ensuing years. Finally, Chapter 9 will examine how the case fits into the development of constitutional jurisprudence in the areas of free exercise, separation of powers, and federalism.

## Chapter 1

# The Road to RFRA

The First Amendment to the Constitution begins, "Congress shall make no law respecting an establishment of religion, or prohibiting the free exercise thereof." Although the first segment, the "establishment clause," was raised by Justice John Paul Stevens in his dissent in *City of Boerne v. Flores*,[1] it was the line of cases decided under the second portion, the "free exercise clause," that landed the case on the Supreme Court's docket.[2] When Congress reacted to the court's 1990 decision of *Employment Division of Oregon v. Smith*[3] by passing the Religious Freedom Restoration Act (RFRA) in 1993, it was attempting to claim a role in a stream of jurisprudence that stretched back to 1879 and the case of *Reynolds v. United States*.[4]

### *Reynolds v. United States*: Belief versus Action

This case arose from the attempt of the Mormon enclave in Utah territory to protect its practice of polygamy.[5] The church had adopted a teaching that polygamy was a religious duty, and no one doubted that this was a sincerely held belief by its members. Most Americans, however, were hostile to the sect, and Mormons had encountered discrimination and even violence in the Midwest before moving to Utah. While several aspects of Mormonism engendered these ill feelings, nothing touched raw nerves like polygamy. In the press, it was labeled, along with slavery, as one of the "twin relics of barbarism."[6] For a country that had recently completed a wrenching civil war to eradicate the latter, the former was naturally considered odious.

Because Utah was a territory, Congress was responsible for its governance. Responding to anti-Mormon agitation, in 1862 Congress passed the Morrill Anti-Polygamy Act. It struck at the church not only by banning polygamy but also by voiding the church's corporate charter and limiting the amount of property any religious body could own in a territory. The antipolygamy provision, though, proved unenforceable. Since Mormons made up almost all the population of Utah territory, grand juries could not be found to indict people for violating the act. A few years later, after it had settled most Reconstruction issues, Congress once again turned its attention to "the Mormon question." In 1874, it passed the Poland Act, which turned the federal judicial system in Utah over to appointed federal authorities. Mormon leaders decided it was time to use the free exercise clause to mount a challenge to the federal government's actions. George Reynolds, a young employee of the church who had recently married his second wife, was selected to put his name on the case.

The case was decided by the Supreme Court in 1879, with Chief Justice Morrison Waite writing the opinion for the court. Waite began by acknowledging that Mr. Reynolds was entirely sincere in attempting to follow the teachings of a legitimate religion. However, that was not the question: "the question is whether religious belief can be accepted as a justification of an overt act made criminal by the law of the land." Waite quickly answered "no" to this proposition. Nevertheless, that did not end the matter, as the law in question might be unconstitutional because it lay outside Congress's authority: "Congress cannot pass a law for the government of the territories which shall prohibit the free exercise of religion. The first amendment to the Constitution expressly forbids such legislation. Religious freedom is guaranteed everywhere throughout the United States, so far as congressional interference is concerned. The question to be determined is, whether the law under consideration comes within this prohibition."

Although we do not know why, Waite felt the best approach for elaborating the free exercise clause was to examine the intentions of the amendment's drafters.[7] For guidance in this endeavor he turned to a friend of his, the eminent historian George Bancroft. Bancroft told Waite that James Madison and Thomas Jefferson were the chief architects of the amendment and helpfully supplied him with a number of pertinent books and documents, which Waite analyzed carefully. (He had a well-deserved reputation for thorough research. He once spent months studying electricity before deciding a case, for example.)

The chief justice's mind fixed on two documents in particular. One was a statute supported by both Madison and Jefferson, which passed the Virginia legislature only two years before the Constitution was drafted. Part of its wording was that "to suffer the civil magistrate to intrude his powers into the field of opinion . . . is a dangerous fallacy which at once destroys all religious liberty . . . [I]t is time enough for the rightful purposes of civil government for its officers to interfere when principles break out into overt acts against peace and good order."[8] The other was the famous 1802 letter that Jefferson wrote to the Danbury Baptist Association, saying "that the legislative powers of the government reach actions only, and not opinions." From these statements, Waite drew the central conclusion for which the case stands: "Congress was deprived of all legislative power over mere opinion, but was left free to reach actions which were in violation of social duties or subversive of good order." In short, there is a sharp distinction between opinion and actions, and while one is free to believe whatever he or she chooses, government has ample power to regulate actions, even if they flow from sincere belief, if those actions violate fundamental societal principles.

In order to decide this particular case, it was only necessary then to determine if polygamy was "in violation of social duties or subversive of good order." Citing historical evidence, he concluded that it was, in that it violated a fundamental precept of Western society. Still, though, could Reynolds claim an exemption from the statute on religious grounds? Waite answered in the negative, for "to permit this would make the professed doctrines of religious belief superior to the law of the land, and in effect, to permit every citizen to become a law unto himself. Government could exist only in name under such circumstances."

## INCORPORATION: *CANTWELL V. CONNECTICUT*

The text of the First Amendment explicitly limits its application to Congress. While the wording of some of the other amendments that make up the Bill of Rights, numbers two through eight, is more ambiguous, the Supreme Court held in 1833, in the case of *Barron v. Baltimore*,[9] that none of these amendments applied to the states. This ruling was reaffirmed in 1845.[10]

The adoption of the Fourteenth Amendment in 1868, though, has changed this. After granting citizenship to everyone "born or naturalized in the United States," section 1 of the amendment reads, "No State shall make or enforce any law which shall abridge the privileges or immunities of citizens of the United States; nor shall any State deprive any person of life, liberty, or property, without due process of law; nor deny to any person within its jurisdiction the equal protection of the laws." As we shall see later, it seems clear that most, if not all, of the framers of the amendment intended the Bill of Rights to henceforward apply to the states. Some believed they were accomplishing this through the "privileges or immunities" clause while others leaned on the "due process" clause; nevertheless, the result was the same.[11]

The Supreme Court, however, turned its back on that interpretation when it issued its first decision on the matter in the famous *Slaughterhouse* cases of 1873.[12] The majority, over the vigorous dissent of Justice Stephen J. Field, held that the provisions of section 1 did not make the Bill of Rights applicable to the states. In the following years in a number of cases mostly involving criminal procedure, the Supreme Court held to that view.[13] In one 1884 case, Justice John Marshall Harlan endorsed Field's view in a dissent, but he could not persuade the majority of his brethren. This position was underscored again in 1922 when the court said in *Prudential Insurance Co. v. Cheek* that "the Constitution of the United States imposes upon the states no obligation to confer upon those within its jurisdiction . . . the right to free speech."[14]

However, a mere three years later, the position of the court began to change. Benjamin Gitlow was arrested in New York for violating its Criminal Anarchy Act when he published a document that contained a veiled call for a Communist revolution. Although it was not essential to the decision in *Gitlow v. New York*, Justice Edward Sanford added an important dictum: "For present purposes we may and do assume that freedom of speech and of the press—which are protected by the First Amendment from abridgment by Congress—are among the fundamental personal rights and 'liberties' protected by the due process clause of the Fourteenth Amendment from impairment by the States. We do not regard the incidental statement in *Prudential Insurance Co. v. Cheek* that the Fourteenth Amendment imposes no restrictions on the states concerning freedom of speech, as determinative of this question."[15] Although Gitlow arguably won an important victory with this statement, his conviction was nonetheless upheld. This was followed in 1931 by another ruling involving freedom of the press, *Near v. Minnesota*.[16] The justices held that a state law restricting what could be published was "an infringement of the liberty of the press guaranteed by the Fourteenth Amendment." The next case, *Hamilton v. Regents of the University of California*,[17] decided in 1934, was the first one involving the possible incorporation of the free exercise clause. The University of California, in common with all land-grant colleges at the time, required that its male students take courses in military training. A group of pacifist religious students objected, and when their request for an exemption was turned down by the university, brought a suit. The Supreme Court quoted the Fourteenth Amendment, then said that the students' "contentions are that the enforcement of the orders prescribing instruction in military science and tactics abridges some privilege or immunity covered by the first clause and deprives of liberty safeguarded by the second." The justices first held that any privilege or immunity guaranteed by the amendment derives its force from the due process clause; consequently, they need only deal with the latter. Specifically, "There needs be no attempt to enumerate or comprehensively to define what is included in the 'liberty' protected by the due process clause. Undoubtedly it does include the right to entertain the beliefs, to adhere to the principles, and to teach the doctrines on which these students base their objections to the order prescribing military training." In neither *Near* nor *Hamilton*, it might be noted, did the court state categorically whether the liberty interest flowed from an independent substantive guarantee of the due process clause itself, or whether it was manifested through incorporation of the First Amendment. Incidentally, Mr. Hamilton and the others lost their case, as the court upheld the university's action as a legitimate exercise of governmental power.

The free exercise clause finally won explicit incorporation in 1940 when the Supreme Court decided *Cantwell v. Connecticut*.[18] Norman Cantwell and his two sons, devout Jehovah's Witnesses, were going door to door in a heavily Roman Catholic neighborhood of New Haven, Connecticut. They were distributing pamphlets, soliciting contributions, and playing a phonograph record to anyone who agreed to listen. The record was basically an abrasive attack on the Catholic Church. The three were arrested and charged with unlawful soliciting and a breach of the peace. They claimed that both their free exercise and free speech rights had been violated by the city. In its opinion, though, the court focused almost exclusively on the free exercise right. Its central holding, not only endorsing the clause's incorporation, but also restating Justice Waite's distinction between belief and action, read,

> We hold that the statute . . . deprives [the Cantwells] of their liberty without due process of law in contravention of the Fourteenth Amendment. The fundamental concept of liberty embodied in that Amendment embraces the liberties guaranteed by the First Amendment. The First Amendment declares that Congress shall make no law respecting an establishment of religion or prohibiting the free exercise thereof. The Fourteenth Amendment has rendered the legislatures of the states as incompetent as Congress to enact such laws. The constitutional inhibition of legislation on the subject of religion has a double aspect. On the one hand, it forestalls compulsion by law of the acceptance of any creed or the practice of any form of worship. Freedom of conscience and freedom to adhere to such religious organization or form of worship as the individual may choose cannot be restricted by law. On the other hand, it safeguards the free exercise of the chosen form of religion. Thus, the Amendment embraces two concepts—freedom to believe and freedom to act. The first is absolute, but, in the

> nature of things, the second cannot be. Conduct remains subject to regulation for the protection of society.

Here, the court held, Connecticut had gone too far in restricting the Cantwells' actions. But the central point for our purposes was that the free exercise clause was now applicable to the states as well as Congress.

### THE COMPELLING INTEREST TEST

In 1963, the Supreme Court took the first step on the path to the Religious Freedom Restoration Act being passed 30 years later, and then to *City of Boerne v. Flores*. For in that year, the justices fashioned a test that was to become the standard for deciding free exercise cases for the next 27 years, the compelling interest test.

In 1961, Justice William Brennan had dissented in the case of *Braunfield v. Brown*,[19] which involved a challenge to a Pennsylvania law that demanded that all businesses close on Sunday in order for the public to enjoy a general day of rest. The majority saw the law as fulfilling a general secular purpose, but Brennan thought that they were not even giving "so much as a deferential nod towards that high place we have accorded religious freedom in the past" and that now "any substantial state interest will justify encroachments on religious practice, at least if those encroachments are cloaked in the guise of some seemingly public purpose." Instead, he argued the proper question was "what . . . is the compelling state interest which impels . . . Pennsylvania to impede the appellant's [i.e., a Jewish business owner who wished to close on Saturday instead of Sunday] freedom of worship?" Here he could find none and hence would have found the law unconstitutional.

When *Sherbert v. Verner*[20] came to the court two years later, Brennan convinced his colleagues that his test was the appropriate one, and he was assigned to write the opinion. When Adell Sherbert was laid off from her job in a South Carolina textile mill, she applied for unemployment benefits. She was offered several other jobs, but they all entailed Saturday work. As a devout Seventh Day Adventist, she was required to attend worship services on Saturday and refused the positions. The state then denied her unemployment payments. Brennan noted that Ms. Sherbert was being forced by the state "to choose between following the precepts of her religion and forfeiting benefits, on the one hand, and abandoning one of the precepts of her religion in order to accept work, on the other hand." This was tantamount to a fine for worshiping on Saturday. As he had argued in the earlier case, he maintained that the question was "whether some compelling state interest enforced in the eligibility provisions of the South Carolina statute justifies the substantial infringement of [Ms. Sherbert's] First Amendment rights?" Thus the "compelling interest test" was now endorsed by the court's majority and stood available for later use. (Incidentally, Brennan found South Carolina's claim that the policy discouraged fraud to be wanting.)

The next case to utilize the concept, if not the name, of the compelling interest test was *Wisconsin v. Yoder*,[21] decided in 1972. Amish parents objected to sending their children to school beyond the eighth grade, a violation of the state's compulsory school attendance law. In establishing the framework for deciding the case, Chief Justice Warren Burger wrote that only a "state interest of sufficient magnitude" would justify impinging on a citizen's free exercise of religion and that those were "only those interests of the highest order" (citing *Sherbert* for support). Further, if a state policy "unduly burdens" free exercise, it is invalid. He did turn to Brennan's phrasing when he took up the conflict involved in this case: is the state's interest, a legitimate interest everyone acknowledges, in these children's education "so compelling that even the established religious practices of the Amish must give way"? Burger's answer was "no." Wisconsin thus now joined South Carolina in failing to convince the Supreme Court that one of its policies was important enough to satisfy the compelling interest test.

In the years that followed, the court reflexively reached for the compelling interest test when free exercise cases ended up on its docket. However, litigants had no success outside the unemployment compensation field when they challenged governmental action.

First, the court limited the reach of the test by holding it inapplicable in two important areas of public policy. The first was special institutions such as the military and prisons. Regarding the former, in *Goldman v. Weinberger*,[22] involving the denial by the Air Force of a Jewish officer's request to wear a yarmulke, the court held that military regulations were not subject to the test. As for the latter, in *O'Lone v. Estate of Shabazz*,[23] prison rules, here a refusal to reschedule work shifts to accommodate Muslim prisoners' needs to attend worship services on Fridays, need only be "reasonable," the court said, even when they infringed on free exercise rights. Second, the court held that when government's internal operations were at issue the constraints of the compelling interest test had to give way to a more flexible approach. For example, in *Bowen v. Roy*,[24] parents were told that they had to apply for a social security number in order to obtain welfare benefits for their child despite their religious objections to doing so. The court said that government need not reorder its procedural requirements in order to meet the compelling interest test. A lower level of review was also applied in *Lyng v. Northwest Indian Cemetery Protective Association*.[25] The Forest Service planned to build a road that ran close to a Native American religious cemetery. Nevertheless, the Supreme Court ruled, following *Bowen*, that since the road was on public land, this was a matter of internal governmental operations.

When it came to applying the *Sherbert* test, an interesting dichotomy developed. Three cases came to the court in the 1980s involving denial of unemployment benefits, and the individuals involved won all three. In other areas of public policy, though, governments fared much better. Regarding the first category, in the 1981 case of *Thomas v. Review Board of Indiana Employment Security Division*,[26] the justices ruled that a pacifist could not have his application for benefits rejected because he refused a job in an armaments factory. Likewise, six years later the court held in *Hobbie v. Unemployment Appeals Commission of Florida*[27] that the compelling interest test was to be applied even if the applicant had a religious conversion during his period of employment. Then, in 1989, the court handed down *Frazee v. Illinois Department of Employment Security*,[28] saying that even if the person's faith had no specific doctrine regarding work on the Sabbath, his individual belief was enough to trigger the compelling interest test.

As for the second group, despite the *Yoder* holding, people claiming exemption from other government actions on religious grounds generally failed. For example, *United States v. Lee*[29] was another case involving the Amish. An Amish business owner claimed that he should not have to pay social security taxes since, because of their religious beliefs, the Amish did not draw benefits from the system. Operating a sound social security system was, however, a compelling enough interest, the court asserted, to warrant making Mr. Lee pay the tax. When Bob Jones University, which had racially discriminatory policies in place, lost its tax-exempt status via an Internal Revenue Service (IRS) ruling, it claimed a violation of its free exercise rights. The Supreme Court held, though, in *Bob Jones University v. United States*,[30] that ending racial discrimination was a compelling governmental interest and sided with the IRS. The IRS cleared the compelling interest hurdle in another case, *Hernandez v. Commissioner of Internal Revenue*.[31] This time it was members of the Church of Scientology who wanted to claim special "deductions" from their income taxes. In short, aside from *Yoder* and the unemployment compensation cases, governments seldom found the compelling interest test much of a hindrance to their activities.

### *EMPLOYMENT DIVISION, DEPARTMENT OF HUMAN RESOURCES OF OREGON V. SMITH*: THE COMPELLING INTEREST TEST OVERTURNED

The case of *Employment Division, Department of Human Resources of Oregon v. Smith*[32] was the first direct step toward *City of Boerne v. Flores*. Justice Antonin Scalia's opinion for the majority announced that henceforward the court would discard the compelling interest test and that any exemptions from generally applicable laws would have to be granted by the legislature. The case presents several ironies, but the chief one is that this issue was not even argued by the parties to the case. Had Justice Scalia confined himself to the matters at hand, the whole controversy over RFRA would have never occurred.

Alfred Smith and Galen Black were members of the Native American Church, the ritualistic practices of which involved ingesting small amounts of peyote, a mildly hallucinogenic drug that was illegal in Oregon.[33] Both men were also employees of a drug rehabilitation center, and upon beginning employment had signed a statement promising to remain drug free. When their supervisor learned of their taking peyote (which they voluntarily acknowledged), even as part of a religious ceremony, he discharged them. They filed for unemployment benefits but were turned down on the grounds that they had been fired for cause.

The case had a rather serpentine route through the Oregon and federal courts, finally coming to rest on the docket of the United States Supreme Court in 1990. Both Oregon's attorney general and the lawyer for Smith and Black believed that this would be a standard compelling interest case. Did Oregon have a compelling interest in uniformly enforcing its drug laws that would trump the men's claim to free exercise? If so, then the state could deny them unemployment benefits; if not, then the men were entitled to the benefits.

The state's attorney argued that Oregon had three possible bases upon which it could claim a compelling interest in enforcing its drug laws, any one of which would suffice: the health and safety of the state's population, the need for a policy of uniform enforcement without exceptions, and the requirement in Oregon's state constitution that the state must remain neutral among religious groups. This third point was deemed important because if the state gave an exemption for Native American Church peyote use, it would be favoring one religious group over others.

When the Oregon Supreme Court had considered the case, two consequential rulings emerged: (1) that the state law prohibiting the use of peyote, even when done for sacramental purposes, was valid, and (2) that the fact that the men's conduct was illegal had no bearing on whether or not they were entitled to unemployment benefits. Seizing on the second of these holdings, Smith and Black's attorney took the position that this case was directly analogous to *Sherbert*. Since the criminality of their actions was irrelevant, what they had done was no different from what Adell Sherbert did. Oregon, therefore, had no more compelling grounds to deny them free exercise than South Carolina had had. However, as a fallback position, he also argued that even if the conduct here had been held to be criminal, Oregon had not proved that it had a compelling interest in denying them the right to use peyote for religious purposes. He pointed out that a number of other states and the federal government exempted peyote from their lists of banned drugs. It was this argument that Oregon's attorney general was trying to address when he offered the three justifications for continuing to enforce the law against everyone.

Justice Scalia wrote the opinion for a majority of five. Justice O'Connor wrote a concurring opinion, which made the vote favoring Oregon 6–3. When published, Scalia's opinion took many by surprise, including the attorneys who had argued the case, for he rested the key portion of the opinion on an issue that had not even been briefed: the validity of the compelling interest test. Dave Frohnmayer, the Oregon Attorney General, said that Scalia's effort "came as a total shock . . . [W]e were really surprised at how sweeping this case was, and surprised that the Court had taken the occasion of a very straightforward case that they could have reversed on state interest grounds to revisit [the *Sherbert*] test altogether."[34]

Scalia argued first that it was important to draw a line between laws aimed directly at a religious practice and general purpose statutes that merely happen to impinge on someone's free exercise. Only the former, he said, had been consistently voided by the court. In contrast, the latter had received a more favorable hearing. "We have never held that an individual's religious beliefs excuse him from compliance with an otherwise valid law prohibiting conduct that the State is free to regulate. On the contrary, the record of more than a century of our free exercise jurisprudence contradicts that proposition." He cited two cases as precedent for this holding. The first was *Minersville School District v. Gobitis*,[35] a World War II–era case upholding the state's demand that Jehovah's Witness children salute the flag. However, that ruling was explicitly overturned a few years later in *West Virginia v. Barnette*;[36] thus, its precedential value should have been inconsequential. The other case was *Reynolds*. As we have seen, though, Waite's opinion held that polygamy could be banned because it was so at variance with society's fundamental moral values. He did not hold that all religiously inspired conduct must give way to the demands of the state. In any event, even if we read *Reynolds* to stand for the proposition that there is a universal and sharp belief-action dichotomy, that notion had been substantially modified by subsequent holdings, as already discussed.

Ignoring these matters, Scalia declared next that the only instances in which the court had sided with a free exercise claimant was in what he called "hybrid cases": that is, when a free exercise claim was combined with a another constitutional right, specifically free speech or the right of parents to determine their children's religious upbringing. Here, no such link existed; instead, this was merely "a free exercise claim unconnected with any communicative activity or parental right." But the whole idea of the need for free exercise to be connected to another constitutional right is of questionable validity. For example, for support of his "hybrid" thesis, Scalia cited several previous rulings, including the substantive holding in *Cantwell v. Connecticut*. There, after the court had held that states were to be held to the First Amendment, the majority took up the question of whether the Cantwells' constitutional rights had been violated. The court noted that the Constitution requires "that the free exercise of religion be not prohibited and that freedom to communicate information and opinion be not abridged." However, no reasonable reading of that sentence implies that free exercise rights are dependent on their being linked with free speech rights. Each right clearly stands on its own. In any event, the Constitution's text plainly puts free exercise on an even footing with all other rights.

Applying his framework, Scalia wrote that Oregon's law was not designed to regulate a religious practice and that the men's claims did not present either of the hybrid situations. Therefore, the belief-action dichotomy dictates a victory for the state.

But it was Scalia's renunciation of the compelling interest test that provoked the ensuing angry reaction in Congress and among the faith and civil rights communities. When he took up this question (again, recall, unbriefed by the parties to the case), he noted first that the test had only proved successful for individuals in the unemployment compensation field. In other areas, the government had won. Thus the test was inapplicable to most government policies. This is a most curious position. How can it be relevant that any particular judicial test results in victories for one side or the other? This is most likely simply a function of the type of cases that come to court. Besides, the fact that the government won on a variety of fronts completely undermines the logic of the most-quoted section of the opinion:

> If the "compelling interest" test is to be applied at all, then, it must be applied across the board, to all actions thought to be religiously commanded. Moreover, if "compelling interest" really means what it says (and

> watering it down here would subvert its rigor in other fields where it is applied [free speech and equal protection]), many laws will not meet the test. Any society adopting such a system would be courting anarchy, but that danger increases in direct proportion to the society's diversity of religious beliefs . . . Precisely because "we are a cosmopolitan nation made up of people of almost every conceivable religious preference," . . . we cannot afford the luxury of deeming *presumptively invalid*, as applied to the religious objector, every regulation of conduct that does not protect an interest of the highest order [emphasis in original].

Whatever the abstract merits of this argument, surely no one would seriously contend that between 1963 and 1990, when the *Sherbert* test was in effect, the United States was "courting anarchy" because it had to give in to religious free exercise claims.

In his wrapping up, Scalia stressed that the court was not holding that religious exemptions from generally applicable laws were not sometimes warranted. It was merely that any exemptions had to be granted by the legislative branch, not the courts. Judges are ill-equipped to assess the centrality of religious practices to professed theological beliefs, analyze how much burden particular policies impose on religious adherents, and weigh the needs of society against free exercise claims. Legislators are in a much better position to perform those balancing exercises. Of course, he granted, "leaving accommodation to the political process will place at a relative disadvantage those religious practices that are not widely engaged in." Nevertheless, "that unavoidable consequence of democratic government must be preferred to a system in which each conscience is a law unto itself or in which judges weigh the social importance of all laws against the centrality of all religious beliefs."

Justice Sandra Day O'Connor wrote a concurring opinion that was all but a dissent. She did not think the compelling interest test should be abandoned and said so in strident terms: "In my view, today's holding dramatically departs from well settled First Amendment jurisprudence, appears unnecessary to resolve the question presented, and is incompatible with our Nation's fundamental commitment to individual religious liberty." She then proceeded to pick Scalia's logic apart. As for banning only those laws specifically targeting a religion, she noted that no legislative body is going to "be so naïve as to enact a law directly prohibiting or burdening a religious practice as such." This is an "extreme and hypothetical situation" that should not guide First Amendment principles. She also attacked the "hybrid case" conclusion, arguing that this is just a sleight of hand to escape *Cantwell* and *Yoder*. "Moreover," she went on, "we have not 'rejected' or 'declined to apply' the compelling interest test in our recent cases." Instead, the test had been repeatedly affirmed. Altogether, Scalia had simply wandered off base:

> The Court today gives no convincing reason to depart from settled First Amendment jurisprudence. There is nothing talismanic about neutral laws of general applicability or general criminal prohibitions, for laws neutral toward religion can coerce a person to violate his religious conscience or intrude upon his religious duties just as effectively as laws aimed at religion. Although the Court suggests that the compelling interest test, as applied to generally applicable laws, would result in a "constitutional anomaly," the First Amendment unequivocally makes freedom of religion, like freedom from race discrimination and freedom of speech, a "constitutional nor[m]," not an "anomaly."

Her displeasure with Scalia's conclusions expressed, the last part of her opinion explained why she felt Oregon had met the compelling interest test. Justices William Brennan, Thurgood Marshall, and Harry Blackmun joined her critique of the majority's logic. They, however, thought that Oregon had not met the compelling interest test and that, therefore, Smith and Black should receive their benefits.

Scalia, it should be noted, replied to O'Connor's fusillade with several biting footnotes. It was a dispute that would not mellow with time and would resurface in *Boerne.*

## THE RELIGIOUS FREEDOM RESTORATION ACT

Almost immediately after *Smith* was handed down, a number of religious and civil rights leaders met with sympathetic members of Congress and their staffs to explore what, if anything, could be done to restore the compelling interest test.[37] By June 8, 1990, an ad hoc working group decided that legislation was the best approach and that such legislation could be based on section 5 of the Fourteenth Amendment. Soon thereafter the Coalition for the Free Exercise of Religion (CFER)—composed of a heterogeneous grouping of religious and civil rights organizations, including the American Civil Liberties Union and People for the American Way from the secular left; the National Council of Churches, representing mainline ecumenical denominations, the National Association of Evangelicals, and the Home School Legal Defense Association from the Christian right; and various Jewish groups such as the American Jewish Committee—sketched together the outline of what was to become the Religious Freedom Restoration Act (RFRA) and had their congressional allies, Representative Stephen Solarz of New York and Senators Edward

Kennedy of Massachusetts and Orrin Hatch of Utah, introduce it in the House and Senate, respectively. A number of representatives and senators quickly stepped forward to become cosponsors. Solarz spoke confidently at the initial hearings on the bill: "It is perhaps not too hyperbolic to suggest that in the history of the Republic, there has rarely been a bill which more closely approximates motherhood and apple pie than the legislation before you."[38] At first glance, it would seem that with a coalition of this magnitude backing the bill and with cosponsors from across the political spectrum in Congress supporting it, coupled with the fact that it was a fairly simple bill, merely restoring the longstanding compelling interest test as the framework for judicial decisions in free exercise cases, Solarz was right and it would glide to passage. In the end, it did pass overwhelmingly, 97–3 in the Senate and unanimously in the House, but it took three years to accomplish this feat. During this time, the Subcommittee on Civil and Constitutional Rights of the House Judiciary Committee held two hearings on the bill,[39] the Senate Judiciary Committee held its own hearings,[40] the Congressional Research Service issued a lengthy legal analysis of the proposed law,[41] and intense politicking occurred behind the scenes. Although our major concern here is with the constitutional question of Congress's power to enact the law, it will be helpful to pause and briefly summarize the issues that stalled the bill. There were two major and two minor matters at fault: abortion and prisoner rights being the former and religious institutions' participation in public social programs and the tax-exempt status of religious property the latter.

The abortion controversy placed a couple of interest group elephants in the room: the Catholic Church and the National Right-to-Life Committee.[42] Their position was heavily shaped by the fact that the Supreme Court was set to decide the case of *Planned Parenthood of Southeastern Pennsylvania v. Casey*[43] in 1992. *Roe v. Wade*,[44] the seminal 1973 abortion case, had based a woman's constitutional right to obtain an abortion during the first trimester of pregnancy on an inferred right of "privacy." *Casey* dealt with several restrictions that Pennsylvania had adopted to impede a woman terminating her pregnancy. Many observers thought that the court might well use this case to overturn *Roe*. Before the case was decided, prolife groups feared that if *Roe* were overturned, RFRA might provide a new avenue for women demanding abortion rights. In the end, the court refused to overrule *Roe* but did allow most of the state's strictures to stand because they posed no "undue burden" to a woman exercising her right to have an abortion. While disappointed that the court retained *Roe*, abortion opponents were cheered by the standard of review the court had used to uphold the state's actions. They were now set to campaign for additional restrictions in other states and wanted nothing that might make challenges to those hoped-for new laws any easier. RFRA, they thought, might provide just such a basis.

Thus there were before and after *Casey* concerns voiced in relation to RFRA and abortion. First, there was the fact that several prochoice groups, including some who were members of the CFER (such as the ACLU), had argued that a woman should be able to assert a free exercise right to an abortion. That is, if her religious beliefs allowed her to have an abortion, the state would be denying her free exercise if they prohibited her from doing so. Jewish teaching was alone in mandating an abortion if the life of the mother was in danger; however, many other religious bodies' beliefs allowed abortions in a wide variety of circumstances. Additionally, it is important to remember that under the *Frazee* case already cited, there need not be any specific teaching from one's religious community that directed the action in question when a free exercise claim was made. Consequently, any woman might conceivably claim that her own religious beliefs led her to choose to have an abortion. For example, in one case from Utah, a plaintiff (supported by the ACLU) made such a claim by saying, "I am a practicing Christian and I have talked to my minister about how to handle this unintended pregnancy. He helped me come to the conclusion that terminating this pregnancy was the choice consistent with my faith. It would be wrong for me to give up my goal of independence for myself and my children."[45] (The trial court dismissed this argument, incidentally.) What prolife advocates feared was that RFRA would strengthen such free exercise claims because it put such an emphasis on free exercise rights. Should the court read the statute broadly (and they contended that the current court was moving in the direction of broad statutory construction), then such arguments might carry the day in some places. Adding to their worries, some groups supporting RFRA had said explicitly that if it were enacted they planned to use it as an argument in making such claims. Thus, even if *Roe* were one day overturned, RFRA could open the door to another constitutional basis for abortion rights.

Second, according to *Casey*, states could adopt a welter of policies regulating abortion so long as they did not put an "undue burden" on the right to an abortion itself. However, if RFRA were adopted, then states would have to meet the compelling interest test for such restrictions, and this would be a higher barrier.

RFRA's supporters, which included many prolife groups, tried to turn back these arguments.[46] First, they pointed out that it was illogical to think that a court that would overturn a privacy right to an abortion would turn around and grant a free exercise right to one, whether RFRA was enacted or not. Second, in any event, protecting unborn fetal life would surely be a compelling interest, and that would override any claim made under RFRA. In short, the Congressional Research Service concluded, "It seems doubtful that most such claims [under RFRA] would have any likelihood of success."[47] Furthermore, as a practical consideration, if language excluding abortion were added to the bill, it would never pass. If so, that would be tragic, as many cases are now going against religious rights, including ones affecting doctors refusing to perform abortions in Catholic hospitals. During the House hearings Solarz told Representative Henry Hyde (the main abortion opponent), "The dangers which concern you are extremely remote, whereas the dangers of the *Smith* decision are palpably real."[48] Voicing similar sentiments at the Senate hearings, an exasperated Oliver Thomas of the Baptist Joint Committee on Public Affairs said, "While we have been haggling over a hypothetical abortion question, more than 50 cases have been decided against religious claimants. That is what we know."[49]

In the end, after *Casey* was handed down, some compromise language was worked out and inserted into the bill. It did not mention abortion directly and did not change the thrust of the measure. This was enough, however, for the Catholic bishops and the National Right-to-Life Committee both to withdraw their opposition, and everyone seemed satisfied. The House Judiciary Committee Report merely noted that "the abortion debate will be resolved in contexts other than this legislation."[50] Then, to underscore the point, it added, "To be absolutely clear, the bill does not expand, contract or alter the ability of a claimant to obtain relief in a manner consistent with free exercise jurisprudence, including Supreme Court jurisprudence, under the compelling interest test prior to *Smith*."

Senators Alan Simpson of Wyoming and Harry Reid of Nevada were the chief doubters regarding the act's application to prisoners, although they were acting on behalf of the attorneys general of 26 states and of prison administrators in every state. Recall that the Supreme Court had declined to apply the compelling interest test to prisons in *O'Lone v. Shabazz*, which held that prison regulations need only be "reasonably related to legitimate penological interests." Without a carve out for prisons, the compelling interest test would now apply to all governmental activities, including prisons (state and federal). Simpson and Reid argued that prisoners would concoct offbeat and absurd religions—and offered several colorful examples—in order to claim special privileges. At a minimum, such claims would absorb the time and resources of prison administrators and the courts. As a result, "the nation's prisons will not only become more expensive to administer, they will become infinitely more dangerous to operate."[51] Supporters of RFRA countered that the courts would easily dismiss inflated inmate claims and that the compelling interest test would not unduly hamper prison administration. Simpson sat on the Judiciary Committee and voted against reporting the bill out favorably. On the Senate floor Reid offered an amendment excepting prisons from RFRA, but it failed 41–58.[52]

The other two issues were merely sideshows. The Catholic Church raised both but was supported by several others. It was very unlikely any successful suit could have been instituted on free exercise grounds on either score, as historically such suits were always filed on establishment clause grounds. To make sure, though, language was inserted into the final draft to prohibit plaintiffs using RFRA to challenge either church participation in public welfare programs or tax exemptions for religious property.

We turn now to the most important constitutional issue, the basis for Congress to enact RFRA. As has been said many times, the United States Constitution is one of delegated powers, meaning that there must be a specific authority within its provisions for each piece of federal legislation. As the initial discussions in the wake of *Smith* unfolded, it was Morton Halperin, an ACLU attorney, who first suggested they turn to section 5 of the Fourteenth Amendment. Several additional meetings among the leaders of the CFER, Solarz's staff, and legal consultants (including those in the Department of Justice) ensued; although some expressed qualms, a consensus emerged that section 5 was the surest foundation for the act.

The Thirteenth, Fourteenth, and Fifteenth Amendments constitutionalized the North's victory in the Civil War. The thirteenth outlawed slavery; the fourteenth protected certain rights against state infringement and demanded that the states deny no one equal protection of the laws; and the fifteenth guaranteed voting rights to the newly freed slaves. Not entirely trusting the Supreme Court to interpret these amendments in the spirit intended (it was a court, after all, that still had Southern members and in 1857 had issued the infamous *Dred Scott* decision), Congress added an enforcement clause to each of the three amendments. The Thirteenth and Fifteenth Amendments have only one substantive section each, making their enforcement clauses section 2. The wording is identical, save for the definite article: "Congress shall have power to enforce this article by appropriate legislation" (thirteenth) and "The Congress shall have power to enforce this article by appropriate legislation" (fifteenth). The Fourteenth Amendment contains four substantive sections, making its enforcement clause section 5. The words are simply moved around: "The Congress shall have power to enforce, by appropriate legislation, the provisions of this article." Inasmuch as it is the Fourteenth Amendment's due process clause, from its first section, that makes the free exercise clause applicable to the states, Congress's power to affect the free exercise clause had to be found here. Little attention was devoted to the basis for making RFRA applicable to federal statutes (although there was a brief mention of the necessary and proper clause [Article I, Section 8]), the assumption being presumably that Congress could tie its own hands any way it chose.

The Report from the Congressional Research Service offered only cursory coverage of the section 5 issue, and neither of the reports from the two judiciary committees provided any careful analysis. Moreover, there was remarkably little sustained discussion regarding section 5 during the committees' three hearings. A few members of the House and Senate committees queried witnesses a couple of times, but not in any depth. Professor Douglas Laycock of the University of Texas law school (who would later represent the archdiocese at the Supreme Court in *City of Boerne v. Flores*) submitted detailed letters to both the House and Senate committees laying out the argument for using section 5 to justify RFRA, and he offered a brief summary during his oral testimony.[53] The only people to challenge his views were Professor Ira Lupu of the George Washington University Law School and Bruce Fein, an attorney in private practice.[54]

Laycock began by stressing that technically RFRA would not overturn *Smith*. Under Article III only the courts have the power to adjudicate particular cases. What Congress was doing in RFRA was creating a *statutory* right. According to Laycock, "the express Congressional power to 'enforce' the amendment is independent of the judicial power to adjudicate cases and controversies arising under it . . . Thus, Congress may sometimes provide statutory protection for constitutional values that the Supreme Court is unwilling or unable to protect on its own authority."[55]

A clear example of a previous use of this power was the Voting Rights Act of 1965. The Supreme Court had held some years before that a state's requiring a literacy test before someone could register to vote did not violate the equal protection clause of section 1 of the Fourteenth Amendment. The 1965 act prohibited states from using literacy tests for this purpose, however, and when its constitutionality was tested the Supreme Court upheld it as a valid exercise of section 5 powers. (These cases will be discussed in more detail in Chapters 5 and 6, as they formed a critical backdrop to both the court of appeals and Supreme Court decisions in *Boerne*.) The same had been true concerning the drawing of local electoral districts that have a racially discriminatory effect (as opposed to those that were purposely designed to perpetuate discrimination). The court had said that these policies "do not violate the Constitution, but that

Congress may forbid such practices pursuant to its section 5 powers [citations omitted]."[56]

Adding strength to the argument was the fact that the Supreme Court has upheld Congress's power to ban private discrimination under the parallel provision of section 2 of the Thirteenth Amendment. Using that grant of power, Congress passed statutes banning racial discrimination in housing and the selection of students at private schools, both of which were upheld by the Supreme Court.

Returning to section 5 of the Fourteenth Amendment, Laycock noted that the court had recently used it to justify Congress's ability to enact a system of racial preferences without a specific finding of past discrimination while denying that same power to states.

On the practical front, he pointed out that all the currently sitting justices had endorsed use of section 5 to grant rights that transcended the court's own holdings. They disagreed, to be sure, on how far Congress could go down this path, but they did not deny that the option existed. Importantly, though, what he did not say in his letter was that all the cases examined involved efforts by Congress to overcome racial discrimination.

Moreover, *Smith* itself, Laycock further observed, seemed to invite congressional action. That is, Justice Scalia had specifically said that any exemptions to generally applicable laws needed to be made by the legislative branch. If Congress wished to make a blanket exemption, then surely it was merely following the logic of Scalia's recommendation. To be consistent, the court would have to uphold congressional action on this score.

Professor Lupu's analysis proved to be more prescient. He, too, believed that *Smith* was an unfortunate decision, "both in its reasoning and in its result."[57] Nevertheless, he thought that RFRA had several defects, among them the questionable basis of section 5 authority.

He noted, first, that there were two possible alternatives to section 5: the spending power and the commerce power. Both of these, however, had serious problems: "The case for federal power to enact the Religious Freedom Restoration Act is thus thrown back on the scope of congressional power to enforce the fourteenth amendment."[58] (Interestingly, Congress would turn to these two sources of power, and debate them thoroughly, in its 2000 response to *City of Boerne v. Flores*, the Religious Land Use and Institutionalized Persons Act [see Chapter 7]).

However, turning to section 5 posed problems he thought nearly insurmountable. First, the precedent of *Katzenbach v. Morgan*,[59] upholding the Voting Rights Act, was weaker than Laycock's argument implied, inasmuch as it "was the product of a Court far more attuned to the expansion of rights and far less concerned with insulating the states from federal power than is the current Court."[60] That is, Congress was then swimming with the judicial tide of the day, not against it. The decision upholding a congressional statute casting aside the need to show discriminatory intent in the drawing of electoral districts despite a Supreme Court ruling demanding that such intent be shown was, he acknowledged, a stronger precedent. However, RFRA would have much greater implications for federalism, in that it would affect so many areas of public policy and would likely, therefore, be viewed more skeptically by the court.

Two institutional arguments are stronger, but even they are wanting. The Supreme Court seemed to be saying in *Smith* that the courts are not qualified to make the delicate judgments required to assess the balance between free exercise claims and the needs for uniformity in the enforcement of generally applicable laws and that therefore such decisions should be made by the legislature. Consequently, regarding the first proposition, Congress could assert that it has superior fact-finding ability and that in its judgment RFRA is necessary to correct a pattern of clear violations of free exercise. However, "the Act does not rest on any claim, general or particular, of legislative superiority in fact-finding, and thus cannot draw upon that line of reasoning."[61] (Again, Congress would pay particular attention to this question in 2000.) As for the second proposition, Congress could say, in line with what Laycock argued, that the legislative branch is merely following Scalia's suggestion and enacting a way for future exemptions to be measured, the compelling interest test. Lupu, though, maintained that there was a significant difference between particular exemptions and a generalized one such as that established by RFRA. It would constitute handing back to the courts what they said in *Smith* that they did not wish to have: the responsibility for drawing up the balance sheet in specific cases.

Given these defects, Lupu offered three alternatives. The first was to do nothing. Part of the justification for this was that the case of *Church of the Lukumi Babalu Aye v. City of Hialeah*,[62] involving the legitimacy of local regulations on animal sacrifices, was then pending before the Supreme Court. It was possible that the court might retreat from *Smith*, making RFRA seem less necessary. (The court instead reiterated its support for *Smith* in this case, even though it ruled for the church.) The second was to avoid the terms the justices had used. That is, the compelling interest test could be rephrased in some way, to avoid stepping on judicial sensitivities about its authority as the sole legitimate interpreter of the Constitution. Lupu suggested, "Except on a showing of extraordinarily good cause, no person acting under color of federal or state law may take any action which seriously injures any person in his or her religious practice."[63] Finally, he recommended Congress might propose a constitutional amendment overturning *Smith*.

A brief oral exchange followed between Laycock and Lupu. Laycock, for his part, reiterated that the Supreme Court had on several occasions indeed recognized Congress's power under section 5 to create statutory rights that exceeded those granted by the court as constitutional. Turning to the Voting Rights Act once more, he said, "Now, Professor Lupu said . . . that Congress can't simply reverse the direction the courts have been going in. Well, we will see, but the Supreme Court flatly said literacy tests for voters in the South are permitted, and Congress said they are forbidden, and the court enforced that statute."[64] Further, he mentioned that some people contended that the court smiled favorably on the Voting Rights Act because Congress had compiled a number of relevant facts regarding the abuse of the tests, facts not considered by the court when it decided the previous literacy test cases. He was "not sure if congressional factfinding is essential to an exercise of section 5 power, but the Voting Rights Act and the cases construing them certainly indicate that finding of fact is helpful."[65] Therefore, he recommended that Congress offer up three facts: that religious minorities have been persecuted throughout American history; that Congress, being "the expert on the political process," state that legislating case-by-case exceptions is too unwieldy to be a useful approach; and that litigating motives one case at a time is also singularly impractical.

Lupu agreed that if Congress offered up such a set of findings that the possibility of judicial invalidation of RFRA would be reduced, but not eliminated. However, he thought that the doctrinal positions of the contemporary court regarding federalism and separation of powers were simply too strong to be overcome by even significant congressional fact-finding:

> I am reminded of two things about the current Court. No. 1, as compared to the Court of 20 years ago, which decided the major cases involving section 5 of the 14th amendment, this Court is much more hospitable to the interests of States. The Chief Justice of the United States [William Rehnquist] is the author of a major opinion having with to do with State sovereignty and immunity from Federal legislation.
>
> Second, this is the same Supreme Court . . . that decided *Smith*, that said, we don't want to apply the compelling interest test across the board to State laws. We are not going to do it under the 1st and 14th amendments. For Congress to turn around and say, oh, yes, you are. We tell you you have to do it, I think will not sit too well with the folks who voted in the majority in *Smith*.[66]

While Lupu's argument was grounded in prediction, sharing the goals of RFRA's supporters, Bruce Fein was opposed to the statute. He offered several objections, but the chief one seemed to concern federalism. He suggested that neither the commerce clause nor section 5 provided ample congressional authority for the act, and it would therefore likely be held unconstitutional. But he said there was even more to fear if the act were upheld: the power of the states would almost become a nullity. If this exercise of section 5 power were sustained, Congress could virtually overturn any state policy. In short, "It seems difficult to conceive of any constitutional theory that would validate the RFRA and yet avoid sounding the death knell of federalism."[67]

During the hearings, a good bit of evidence was presented about the effects of *Smith*. Lower courts, several witnesses stressed, were indeed following its guidelines and bowing out of the business of deciding which claims for exemptions from generally applicable laws met the compelling interest test. As a result, religious claimants were losing much more often. J. Brent Walker of the Baptist Joint Committee on Public Affairs presented a list of 48 lower court cases decided through June 15, 1992, in which religious plaintiffs had lost.[68] One particularly heart-wrenching case was detailed for the committee, involving the performance of a compulsory autopsy on a member of the Hmong. Even the federal district judge deciding the case expressed his own sorrow at the outcome he felt he had to deliver: "While I feel constrained to apply the majority's opinion [in *Smith*] to the instant case, I cannot do this without expressing my own agreement with Justice Blackmun's forceful dissent."[69]

Apparently persuaded that the bill was needed and that section 5 provided the required constitutional authority, both judiciary committees reported the bill out in May of 1993. The vote was unanimous in the House body, while Senator Simpson was the lone dissenter over in the Senate. After Senator Reid's futile floor attempt to add an amendment exempting prisons, the Senate passed the bill 97–3 on October 27, 1993. The House followed suit on November 3, 1993, with a unanimous voice vote. Having previously expressed his support for the measure, President Bill Clinton signed it on November 16, 1993.

The structure of the law will be presented in Chapter 5, as we take up the court rulings.

Chapter 2

# Boerne, Texas, and St. Peter Apostolic Catholic Church

An early-nineteenth-century visitor to the Cibolo Valley, which comprises the area west of San Antonio that is now Kendall County, described it as "a delightful prairie with occasional groves of trees of 10 to 12 varieties of oaks. The whole valley resembles a park, whose diversity and rarity cannot be easily duplicated elsewhere."[1] Whether or not this was a bit of typical nineteenth-century real estate puffery designed to entice settlers is not known. But for whatever reason, in 1847 a small group of young idealistic German socialist intellectuals, part of a large group of German immigrants from the "Adelsverein" who had earlier settled New Braunfels and Fredericksburg, Texas, established an experimental community at Bettina, near where Boerne now sits. Within a year, dissent within the community led to its breakup. Eight of the dissidents decided to set up another community at present-day Boerne in 1849 and called it Tusculum. By 1851 fresh like-minded immigrants from Germany had arrived, and a surveyor was engaged to lay out a town. The residents renamed their settlement for a German journalist, Ludwig Boerne, who had had to flee to France from his native Frankfurt because of left-wing articles he had written.[2] Along with farming, the people quarried limestone in the nearby hills and fabricated shingles from the cedar trees that grew in the area. Prosperity came soon, and a stage stop and a post office were set up in 1856. Maintaining their German heritage was important to the local residents, as can be witnessed by the organization of the Boerne *Gesang Verein*, a singing society, in 1860. Equally important, retaining their secular socialist leanings, was that neither clergy nor churches were welcome. In legend, a sign in the town said, "Priests and ministers, don't let sundown catch you in this town."

Meanwhile, a journalist named George Kendall (1809–67) had been sent to France as a correspondent for the New Orleans *Picayune.* [3] There he met and married Adeline de Valecourt. Kendall became interested in sheep raising and began studying how farmers in France were going about it. He also traveled to England and Scotland to investigate techniques used there. In 1855, he came to Texas and bought 15,000 acres near Boerne, where he began his sheep-raising operation. The venture proved highly successful, and Kendall became a prominent citizen. When a new county was organized by the legislature in 1862, it was named after him. Although Kendall had no particular interest in religion, his wife was a devout Roman Catholic. To allow her to continue to practice her faith, he built a log chapel on his land and paid priests from San Antonio to come out periodically to conduct services and celebrate the sacraments.

Emil Fleury (1845–1929) was the youngest son born to a wealthy family in Maiche, France.[4] He studied philosophy and theology at the University of Fribourg, and showing a lifelong aptitude for languages, became fluent in Latin, Spanish, Italian, and German in addition to his native French. When he announced that he wanted to become a priest, his father disowned him and froze him out of any inheritance. Undeterred, Fleury enrolled at the St. Irenaeus Seminary in Lyon. In June 1866, the Bishop of Galveston visited St. Irenaeus seeking volunteers for mission work in Texas. Fleury enlisted and arrived in Galveston in late 1866. To test the young man's stamina, the bishop sent him to Boerne with instructions to build a church to serve the scattering of German Catholics who had ventured to the area (settling mostly outside the town to avoid trouble). The bishop knew this was going to be no small challenge, given the town's hostility to religion.

Welcomed by Kendall, Fleury's first move was to acquire a tract of land on a small hill outside the town. Then he studied up on construction techniques. Following that, he went to Fredericksburg, Texas, and found two stone masons willing to teach him how to quarry and mortar limestone. Gathering funds from George Kendall and the few potential parishioners (the predominantly German character of the area, even among its Catholics, can be gleaned from the names of almost all these people: Sultenfuss, Phillip, Scherz, Staffel, Dienger, Daizer, O'Grady, Kunz, Acker, Beek, Riley, and Kaiser), he enticed them to Boerne to help him with the church. He also built a kiln and dug a well himself. He even survived an Indian attack one night by wrapping himself in a blanket and lying still on the scaffolding of the half-built church, although his horse was killed by the intruders. The church was completed (debt free, it might be added) in 1867 and served the parish until 1923. After that, it was maintained and used for a variety of purposes, including CCD (Confraternity of Christian Doctrine, religious education for Catholic youth) classes, social gatherings, Boy Scouts, and youth group meetings. By 1948, although it had been patched regularly, the building was in need of substantial repair. A letter from the priest at St. Peter at the time, Fr. A. J. Kraus, to the Archbishop of San Antonio is especially interesting in light of what happened in the 1990s: "While the more urgent repairs have been made from time to time, the building is not at present in first class condition . . . To help you visualize the situation let it be noted that the building is one of the older in Boerne, certainly the oldest church building . . . The work will serve a two-fold object—preserving an old historic landmark of the parish, town and county, and also putting it into such condition as will make it serve present needs of the parish."[5] The archbishop gave his consent for the work to be done, and the repairs were made. In 1986–87, a new round of restoration work was done to preserve the "old" church. It still stands today, and in 1987 was designated an official Texas Historic Landmark.

In 1869, Fleury was assigned to a church in New Braunfels, Texas, and after that served parishes in other towns in Texas, New Orleans, Nebraska, Alaska, and the French colonies in Africa. He taught Romance languages at the University of Denver in 1911–12, at age 66 and 67. In 1916, he was called back to Galveston to become the spiritual director of an orphanage. During the next few years, he visited Boerne frequently, and in 1923, at age 78, he was asked to lay the cornerstone of the "new" church, the building that would become the subject of the Supreme Court case.

The railroad came to Boerne in 1877, and the town continued to grow. As the initial hostility to religion softened, additional Catholic families came to the area, and St. Peter grew also. In time, too, a Lutheran, a Methodist, a Baptist, and an Episcopal church were also built on the town's outskirts, although in different directions from St. Peter. Eventually, all these churches were brought within the city limits. In 1896 the Sisters of the Incarnate Word opened a school near the church, and in 1898 a sanatorium was built. (These closed in 1929 and 1930 respectively because of financial difficulties induced by the Great Depression.) In 1918, with Fleury's church unable to accommodate the slowly but steadily growing number of worshipers on Sundays, planning began for the building of a new church. Since the church owned the property adjacent to the old church, it was natural to build the new facility there. It was decided to build it of local limestone and make it a replica of Mission Concepcion in San Antonio. Construction began in 1920, with parishioners, as before, doing much of the work themselves. A local judge, for example, whose property contained a long stone fence, agreed to let the church have the stones if they would build him a new wire fence. They did so and hauled the stones to the building site.

The church was dedicated on December 23 and consecrated on December 30, 1923. Although numerous Catholic dignitaries attended both ceremonies, Fr. Fleury was the most applauded. While there, he sat under an oak tree he had planted as a sapling when he was building the original church. *The Southern Messenger*, Texas's Catholic newspaper, described the new church in these terms: "The church is built of stone. It measures 38 by 85 feet and is 21 feet high. The church may be seen at Honey Creek, a distance of twenty-one miles. The approximate cost of the church is $8,000. It would have been materially greater but several of the parishioners who assisted in the construction generously donated their services." Bishop A. J. Drossaerts praised the "wonderful zeal and effort" the parishioners exhibited in building "this magnificent new church." He added, "As the famous St. Peter's [in Rome] has served as a haven for thousands so I hope St. Peter's, Boerne, will serve a similar purpose."[6] Perhaps the most prescient observation, though, came from the reporter for the *San Antonio Express*:

> The new edifice was necessary to handle the ever growing congregation which could no longer find room in the little church on the hill, built near three score years ago. The little church still stands and is used but it is "too small" and the congregation has built a stone edifice with two towers, a facsimile of one of the San Antonio missions. It is located south of and near the old church and standing on a hill fronting the Boerne-San Antonio Road cannot fail to attract notice by passers by.[7]

Indeed, attract notice it did. In time, in fact, rather ironically given Boerne's early history, the church came to symbolize the town for both local residents and visitors alike. A public park was built across the street from the church, with pleasant views of the structure from numerous angles. For many people in the town, therefore, it had become almost a semipublic building. It was "an absolute landmark in Boerne. Anybody giving directions to a place on Main Street, that's the main point of reference. And it's not St. Peter's Catholic Church, it's 'the church on the hill.'"[8] Bettie Edmonds, president of the local Historical Preservation Society and an artist who had painted the church (as well as many other historic buildings in the area), said in 1992, "This building is one of the most inspirational sites in Boerne to anyone who visits our town, Catholic or not."[9] Another local preservationist quoted by the local newspaper added, "Artists, photographers and sightseers are drawn to Boerne for our historic buildings and St. Peter's is one of them. It is a landmark and it shouldn't be changed."

As for the parishioners of St. Peter in the 1990s, particularly those of long standing, it is small wonder that they would have an extremely strong attachment to this building. After all, their parents and grandparents had left their handprints on its walls and the major milestones of their and their children's lives had been celebrated there. (Incidentally, the continuing German character and heritage of the parish are evident from the names of those 1923 laborers: Kronkosky, Schwarz, Sotello, Lamm, Hugman, Kaiser, Cole, Pfeiffer, and Klar.) Standing across the street in Veterans Park or driving through Boerne on Highway 46, it is also easy to see how non-Catholics came to admire and cherish the building. A lovely grotto was built with donated rock and labor in 1960–63; a new parish hall was constructed in 1974; adjacent lots were purchased for more parking space in 1983; and an outdoor pavilion was also added in 1984.

All these additions were evidence of the parish's steady growth. Most of this came as a reflection of the significant population increases that both Boerne and Kendall County witnessed between 1960 and 1990. The census tabulated 2,169 people in Boerne and 5,889 in the county in 1960; 2,432 and 6,964 in 1970; 3,229 and 10,631 in 1980; and 4,274 and 14,589 in 1990. Fr. Joseph Manning came to St. Peter in 1969, and it was on his watch that much of the growth occurred. By 1987, two hundred more families were added to the rolls. By the time Fr. Tony Cummins came to the parish in 1990, overcrowding at services had become a serious problem, so much so that a number of communicants were forced to stand at the main Masses. Significantly, as much of the growth came from people moving out from San Antonio, many of the newcomers did not have the strong emotional investment in the building—and often were not of German background. (Even as late as the 1960s, German was still spoken in many places in Boerne.)

The cleavage that developed in the church did not precisely mirror an "old timers" versus "newcomers" fault line, but that was part of it.[10] Further, any time a new pastor of any denomination replaces a popular and long-serving minister (and Fr. Manning was extremely popular among both the parishioners of St. Peter and the people of Boerne, being appointed, for example, chaplain to both the city police and fire departments), there are bound to be difficulties of one sort or another. Soon after he came, Fr. Cummins reorganized some of the internal operations of the parish, and the result was a lessening of the position of a Men's Club that Fr. Manning had established in 1971, a dedicated group that had been active in raising funds for a variety of projects.[11] Naturally, this led to some grumbling. The new priest also felt that it was inappropriate to have an American flag flying in the front of the building, a position shared, of course, by many Christians of all denominations. Nonetheless, some veterans were upset by its removal. But it was primarily a dispute over what to do about the overcrowding, and consequently what that might mean for the 1923 church, that began to divide the congregation. As the discussions within the parish became known in the wider community, the non-Catholics in the town seemed to fall into three groups. One portion, which included most of the ministers of the other churches, felt that the needs of the church took priority over the beauty of the building. A second segment deeply regretted that the church might be sacrificed to growth but were willing to let the officials of the church make the decision. A third group vehemently opposed tampering with the historic architecture of the 1923 church, and while the size of this group is impossible to measure, it was substantial; and they were clearly the most vocal.

In January of 1991, Fr. Cummins issued an invitation to the parish to serve on a Physical Plant Planning Committee. In September, the committee selected architect Greg Davis to help them develop a ten-year master plan. A sense of unease was sprouting among some members of the parish, and a note in the October 6, 1991, church bulletin tried to allay their concerns. "The important point to be made," it said, "is at this time no decisions are being made—other than to hire an architect to assist the Committee to develop the Master Plan."[12] In March of 1992 several possible expansion plans were discussed, some envisioning keeping more of the 1923 church than others.

A committee was established to conduct a survey of the parishioners, and Dr. Jerome Matz, a professor of sociology at St. Mary's University in San Antonio, was asked to help with its construction.[13] It was handed out to all those age 13 and over attending the April 4 and 5, 1992, Masses. In all, 492 members completed the survey. (The parish registry contained 2,200 registrants; however, the number of regular Mass attendees was markedly fewer than that, but more, as the critics were quick to point out, than 492. In fact, the church itself later gave a figure of 1,100 regulars, as noted in what follows.) Demographically, 38 percent of the respondents had attended St. Peter five years or less, while 48 percent had been there for ten years or more. On a question soliciting their personal commitment to the parish, 25 percent said they were highly committed, 59 percent moderately committed, with 11 percent indicating only a low commitment (the remainder either had no commitment or did not answer). As for satisfaction with how the parish was currently operating, 38 percent said they were very satisfied and 49 percent satisfied. But the key questions were about expansion. A section headed "Physical Facilities" offered this preface to three questions:

> During the past 5 years, the numbers of persons attending Masses at St. Peter's, has steadily increased and our worship space has become very limited. This growth pattern is expected to continue. Hence, Phase I of our parish Master Plan addresses this growth pattern.
>
> To increase our worship space, the existing Church will be enlarged while preserving the front appearance of the Church with the 2 towers. This decision to enlarge the existing Church has been made because the construction of a new Church building, [*sic*] would require the destruction of the existing Church building due to the limited size of the lot.

Then came the critical questions:

> How do *you feel* about the idea of enlarging the existing Church while preserving the front appearance of the Church? [Answers: Strongly Favor, Favor, Oppose, Strongly Oppose, Undecided, or Don't Know.]
>
> If the majority of parishioners approved of the idea of enlarging the existing Church while preserving the front appearance of the Church, *would you favor/oppose* the idea? [Same reply possibilities as before.]
>
> Would *you* be willing to *help financially support* an enlargement of the existing Church through additional contributions? [Answers: Yes, definitely, Yes, maybe, No, not at all, and Undecided.]

The answers to the first question were Strongly Favor, 48 percent; Favor, 26 percent; Oppose, 7 percent; Strongly Oppose, 8 percent; and Undecided, 7 percent, with the rest not knowing or not answering. For the second question, the tabulation showed 45 percent Strongly in Favor, 31 percent in Favor, 8 percent Opposed, and 7 percent Strongly Opposed [the remainder, as before, either being undecided or giving no answer.] (This is a curious result, as more claimed to be strongly in favor of enlargement than were strongly in favor of doing so if a majority of their fellow parishioners approved of the plan. Normally, one would expect the opposite.) On the financial question, 41 percent responded Yes, Definitely; 29 percent Yes, Maybe; and 10 percent Not at All [with undecided and no answer composing the balance].

Pointed discord began to emerge, as an ad hoc group of parishioners mobilized to oppose the implications of the survey. The wording of the questions, they felt, was stacking the deck in favor of making substantial modifications to the church, demolishing, that is, all but a small area around the front towers. At this point, it is worth noting that most experts felt that building a new freestanding building would have been difficult if not impossible (as hinted at in the second question) because of the lay of the land. Some countered, however, that this option was not explored enough and that the city should be approached about closing an adjacent street to make room for an entirely new edifice.[14] Even if this had been practical, though, the parish would have then had two historical structures to maintain, which would have imposed a significant financial burden. The option of opening a second parish in Boerne was not seriously explored either, as there was already a shortage of priests in the diocese.

Anna Marie Davison, who had written the 1987 history of the parish, Bertie and Richard Sciaraffa, Freeda and Johnny Granato, who had done much of the 1986 restoration work himself, and Thomas Sullivan took the lead at this point. They quickly enlisted the help of Bettie Edmonds, in light of her expertise in historic building preservation. Somewhat later, Dub Smothers, a wealthy retired businessman who had actually been a parishioner of Fr. Cummins in San Antonio before moving to Boerne, joined them. Throughout, though, they had a significant number of backers and sympathizers in the parish—and outside it. The dissidents' first move was to circulate a petition among both members of the congregation and the townspeople urging that the church building not be destroyed. Copies of the petition could be found at the public library, a grocery store, and a restaurant. By April 15, 552 people had signed.[15] Church officials contended that only 10 percent of them were members of the parish; backers of the petition, though, counted 176 parishioners, or 32 percent. It was directed to Msgr. Lawrence Stuebben of the archdiocese office, whose portfolio included approving new building projects. Bettie Edmonds was asked to first take the petition to Fr. Cummins, which she did. However, it garnered only a cool reception.

Fr. Cummins told the local newspaper, "I was stunned when I learned about the opposition. They [the planning committee] have worked so hard and been so open." The chair of the planning committee, Bob Weiss, added, "We will proceed slowly. A lot of time, a lot of soul-searching has gone on as to what we are going to do." In an attempt to allay some of the discontent, Fr. Cummins emphasized, "There is absolutely no decision made as to what we are going to do. We have ideas, and we will present these ideas, but if the parishioners do not like what we suggest, we will begin all over again. No decision has been made because there has been no input back from the parishioners."[16]

Msgr. Stuebben responded to Mrs. Davison on May 8. After acknowledging the 552 signatures, he tried to move the discussion back to the local level while stilling the waters:

> The kinds of questions and concerns that are raised in your letter need to be dealt with at the parish level where there are appropriate structures already in place . . . where the concerns, questions and different views of parishioners can be expressed and listened to so as to arrive at decisions that will meet the needs of the parish and preserve parish unity . . .
>
> At this stage, I have no idea as to what is the best plan or approach to take to meet the needs of the growing Catholic community in St. Peter's Parish in Boerne. I also think that the last thing that any of you in the parish would want to happen is for the Archbishop or the Archdiocesan Building board or some other agency of the Archdiocese to come to Boerne and simply tell the pastor and parish community what to do. It has long been the policy of the Archdiocese that these matters are best dealt with on the local level through a process of working together, listening to one another, doing the necessary negotiating so as to arrive at decisions that truly serve the community, maintain the unity that is so much a sign of God's presence and God's blessings and finally serve as an example and witness to the wider community in which you live and the entire Archdiocese.[17]

On June 15, Mrs. Davison wrote to the Texas Historical Commission (enclosing 15 photographs) asking for help in designating the church a historic landmark. The commission's director of National Register Programs replied encouragingly on June 23. "The 1923 St. Peter's church," he wrote, "is certainly eligible to be a Texas Historic Landmark." He added that also "both the 1867 and 1923 churches could be nominated together for listing in the National Register of Historic Places." After analyzing and praising the architectural style of the building, he said that "its presence is no doubt a local landmark, familiar to residents and visitors to the city." Most important, perhaps, the commission stood ready to help with the preservation efforts: "Obviously we encourage your congregation and its leadership to preserve this important complex, and to recognize the significance of the 1923 church. We will be glad to provide you with technical assistance in maintaining these buildings, and to consult with you on alternatives to accommodating a growing congregation."[18]

On Sunday evening, May 31, the Pastoral Council presented several options for a master site plan to the chairs of the various parish committees; the following Sunday evening, June 7, they did the same for the general congregation. These plans called for the preservation of the towers only, as the dissidents had feared. The quarterly parish newsletter for June 1992 summarized the presentations and the questions raised afterwards. In the introduction, it said that "the Pastoral Council will establish sub committees for the expansion of the church while keeping the towers." The building committee had considered building a new church on property already owned by the church but had opted instead for expansion of the current building. Not only would the lay of the land make this difficult, but the resulting church could not be as large as could an expanded facility. Thus five rationales were offered for this decision: adequate parking, seating space, evangelization, meeting parish growth, and minimizing fracturing St. Peter's community (by offering ever more Masses). The newsletter paraphrased five concerns raised by congregants and the answers provided by the Parish Council. Two of them are especially pertinent (question in regular type, answer in italics):

> Not fully understanding the direction the church was being expanded, some parishioners thought the expansion would be to the rear of the church leaving the front and the sides as is. *The Site Plan used to show the expansion prior to the survey is an architect's concept of the expansion given the elevation of the ground and the desired community goals. It is not the actual church design.*
>
> Since the concept of the church's design, an old Spanish mission, may be considerably altered, why bother to keep any aspect since renovation costs more than new construction. *A design committee will work out the appearance and size of the expanded church carrying forward something of the past into the future. Ultimately, the financing will determine the scope of the enlargement.*

Fr. Cummins closed the meeting with the following comment: "The Church is something to be handed on, a tradition in a dynamic sense, more like a library than an ancient museum. Tradition is not merely a piece of the past brought into the present—but rather the dreams and hopes of the past and present brought into the future."[19]

With it now clear that more of the church building was in jeopardy than some of the previous drawings had indicated, the rumblings became more serious. Fr. Cummins felt the need to put the following note in the June 14 bulletin:

> Everyone's views and opinions are important and the decision to move forward is based on the majority view. The recently completed survey reflects 76% of the respondent [*sic*] said favor to the question: "If the majority of parishioners approved of the idea of enlarging the existing Church while preserving the front appearance of the Church, . . ."
>
> It's certainly my hope that the minority view will respect the wishes of the majority and work with them as I'm sure would be the case if the vote had been reversed.
>
> We have a long journey ahead of us—the next step is to put together a schematic and building committee. If you are interested in serving on

> this committee, please submit your name and a short paragraph describing your vision of St. Peter parish.[20]

On June 22 and July 9, as tensions within the parish escalated, the dissidents met with Charles Wilson of the St. Joseph Foundation.[21] This was a San Antonio–based organization devoted to representing the rights of Catholics in a variety of forums. Mr. Wilson suggested that Mrs. Davison obtain a procurator's mandate, which is a document that allows one person to represent others in a church proceeding. She hoped thereby that she could not only speak with greater authority within the church but also start the state historical commission's paperwork. While Mrs. Davison was asking people to sign the document, she, Thomas Sullivan, and Richard Sciaraffa wrote a highly critical letter to the editor of one of the local papers:

> It was interesting to read the results of the recent survey conducted by St. Peter's (Catholic Church) in regard to replacement of the present church. However, no mention was made of the fact that only 40.7 percent would be willing to financially support this.
>
> Also, since that time, at two additional meetings the building committee stated that all of the church is to come down with the possible exception of the towers. Several people have said that had they understood this, they would have opposed the proposal.
>
> We wonder what a current survey would show in the light of this new information. It would appear to us that Kendall County is threatened with the loss of a local landmark.
>
> We are publicly asking the pastoral council, planning committee and leadership of St. Peter's Church of Boerne, to reconsider the plans to partially destroy the existing church. This is totally ignoring the value of a historical complex.[22]

At the same time, Mrs. Davison wrote Roy Graham of the architecture department of Catholic University of America asking his opinion of the situation. He responded on August 5, "I am frankly shocked that your congregation and its leadership would consider the demolition of this important historic complex. It is not only important to save the structures for the patrimony of the Catholic Church, but it would be difficult to explain the loss of such a symbolic edifice to the entire population of Boerne and south Texas."[23] He offered to forward the material she sent to the United States Council of Bishops and the appropriate office in Rome.

Fr. Cummins felt that Mrs. Davison and the others were now stepping over the line, especially in seeking the procurator's mandate. In the July

18–19 church bulletin, he took a rather sharp tone. (Although he called the document a "petition," technically under Canon Law it is not that, in that no specific request is made.) "This petition," he wrote, "has no place in a Christian community, it is divisive, and combating it potentially sets people against people. It is a for or against invitation, spelled out in arbitrary language. It is an agent causing confusion, and confusion is the devils [*sic*] handy work."[24]

When told of Fr. Cummins's comments, the St. Joseph Foundation's Mr. Wilson sought the opinion of Kelley O'Donnell of Bakersfield, California, an expert on Canon Law. Along with his letter, Wilson enclosed a stack of material on the evolving controversy. On July 30, O'Donnell replied with a six-page, single-spaced letter to Wilson. He was critical of the decision-making process at St. Peter's, in that the plans for demolishing all but the towers moved too quickly from being "considered" to a "definite undertaking." Additionally, he felt the dissidents were on strong grounds substantively. Canon 1216, he noted, provides that "the principles and norms of the liturgy and of sacred art are to be observed in the building and repair of churches; the advice of experts is also to be employed." Given the letter from the Texas Historical Commission, he felt that there was a strong case that the building needed to be protected: "The letter written by Jim Steely, the Director of the National Register Programs, leaves little room for debate concerning the *significant impact* the church structure has in the *development of architecture for the Catholic community* as well as the *community at large* in Boerne" (emphasis in original). For further support, he quoted a provision of the *General Instruction of the Roman Missal* (Number 254): "The Church is intent on keeping the works of art and the treasures handed down from the past and, when necessary on adapting them to new needs." Finally, he felt that Mrs. Davison had followed the proper steps in seeking the procurator's mandate and that Fr. Cummins' criticisms were therefore not valid.[25]

Back in Boerne, an irate Anna Marie Davison wrote a letter to Fr. Cummins demanding that he make an apology for his July 19 bulletin comments in writing and that it be printed in the bulletin.[26] Failing that, she requested a meeting to discuss an apology. At 2:30 on August 14, a meeting was held at the rectory. Fr. Cummins was accompanied by two members of the Pastoral Council. Coming along with Mrs. Davison were Richard Sciaraffa, Thomas Sullivan, and Freeda Granato.[27] They also asked Charles Wilson to attend, which he did. According to Mrs. Davison's notes of the meeting, no apology was forthcoming. A little later, however, Fr. Cummins sent a letter to all members of the parish. In it he indicated that he now had more information regarding the procurator's mandate. Although he said he was still convinced the church should be enlarged, he acknowledged that others disagreed, but felt that "if we can handle our differences in a prudent, constructive and charitable manner, then the entire parish will benefit, whatever becomes of the building." In that spirit, he offered the hand of fellowship: "in view of this, I wish to withdraw the comments I made in the July 19 bulletin. Also, I have extended an apology to Mrs. Davison, and she has accepted. I hope and pray that all of us can put this incident behind us and move forward together in forming a stronger community of faith."[28]

In August and September fund raising began, with $660,000 eventually pledged by May of 1993. Discussions on plans continued among the building committee, the Pastoral Council, and the architect. On September 19 and October 25, 1992, parish meetings were held to discuss and approve floor plans and other matters. On Sunday, February 7, 1993, a model and sketches of the proposed building plan were presented at a church reception. As the dissidents feared, the twin towers would be all that would remain of the old church (see photos following Chapter 9).[29]

The controversy now spilled directly out into the community, while still engaging the dissident parishioners. The San Antonio Conservation Society sent a letter offering their help in developing alternatives, but the offer was turned aside by the church. Fr. Cummins attended a meeting of the Boerne Area Historical Preservation Society to explain the church's position, stressing that the towers would continue to be an attractive amenity for the town, and told the *San Antonio Express-News* that "the view from the park will be virtually the same. You'll have to look very hard to see any difference from there."[30] Meanwhile, Thomas Sullivan prepared the appropriate documents to have the Texas Historical Commission designate the building a historic landmark and sent them to Archbishop Flores for his signature. The archbishop, however, declined to sign them. Richard Sciaraffa even sent a letter to Rome, asking authorities there to intervene.[31]

An avalanche of letters to the editor in the two local newspapers reflected all shades of opinion. Most were thoughtful and reasoned. However, a significant number were vitriolic, and the percentage of these seemed to grow as summer turned to fall. At times, they even contained embarrassingly sharp personal attacks of one sort or another. (Both papers, incidentally, said that they received far more letters than they could possibly print.) Setting aside those from members of the church, the most interesting ones demonstrated how much the building meant to the community. The following paraphrases and quotations are a mere sample:[32]

> The church "means a lot to Boerne and I would hate to see it ruined."
>
> It is "foolish" to say St. Peter's belongs to the parish alone. "The building is a concern of all citizens in the area. It is a landmark of historical value."
>
> "Boerne is a town that is known and admired for its historic preservation."
>
> An artist who had visited the city said that it was the "ultimate landmark of Boerne, Texas."
>
> An amateur photographer from New Zealand who had visited the town wrote to say that he was "devastated to learn that there is a plan to tear down this building to erect a newer, more modern facility."
>
> A local five-year-old begged the parish not to tear down "my castle."

On the other side, a number of people wrote in to say that while they would like to keep the building, the needs of the church, as defined by the members themselves, had to take priority. It is, after all, many of them said, a vibrant, living church, and its needs trump those of historical preservation. Nevertheless, if the number of letters to the editor is any measure (and it is, of course, not a perfect method of score keeping, but since both papers strove to publish a representative sample of what they received, it is a reasonably fair one), then the majority sentiment clearly favored keeping the church as much intact as possible.

The Boerne Area Historical Preservation Society and the Kendall County Historical Commission were both divided on the issue, especially since both groups contained members of the parish. After extensive discussions, they issued a joint statement on August 25, 1993:

> Because our members are so diverse, we find ourselves on every side of this issue. We are grateful for this diversity, for it gives our groups greater knowledge, vision and balance.
>
> Since the property is wholly owned by the Catholic Diocese, only its congregants can know what is best for themselves. We historical organizations are not in a position to be able to pronounce to the owners [and not in a position to buy it as a museum].
>
> Be assured, both of our organizations are available for historical and architectural research and for consultation on these matters upon request.

> It is our joint hope that St. Peter's congregation may come to a wise and amicable decision.[33]

Opponents scheduled a public rally at Veterans Park for September 18. The flyer promoting it urged, "If you're concerned about the planned destruction of St. Peter's Church in Boerne, join other concerned parishioners and citizens of Boerne at a . . . rally." At the bottom of the announcement, bold letters proclaimed, "We Need Your Support."[34] The *Boerne Star* published a picture of the rally on page 1 in the following week's edition. Although it is hard to gauge, it seems to depict a reasonably good turnout for a town of 4,300.

Still convinced that enlarging the sanctuary while keeping only the towers of the 1923 church was the appropriate path, on December 13, 1993, church officials came to city hall to file a request for a building permit.

Chapter 3

# A Building Permit Denied

There is no doubt that Boerne is a charming town and that much of that charm has to do with the architectural integrity of the town's center and the areas immediately adjacent to it. The buildings are mostly made from the limestone that has long been quarried locally, and the late-nineteenth- and early-twentieth-century flavor of these edifices, both mercantile and public, has a pleasing feel to it. Further, the center of town was then and still is a vibrant commercial area. Where Main Street (also labeled Hauptstrasse on signs) and Blanco Road intersect in the city center, a small public park is flanked by Ye Olde Kendall Inn, what was the public library, and a commercial building. Four blocks east on Blanco is the superbly maintained city hall, built in 1909. If one drives south on Main Street from the intersection, the businesses that front it are also mostly of vintage construction. A few blocks down, one crosses Cibolo Creek, after which there is a gentle rise and Veterans Park appears on the left and St. Peter's on the right. It is no wonder that residents and visitors alike find the town picturesque and no surprise at all that many would want to keep it that way.[1]

Between the filing of the application for the building permit in late 1993 and late 1995, when the battle shifted to the Federal Court of Appeals in New Orleans and the questions of federalism and separation of powers assumed center stage, debate continued to rage in Boerne. Looking back from the vantage point of a decade and a half, it seems that surely some kind of compromise could have been worked out. There were, after all, numerous meetings, both formal and informal, between representatives of the church and the city.[2] This feeling is underscored by the fact that when the parties did compromise in 1997 the agreement they hammered out was almost identical to one of the proposals the city had floated at the time. Why this stalemate? The most oft-cited reason, by both participants and observers, was that the parish and city both just dug in their heels, and relations simply soured further with each rejection of the other's offer.

Before embarking on the narrative of what happened during those two years, it will be helpful to identify the major participants. Although the Catholic Church is organized hierarchically, each parish in practice enjoys a good bit of autonomy. Here, the local parish was making the decisions, with the archdiocese offering advice and moral support but not directing the decision-making process. Further, the financial obligations for architects and legal fees were met by the parish. Thus Fr. Cummins, Mr. Bob Weiss, president of the parish council, Mr. Richard Mecke, chairperson of the building committee, and Mr. Henry Friesenhahn, head of the capital-building fund, were the key players. For the city, there was an array of both elected and appointed officials. The mayor (Patrick Heath, a former Methodist minister) and the five members of the city council (Donald Gourley, R. L. Bien, Darrell Street, Bill Lester, and Ann Reissig) were then elected at large.[3] The key members of the city's staff were the city manager, Ron Bowman, and the director of planning and community development, Christopher Turk. Both Mr. Bowman and Mr. Turk are still in their posts and, it should be noted, at the time were parishioners of St. Peter's. The Historic Landmark Commission, whose role will be discussed momentarily, was appointed by the city council.

In 1985 the city council voted to create a Historic Landmark Commission (HLC), but it was not until 1987 that members were actually appointed. Phillip Bell, a local commercial real estate broker, who along with the other members took the post thinking of it as a public service, was appointed chair and remembered all the members thinking, "Oh, this will be simple. Little old lady comes and asks to paint their house blue, green, pink—we say yes, no—go home and sleep well."[4] In 1991, the boundaries of the historic district were drawn and approved; later that same year, these boundaries were slightly expanded. The original district's boundaries bisected St. Peter's, with the towers and roughly the front half of the church within the boundary. The expanded district, however, encompassed the entire church. According to the ordinance, the HLC had to approve significant changes to any structures within the district.[5]

The preamble to the ordinance read as follows: "Whereas, the City Council of Boerne is aware that the City of Boerne has various areas, places, buildings, and structures having significant historical value which reflect the heritage of the city, the State, and its people; and Whereas, it is recognized that rapid change in population, economic functions and land use activities has led and is leading to the increased demolition of these landmarks so that the City, the State and the Nation are thereby losing a part of their heritage." This was followed by a declaration of policy "that the protection, enhancement, preservation and use of historic landmarks is a desirable public good and is needed in the interest of the culture, prosperity, education and general welfare of the people."[6]

After that, seven purposes of the measure were enumerated:

(a) To protect, enhance and perpetuate selected historic landmarks which represent or reflect distinctive and important elements of the City's and State's architectural, archaeological, cultural, social, economic, ethnic and political history and to develop appropriate settings for such places;

(b) To safeguard the City's historic and cultural heritage, as embodied and reflected in such historic landmarks, by appropriate regulations;

(c) To stabilize and improve property value in such locations;

(d) To foster civic pride in the beauty and accomplishments of the past;

(e) To protect and enhance the City's attractions to tourists and visitors and provide incidental support and stimulus to business and industry;

(f) To strengthen the economy of the city;

(g) To promote the use of historic landmarks for the culture, prosperity, education and general welfare of the people of the City and visitors to the City.

When an application for a building permit was made to the building inspector, he first was to determine if the property lay within the historic district. If so, he had two days to forward it to the chairperson of the HLC. The HLC then had 15 days to make a recommendation to the building inspector. It could approve the permit, deny it, or suggest modifications. If the property owner was dissatisfied with the ruling, he or she could appeal to the city council within 60 days. On appeal, the city council was empowered to support or overrule the commission.

In its deliberations, the HLC was ordered to consider six matters:

(a) The effect of the proposed change upon the general historic cultural and architectural nature of the district;

(b) The appropriateness of exterior architectural features which can be seen from a public street, alley, trail or walkway;

(c) The general design, arrangement and material of the building or structure and the relation of such factors to similar features of buildings or structures in the district;

(d) The criteria used shall not be the aesthetic appeal to the Landmark Commission of the structure or the proposed remodeling, but rather its conformity to the general character of the Historic District;

(e) Harmony with adjacent buildings (scale, height and mass);

(f) The value of the historic district as an area of unique interest and character and its not being impaired.

Two legal matters cropped up that engendered some initial sparring between the parties. The first was whether or not the HLC had jurisdiction over the entire building despite the fact that only a portion of it technically lay within the original historic district. In early December the city staff knew that an application for a building permit would soon be filed by St. Peter's; accordingly, they met with the city's attorney, Gordon Hollon, on December 9 to clarify the question. On January 11, 1994, Hollon informed Chris Turk and other city officials that, given the wording of the ordinance, the HLC indeed had control over the entire structure.[7]

That same day, Turk called Bob Weiss to tell him of Hollon's opinion, and the second problem was unearthed. During their conversation, Turk told Weiss that they would have to file for a building permit covering all the building. Somewhat surprised, Weiss said that they had already filed the application for a permit. Puzzled since he had not seen it, Turk said he would check it out but in the meantime would fax Weiss a new application form. Apparently because there had been a staff turnover in the building inspector's office immediately after the December 13 filing, St. Peter's application had not been forwarded to the HLC. On either January 24 or 25 the new building inspector called Turk to tell him that he had found the application in his desk. On January 25 Turk called the church to tell them that they had found the original application and therefore that another was unnecessary. On the same day, he contacted Phillip Bell, the HLC's chair, and asked him to schedule a meeting for February 1.

The problem was section 7 of the ordinance, detailing the procedures to be followed by the city upon receipt of the application for a permit. As noted, the building inspector had two days to notify the chair of the HLC of the application if that body's approval was required. Then, according to the ordinance, "action shall be taken on any application for a Building Permit within forty-five (45) days after the application has been received by the Landmark Commission Chairman. If no action is taken within the forty-five (45) day limit, the Building Permit shall be deemed approved and the City Building Inspector shall immediately so advise the applicant in writing."

Thomas Drought, the church's attorney, argued that Mr. Bell should have received the application on December 15, 1993, two days after it was filed. Therefore, by February 1, 1994, the 45-day time limit had expired; consequently, the permit had to be granted automatically.

On the Saturday before the Tuesday, February 1, meeting, the members of the HLC toured the church and its property. That Tuesday, 63 "guests" signed in for the commission's 6 p.m. meeting.[8] Bell called the meeting to order and invited Fr. Cummins to make his presentation. Before doing so, he announced that Mr. Drought would like to make a statement for the record, whereupon the attorney laid out his position regarding the 45-day question. The commission huddled and decided that this matter would need a legal opinion but that they should go on with the substance of the meeting nevertheless.

The church had prepared a seven-page presentation, accompanied by drawings of the present church and the projected addition.[9] The document began by outlining seven reasons why the new sanctuary was needed, all the while paying careful attention to the sensitivities of preservationists. It stressed that the "expansion keeps the existing towers," that "lighting will enhance the towers [*sic*] statement on Main Street," that the "expansion will insure the future use of the existing church, and guarantee the towers will be preserved and maintained as a Boerne landmark," that the use of high-quality construction materials would complement "the existing architectural detailing," and that "the new facility will be an asset to Boerne and serve the community for future generations." Following a "Fact Sheet" and the architect's drawings, the concluding section made an attempt to address each of the six criteria the HLC was instructed to employ by the ordinance. Its final statement declared that "*the unique interest* of the Historic District will not be impaired by the addition to this building. It will enhance Main Street by focusing on the towers of the existing building and meld the old architecture with the new. It will be a unique addition to the district" (emphasis in original).

Fr. Cummins presented this material, then introduced Weiss, Mecke, Friesenhahn, and Greg Davis, the church's architect. Weiss, Mecke, and Davis testified to the need for the proposed construction and how it would be a part of Boerne life. Davis said, for example, that "the new building will be a canvass to display the towers. They will stand out even more than they do today." Bob Vollmer, a member of the commission and himself an architect, however, challenged that. "I am concerned," he said, "that it will overpower the towers. I disagree that it will be a backdrop. I question its scale." When the group from the church had finished, the opponents were given an opportunity to speak, and several, including Anna Marie Davison and Richard Sciaraffa, gave impassioned speeches urging that the permit be denied.

Despite the fact that Bell voted only in the case of a tie, he felt compelled by the looming legal question and the need for diplomacy to make a summarizing statement. The official minutes record it as follows:

> Chairman Bell said he personally would not like to see the church not be built. His biggest problem personally is wrestling with the fact that the number one mission of the Landmark Commission is to preserve part of history. He does not feel personally that we will be able to make a decision at this time in lieu of the comments from the attorney. He felt that was a point that certainly needs to be clarified and we need to take a look at it with staff and the city attorney's interpretation. With that in mind, he would like to hear a motion from the commissioners that would allow time to consider all the statements. Specifically, in all fairness, to take a look at the legal matters that were brought up.

As events unfolded, Bell would point to this statement several times in order to show that he himself was not opposed to the building of a new church but that he took his role on a public body as his first obligation.[10] A motion was duly made "to ask for an opinion from the city attorney on the 45-day writing of the ordinance. Then if we should act, then we should meet again and act." It carried unanimously. Another meeting was to be held February 15.

On February 10, Hollon wrote to Turk, asserting that in his opinion Bell did not officially "receive" the permit application until the meeting of February 1. Thus the commission legally had until March 18 to make its decision. However, he recommended that the commission render a decision as soon as possible after the February 15 meeting.

Tensions seemed to be growing within the town. Letters to the editors of the newspapers from both camps urged people to turn out on February 15. Further, there were numerous petitions and letters sent and phone calls made to members of the commission. The commission announced that it was moving the meeting to the Boerne Area Community Center in order to accommodate the crowd. This time, 228 people signed in as "guests." Bell opened the meeting by saying that he was going to restrict the number of speakers because of time constraints and out of respect for the applicants. Furthermore, he asked that people act "with respect and in a very orderly process." Bob Weiss was called on first. He provided a general overview of the need for the new church and how their plans were conducive to maintaining the integrity of the historic district. "From the beginning, the building committee asked how much can we retain, not how much can we tear down." Fr. Cummins followed with a brief statement on the history of the church and replied directly to those who were urging that St. Peter's should build a third sanctuary. "We have two churches on our site," he said. "Are we to build a third church and seventy years from now a fourth and then a fifth? Because then they would be considered historic." Opponents then took the floor and largely rehashed all the arguments that had been made previously.

When both sides had spoken, Bell asked if any commission members wanted to comment. None did, and he called for a motion. Bob Vollmer, the architect, moved, "Since the proposed plan will adversely affect the historic district and is inappropriate or inconsistent with the spirit and purpose of Ordinance No. 91-05, that the Landmark Commission should hereby advise the City Building Inspector, . . . that the pending permit application cannot be approved until certain changes to the permit application are made." It carried unanimously. Afterward, Bell told the press, "We only had one issue to deal with. Not what color rock or what kind of roof they were planning to use, but only are we going to let them tear down that building . . . We didn't say they can't build a new church. We want them to build a church to meet their needs. We will work with them as much as we can if [a new plan] is in the historical district. If no part of their plan is in the district, they don't have to come before us at all."

Disappointed but not surprised, the church now decided to appeal to the city council. Before doing so, however, they modified their construction plans in two ways. First, they would "lower the horizon" of the addition, which would allow the towers to be less overshadowed by the new edifice. Second, they would move the new addition back an extra five feet, also giving more prominence to the towers. Opponents, however, were unswayed. Again, before the meeting, scheduled for April 12, both sides marshaled their forces. Petitions flooded city hall. St. Peter's paid for a four-page supplement to the April 6 edition of the *Star* titled "Growing in Grace."[11]

The front page of the insert contained a drawing of the new building; it was similar to the one that had accompanied the presentation to the HLC, but with the modifications in place. Its caption read in part, "Designers have worked carefully with parishioners to preserve and enhance the native architecture of the well-loved existing church in styling the new building . . . By positioning the expansion behind and to the right of the current building, the view from Main Street will continue to focus on St. Peter's towers and entrance." The text of this page stressed how the plans met the needs of both preservation and the congregation. Regarding the former, it pointed out that "the plans for the new church follow the existing proportions of the current building, including matching 'wall heights' on the Main Street side and using stonework to complement the Main Street façade . . . All materials selected for the addition are quality native rock and wood—building materials typical of the Boerne area." The second page was given over to a history of St. Peter's, and included photographs of the old and current (1923) church, concluding that St. Peter's growth and active role in community life was "a testament to the love and faith of Fr. Fleury and his early flock of devoted Catholics." The third page laid out a site plan of the church's property and recited how members of the parish had helped shape the choices that had been made. The final page was a straightforward plea to the city council: "Currently, the planned expansion of St. Peter awaits a decision from the City Council of Boerne. The Council must decide whether to accept the recommendation of the Landmark Commission that the church not be granted a permit for the construction." The church simply does not have adequate room, Fr. Cummins was quoted as saying. There are now 780 families registered in the parish and the church only seats 200 people. Then there was a not-so-veiled threat: "Should the City Council of Boerne fail to grant St. Peter Catholic Church a building permit, the church would be severely burdened in fulfilling its mission. The message to newcomers would be 'there's no room for you here.' It is possible that the church would be forced to purchase enough land elsewhere to continue serving its parish." That would have consequences for both the parish and the city. For the parish, it would mean a huge financial expense. But what would then become of the abandoned 1923 church? It would be far better to allow the parish "to continue serving its faithful where the tradition began," Fr. Cummins stressed, adding that "rather than allowing the building to fall into disuse, I think this plan will preserve its most appealing visual aspects for many years to come."

On April 11, Phillip Bell sent a memorandum to the mayor, council members, and city staff. He stressed that the HLC "did not deny a request to build a new church." Instead, their interest was preserving the existing church. Under "For your consideration," he made two additional notes. First, he attached a letter from the San Antonio Conservation Society to St. Peter's urging that some alternative plans be considered and offering the society's help in the matter. According to Bell's memo, Fr. Cummins had rejected their help. This, said Bell, was "evidence that there are other alternatives . . . but [they] are constantly ignored by the church." Second, he attached the correspondence from the St. Joseph Foundation, discussed in the previous chapter, setting out the position that the church should adhere to the civil law of the jurisdiction.

The agenda for the council's April 12 meeting does not look out of the ordinary. There were 13 items to be discussed, most of which were akin to number three, "Consider awarding bid for purchase of Boerne Fire Department pumper." Number five, though, was "Consider request from St. Peters Catholic Church to appeal the decision of the Historic Landmark Commission concerning the construction/demolition permit for St. Peters Church."

The meeting was moved from city hall, where the council usually met, to the community center. Press estimates put the crowd at around 250.[12] When agenda item number five was called, Mayor Heath called for "civilized discourse." He also emphasized that there would be no discussion of "anyone's character, or . . . anyone's good intentions or bad intentions, anyone's letter to the editor, anyone's telephone conversation." The sole issue on the table was "whether or not the City Council will grant the request from St. Peter's Parish to reverse the decision of the Historic Landmark Commission." Fr. Cummins gave an overview of the church's position and urged that the council overturn the HLC decision. Weiss spoke next and outlined how the church had developed its plans for the building. He also noted that "numerous workshops had been held since that night [the HLC vote] with City Council members and City staff to discuss" various aspects of the plans. He next explained the modifications that had been made to the plans and said that while they would cost the parish an additional $25,000 to $30,000 the members would do it to meet the objections raised to the original design. Davis spoke next and provided more detail about the new rendition and how it preserved the historical integrity of the building. Several questions were asked by council members, but only Darrell Street made known his intention to vote in the church's favor. At one point he said, "I'd rather not be here tonight," a sentiment to which the other members signaled assent.[13] Following those exchanges, opponents were given an opportunity to voice their objections, most of which merely repeated what had been said so often before. At the end of the discussion, Don Gourley made a motion to uphold the HLC; the vote was 4–1. Heath indicated that he would have also voted to uphold the commission had he been called on to do so.

After holding consultations with the archbishop and their attorneys, parish leaders decided that their best course of action was to file a suit. On May 23, 1994, they did so in the San Antonio Division of the United States District Court. Because the property was technically owned by the archdiocese, the suit bore the title of *P. F. Flores, Archbishop of San Antonio v. The City of Boerne.*[14] The May 29 church bulletin contained the following "Note from our Pastor:"

> We don't believe the City of Boerne or any other governing body has the right to deny us use of our parish church building. We also feel renovations planned for St. Peter Church are in compliance with the city ordinance.
>
> On Monday, May 23, 1994, the Archdiocese of San Antonio filed a complaint against the City of Boerne, asking for a declaratory judgement [*sic*]. The complaint was filed in the United States District Court. Careful counsel and consideration was given to the action. The Pastoral Council weighed all the known facts and possible consequences. The Archdiocesan attorney and the Archdiocese offices were also involved in the decision. We have the full support of Archbishop Flores.[15]

Three substantive causes of action were listed. One involved allegations that the ordinance did not meet the requirements of the Texas statute empowering local governments to establish historic districts and that the 45-day window had expired before the HLC's action. For our purposes, these can be set aside. The first of the other two was that the ordinance was unconstitutional because it violated the free exercise clause, the freedom of speech clause, and the Fifth Amendment's taking clause (as well as the free exercise clause of the Texas constitution[16]) while the second invoked the Religious Freedom Restoration Act (RFRA). These complaints are worth detailing, for after the Supreme Court decision the church vowed to continue the suit on grounds other than RFRA. Explicitly, the first complaint said,

> (a) The Ordinance violates the First Amendment to the United States Constitution, as applied to the States by the Fourteenth Amendment, in that it prohibits the free exercise of religion.
>
> (1) The ordinance imposes strict control on the Church's ability to alter its exterior as necessary to accommodate the congregation.
> (2) The ordinance requires that the Church seek approval of a government body before it alters its exterior, whether or not the alteration is for religious purposes.
> (3) The inclusion of the Church in the Historic District reduces the value of the Church property by almost one-half.
>
> (b) The Ordinance violates the First Amendment to the United States Constitution, as applied to the States by the Fourteenth Amendment, in that it violates freedom of speech.[17]
>
> (c) The Ordinance violates the Fifth Amendment to the United States Constitution, as applied to the States by the Fourteenth Amendment,

in that it constitutes the taking of private property without just compensation.

The second, RFRA complaint, was more succinct: "The Ordinance violates Section 3 of the Religious Freedom Restoration Act of 1993 . . . in that it 'substantially burden(s) a person's exercise of religion.'"

The next day the complaint was delivered to city hall. Ron Bowman said the city was "disappointed" but not, Chris Turk would say later, surprised.[18] Representatives of the two sides continued to meet, but each side seemed to be becoming more entrenched. City officials, both elected and appointed, were being pressured by those who wanted no part of the church demolished. On the other hand, the church felt its need for adequate worship space was being entirely neglected in the affair, and in addition continued to feel aggrieved by the whole process of having to submit its plans to governmental authorities. On September 18 in an "Update from the Pastor," members of the parish were told of three offers the church had made, one of which was to sell the property to the city at "replacement cost," estimated at $1,829,000, and build a new church elsewhere. In the same message, Fr. Cummins announced that the church had made arrangements with the Rainbow Senior Citizens Center, near the church, to conduct its Masses there beginning early in the new year.

At the district court, the case was assigned to Judge Lucius Bunton. Appointed by President Jimmy Carter in 1979, he had taken senior status in 1992. His first step was to order a full day of formal mediation before a representative of the Judicial Arbitration-Mediation Service. This was scheduled to be held on October 28 in San Antonio. Should that fail, he said, the trial would commence on January 19 (later moved to February 13 and 14).

Turk reported on the status of the suit at the October 18 meeting of the HLC. Bell said again that he wished the whole matter could be settled out of court. At the same time, he urged the commissioners to make their views known to the elected officials. Important as a measure of how things were moving is that several members said that regardless of how much of the old church was facing destruction, they had serious concerns about the architectural design of the projected addition and its impact on the historic district.

Following Judge Bunton's orders, representatives of the two sides, including their lawyers and architects, met in San Antonio from 9 a.m. to 6 p.m. on October 28.[19] However, at the end of the day, both sides said they were no closer to an agreement than before but that they would nonetheless keep talking. For the church, Bob Weiss sounded slightly optimistic, saying that "we are encouraged by the fact that we can sit down and talk about it. It was a very good session and we will be getting together again." Ron Bowman, on the other hand, seemed to see it the other way: "It was a frustrating day, but we're still working at it. We will keep the lines of communication open, but there are no other steps involved short of going to the court house." Underlining Bowman's pessimism, the city council met in executive session on November 1 to discuss legal strategy with its attorneys.

At the HLC meeting on January 31, 1995, Bell asked Turk for an update on the suit. Turk indicated that there would be a pretrial hearing in Midland but that the trial itself would be held in San Antonio. One member inquired if there was "any consideration [being given] to incorporate the old church into the new one at all?" Turk said "not to the extent that we would like them to." He added at the end that he understood "there were some undertones concerning the separation of church and state."

Turk's comment was particularly apt, for while the city council voted in early February to continue negotiating with the archdiocese, Hollon and his colleague Lowell Denton, whom he had asked to join him in representing the city, had decided that their strategy would be to challenge the constitutionality of RFRA. A ruling in their favor would undercut what they felt was the church's strongest legal position. On March 15, Bunton agreed with the city and held that RFRA violated the Constitution.[20] (We will take up the logic of his opinion in the following chapter.) He then issued an interlocutory decree certifying this question to the Court of Appeals for the Fifth Circuit. An interlocutory decree holds the other issues raised at a trial in abeyance until a higher court can determine whether the lower court has ruled correctly or not on the given question. This meant that none of the other issues raised by the archdiocese would be considered by the court of appeals.

The *Star* quoted unnamed "church officials" as saying that Bunton's decision "does not end the lawsuit, it only defines the way in which it will be tried."[21] For his part, when asked whether a compromise was still possible, Heath replied, "I simply don't know. But I know we didn't bring the suit and we can't withdraw the suit."[22]

Meanwhile, St. Peter's prepared for its April 9 (which was Palm Sunday) move to the Rainbow Center. The bulletin of the Sunday before stressed how unsatisfactory but necessary this move was: "Moving to the gymnasium-like Rainbow Center to alleviate the overcrowding may seem a hardship to many, but we will work together to create a meaningful and satisfying worship service while we wait with prayerful hope for our own church building to accommodate our growing family at St. Peter's!" That same bulletin contained an update on the suit, discussing how important RFRA was for religious freedom in America but pointing to the fact that Bunton's decision and the interlocutory decree would delay the actual trial. It noted, "Until that time, the only possibility for the expansion project to proceed lies in the hands of the City Council of Boerne and a willingness on their part to compromise."[23] Equally stridently, Fr. Cummins told a local paper that the situation was "morally and grossly unjust" and that the church would have to continue to use the Rainbow Center "until the parish either wins the lawsuit it now has before the courts, or city officials agree to discuss a reasonable solution to the permit problem."[24]

At the same time, the church and its architects were working to find something they thought might fly with the city. They now proposed keeping 57 feet of the south wall and 50 feet of the north wall, approximately two-thirds of the old church. Going back any further would necessitate tearing down the parish hall. The parish hall (a nondescript building, everyone agreed) was not in the historic district. At one point, the city had suggested keeping 80 percent of the old church and removing this structure. This had been rejected by the church, however, mostly because of the additional cost involved but also in part because for a year or more they would have no space for the various parish committees to meet. In any event, as of April 2, "City Council representatives have not responded to this offer." The reason the city had not responded is that they had asked their architect, Stan Klein, to look over the new "two-thirds" plans in light of the six requirements of the ordinance. On April 7, he submitted his report to the HLC. Although he was somewhat ambivalent on some of the issues, he was clear on numbers five and six. Regarding the former, he said that "the design of the new church expansion is overbearing in scale, height and massing." As for the latter, he added, "The value of the Historic District as an area of unique interest and character will be affected by the expansion of the church due to the loss of a significant portion of the historic landmark." His conclusion reiterated these points: "Although the revised design is better than the earlier concept, I feel this revised design results in significant loss of historic material comprising external walls and floor plan. An acceptable addition to an historic building should not result in a radical change to the form and character of the historic building."

On the same day, the mayor and city council handed out a press release designed to counter what they regarded as a "propaganda offensive" on the part of the church (specifically the material in the April 2 bulletin saying it was up to the city alone to compromise). For both tone and substance, it is worth quoting in its entirety:

> The City Council of Boerne upholds the morality that has been the foundation of our nation from its beginning. That is, the morality of community life under the rule of law. We believe that the safeguard of our individual and institutional liberties is the willingness of everyone to abide by the laws duly arrived at by the elected representatives of the people.
>
> The question at issue under the lawsuit brought by the Archdiocese of San Antonio against the City of Boerne is whether or not St. Peter's Church should abide by the City's Historic Preservation Ordinance which many other individuals and business owners have complied with for the past three years.
>
> The decisions of the Historic Landmark Commission and the City Council certainly do not mean that the Church cannot build a new sanctuary to meet the needs of its growing congregation. What the city *has* said, however, is that the proposed plan for new construction, which calls for destruction of a large part of the existing 1923 structure, is not appropriate under the guidelines laid out explicitly in the Historic Preservation Ordinance.
>
> For many months the representatives of the City have met formally or informally with representatives of the Church. Each time the Church as presented a new "alternative," the City has reviewed it carefully. But every time, the alternative has been one which still calls for destruction of a large part of the existing 1923 sanctuary, while the parish hall behind the current sanctuary remains untouched.
>
> The City has continued to suggest that a new addition to the 1923 sanctuary, which saves at least 80% of the older building and does not "dwarf" it, would be more appropriate to the scale and character of the historic district. The City has also suggested that a free-standing structure, near the 1923 sanctuary and the parish hall, would also be appropriate. To this end, the City Council has agreed to close a portion of Kronkosky Street to accommodate such a structure.
>
> Since the church has continued for many months to propose essentially the same construction plans as first put forward, the City Council has reluctantly decided that any further conversations should be conducted through the attorneys representing both parties. This is a common practice during litigation. The Church has not withdrawn its lawsuit, so the litigation continues.
>
> In all its actions, the City Council is continually striving to enact ordinances, build streets and public facilities, and sponsor events which will sustain a sense of civic pride and promote the welfare of all our citizens. In a community of mutual respect, tolerance, and cooperation, all of us can live and work and worship freely!

From both the comments in St. Peter's bulletin that the only thing blocking a compromise was the attitude of the city and the invocation of morality by the city, it was clear that both sides were indeed digging in their heels.

St. Peter's went ahead and filed a new application for a building permit based on the two-thirds plan. The building inspector referred it to the HLC, and they set April 17 to take it up. The minutes of this meeting run to seven single-spaced pages. Phillip Bell began by noting that this was a new application and needed to be considered fairly in light of the ordinance. Bob Weiss spoke first, stressing they had met several times with city officials and felt they were making major concessions with this plan. He turned the floor over to Richard Mecke, who handed out sheets contrasting the old and new plans. Greg Davis joined him and together they went through the plan, pointing out not only how it moved the new addition back but also that it lowered the roof by another thirty inches. Also, the new roof would have a plaster finish rather than a rock finish. Several commissioners asked about the need for a tall addition at all, and Davis explained that the acoustics made this necessary. There was then a lengthy back-and-forth concerning the type and color of the rock. Next, there was talk about the sight line. (The drawing did look at the church in a way that minimized the view of the addition, but Davis contended, a point disputed by Bob Vollmer, that a six-foot person standing on Main Street would still see mostly the old church.) Then there was a debate about the problems involved in tying the new building to the old. Near the end of the discussion, Weiss asked if he could address the city's proposed 80/20 plan: "He said they did look at it. He thinks that is what resulted in what you see tonight. If they would have gone with the 80/20 plan, they looked at that plan very seriously, but again if they wanted to maintain the side of the structure, it would push them into the hall. So they had to come back to the next structural point in the existing building and that is the column on the south side. Obviously, that plan had a lot of merit and we think that what we are proposing is really the offshoot of that plan." Weiss was then asked if he would discuss the new plan in terms of each of the six criteria, and he did so. Further exchange of views on various architectural details followed.

After nearly an hour and a half of discussion, Carolyn Chipman-Evans moved that the request be denied, and it carried unanimously.

The HLC agreed to meet a week later to consider a formal resolution to present to the church regarding what steps it could take to meet the commission's objections. The minutes of this gathering also stretch to seven pages. The consensus seemed to move to two possibilities: build an entirely new church or bring forward a plan that incorporated all of the 1923 building. At one point, Bob Weiss asked if they followed option one whether the city would purchase the 1923 church. Bell said that the city's elected and legal personnel would have to decide that but that in his view "it would definitely be considered." In the end, the following wording was adopted:

> BE IT RESOLVED AND DETERMINED, that the HISTORIC LANDMARK COMMISSION makes the following determinations, findings, and recommendations in connection with and in support of its recent denial of the current application:
>
> 1. The proposed structure is overbearing in total mass, as related to or contrasted to the 1923 church structure, as presently proposed to be situated on the site, and as such is inconsistent and incompatible with the other structures in the District, and the adjacent structures in the District.
> 2. It is possible to reevaluate the design alternatives and preserve the 1923 church, while permitting the applicant to build a new facility of the size and character desired and proposed.
> 3. Alternatives that should be considered by the applicant to resolve these objections in any future application are:
>     a. Consideration of a stand alone new structure, on the same site, that would be independent of the 1923 church building.
>     b. Incorporation of the entire 1923 structure, and its sidewalls into the new building, while scaling down (vertically) or moving back the new addition. If the new structure is to be added onto and attached to the 1923 structure, it must be more historically compatible in terms of scale, height, and mass, and sympathetic to the other structure.

For the foregoing reasons, the application fails to meet the criteria set forth in the ordinance for approval.

Soon after this resolution's adoption, Henry Friesenhahn, the building fund chair who also spent a good bit of time taking care of the grounds at St. Peter's, wrote a letter to the *Star*. It sounded sarcastic, but it made a legitimate point: "Since we are often reminded St. Peter's belongs to the community, I always carry extra gardening tools in my pick-up in the event someone wishes to enjoy some of the gardening fun with me. No takers so far."[25]

Dub Smothers was a businessman in San Antonio where he and his family attended St. John Neumann's parish. During several of those years, Fr. Cummins had been the pastor there, and the two had worked together on a variety of projects. When Smothers retired, he moved to Boerne and naturally became active in St. Peter's. He was initially supportive of the building plan but became disenchanted when it became evident that more of the 1923 church was to be demolished than he thought necessary. In mid-1994 he moved closer to the dissidents and wrote a number of letters to people explaining his change of position. In the spring of 1995, he took two steps. First, he engaged an artist to make a drawing of what he called his "dream."[26] It was a new building separate from but compatible with the 1923 church. It would stand on the south side of the property (to the left of the church if facing it from Main Street). Second, he met with Dr. Joseph Doenges, the superintendent of the Boerne Public Schools, and urged that together perhaps they could get representatives from the two sides to meet and work on a compromise, hopefully centering around the 80/20 plan (since it was obvious the church was not going to adopt Smothers's "dream"). On July 25 the two of them met with Weiss and two days later with Heath and Bowman. Both sides seemed open to a meeting. On August 22 the city council voted to approve meetings between city and church representatives. A first meeting was held on September 1 and a second on October 4. Unfortunately, neither produced an agreement. The October 22 church bulletin roundly criticized the 80/20 proposal: "Yes, it is possible to set back the new proposed building an additional 15 feet to accomplish the 80/20 (retain 80%/demolish 20%) plan . . . [T]o do so means demolishing the Parish Hall . . . The 80/20 proposal, because we would need to replace the Hall space, would cost the parish *several hundred thousand dollars* in additional construction costs." Instead, it urged the city to accept "the parish proposal of retaining approximately 60% of the existing church," as a solution. It then added, "A solution would mean: construction could begin, the controversy between the city and the parish would be over, taxpayers would not be burdened with additional legal expense, and all of us could return to our primary business."[27] However, that was not to be, at least for now.

Meanwhile, the case was beginning to attract outside interest. In March 1995, the *Preservation Law Reporter* (a publication of the National Trust for Historic Preservation) ran an article on the dispute.[28] It analyzed Bunton's opinion and ended by noting that it was uncertain what effect this would have on historic preservation efforts, "since historic preservation laws generally do not impose 'substantial burdens' on the free exercise of religion."[29] This was, of course, not a view shared by everyone. In August, the *Houston Chronicle* ran an article on the background of the case and noted how both sides were gearing up for the battle at the court of appeals.[30]

CHAPTER 4

# SEPARATION OF POWERS AND FEDERALISM IN THE REHNQUIST COURT

CONGRESS'S DECISION TO REST ITS AUTHORITY TO enact the Religious Freedom Restoration Act (RFRA) on section 5 of the Fourteenth Amendment meant that when the courts took up the law the central constitutional question would turn away from free exercise and toward separation of powers (specifically the separation between Congress and the courts) and federalism. Consequently, when *City of Boerne v. Flores* entered the federal courts, and the city's attorneys decided to challenge the constitutionality of RFRA, it was the power of Congress to adopt the statute, not its substance, that moved to center stage. Whatever decision the Supreme Court made would, of course, have enormous implications for free exercise jurisprudence—whether or not henceforth the courts would have to apply the compelling interest test, giving the edge in free exercise cases to those wanting an exemption—but the legal arguments were now about separation of powers and federalism. Therefore, it is necessary to set the context for the case by pausing and briefly surveying where the Rehnquist Court's jurisprudence stood in these areas.

## SEPARATION OF POWERS AND THE PROBLEM OF CONSTITUTIONAL INTERPRETATION

The Constitution is both a political and legal document. In its essence, it lays out the structure of political institutions and their interrelationships, specifies how laws are to be made, and catalogs the rights of the citizenry. As with any document, of course, if it is to remain viable its provisions must be interpreted and applied to situations as they develop. Thus it is not, and never has been, subject to dispute whether or not the

Constitution must be interpreted. It is, rather, who shall do the interpreting? In the mid-1990s a rather surprising consensus had taken hold regarding this question: constitutional interpretation was the duty of the Supreme Court alone. Thus this framework formed the basis of judicial thinking when *City of Boerne v. Flores* came to court.

However, this position is by no means obvious from the document itself and certainly not from the broad sweep of American history. And it seems in hindsight that *Boerne* may have had a significant role to play in igniting this debate anew.

In contrast to the judicial supremacy model stands what is usually called the "constitutional dialogues" perspective. According to this model, associated most often these days with Louis Fisher, both the president and Congress, along with state courts and the people, have had and should have a role in constitutional interpretation: Fisher has said that

> The customary identification of the Supreme Court as the exclusive source of constitutional law is far too limiting. The Supreme Court is not the sole or even dominant agency in deciding constitutional questions. For members of Congress to shy away from these issues, claiming that the Court must make the ultimate determination, is tempting but irresponsible. Constitutional issues generally turn not so much on technical legal analysis of particular provisions but rather on a choice between competing sections that contain conflicting political and social values. The Court needs the conscientious guidance and participation of the legislative and executive branches. Equally important are the judgments of state courts and the general public.[1]

Mark Tushnet and Larry Kramer have picked up on this last sentence and argued for popular constitutionalism, defined as the American people themselves playing the primary role in constitutional interpretation.[2] Kramer is more than willing to have the citizenry at large take a direct role in the act of constitutional interpretation, while Tushnet emphasizes the role of political leaders, most specifically those serving in public office. Pointedly, then, on this view Congress and the president can lay as much claim to participate in constitutional interpretation as the Supreme Court. This is not, as many modern Americans might see it, either novel or aberrational.

Presidents Thomas Jefferson, Andrew Jackson, and Abraham Lincoln all advocated a multi-institutional approach to constitutional interpretation. Jefferson, for example, is famous for his departmental theory of constitutional interpretation: "Each of the three departments has equally the right to decide for itself what is its duty under the constitution, without regard to what the others may have decided for themselves under a similar question."[3] And if there is disagreement among the branches on a constitutional question? The first line of defense against deadlock or anarchy is ordinary bargaining and accommodation among the branches. If this fails, the recourse is to the people, which would put a premium on the role of Congress and the presidency.

President Jackson had occasion to consider this issue when a bill rechartering the national bank was sent to him in 1832. Strongly opposed to the bank, Jackson vetoed the bill. Because there was still a debate over whether or not the president should veto bills only on constitutional grounds or could invoke policy objections, Jackson mixed some of both in his veto message. The constitutional issue was considered settled by some of Jackson's contemporaries, since the Supreme Court had previously upheld the constitutionality of a national bank.[4] Jackson strongly disagreed:

> It is maintained by the advocates of the bank that its constitutionality in all its features ought to be considered as settled . . . by the decision of the Supreme Court. To this conclusion I cannot assent.
>
> If the opinion of the Supreme Court covered the whole ground of this act, it ought not to control the coordinate authorities of this Government. The Congress, the Executive, and the Court must each for itself be guided by its own opinion of the Constitution . . . The authority of the Supreme Court must not, therefore, be permitted to control the Congress or the Executive when acting in their legislative capacities, but to have only such influence as the force of their reasoning may deserve.[5]

The political crisis that triggered Lincoln's reflections on constitutional interpretation was much graver than that facing Jackson. The Supreme Court had held in the infamous case of *Dred Scott v. Sandford*[6] that Congress had no power to ban slavery in the territories. While he conceded that the decision of the court in that case was binding on the parties involved (that is that Dred Scott would have to remain a slave), Lincoln denied in his first inaugural address that it settled the issue: "the people will have ceased to be their own rulers [if] the policy of the government, upon vital questions affecting the whole people, is to be irrevocably fixed by decisions of the Supreme Court, the instant they are made, in ordinary litigation between parties in personal actions."[7]

What of the seminal case of *Marbury v. Madison*[8] containing Chief Justice John Marshall's famous statement that "it is emphatically the province and duty of the judicial department to say what the law is"? Kramer argues that this statement must be read in the context of its time period.

Although social contract language is often used to describe the drafting of the American Constitution, in reality the document was deeply rooted in and a product of English constitutional thought and practice. It was but the documentary codification of what Kramer calls the "customary constitution," a set of deep-seated assumptions and ideas about how government was to operate. Because the customary constitution had both political and legal dimensions, the courts, of necessity, had to be involved in its implementation when they decided individual cases: "Read in context, this sentence did not say what, to modern eyes, it seems to say when read in isolation. That is, it did not say 'it is the job of courts, alone, to say what the Constitution means.' Nor did it say 'it is the job of courts, more so than others, to say what the Constitution means.' What it said was 'courts, too, can say what the Constitution means.'"[9]

Nevertheless, by the 1830s advocates of judicial supremacy began making their case. This seems connected, first, to the attempts of the Federalist elites to hold on to some vestige of power through their dominance of the courts and, second, to the growing professionalization of the legal profession. We witness in these years, for instance, more discussion about *constitutional law* rather than *constitutionalism*. The Constitution, that is, was taking on an increasingly legal character. Nevertheless, these ideas did not immediately win universal acceptance but had to contest with the older framework, as can be seen most clearly in Jackson's and Lincoln's assertions. In time, especially after the Civil War, for a variety of reasons the power of the Supreme Court grew. Accretions to its power, despite temporary reverses, continued throughout the three decades following the war, and by the 1890s the court was invalidating federal laws much more often. (Review of state laws, in contrast, had been important from the beginning, and remained so.) When a rigidly conservative court, using a number of dubious constitutional doctrines, struck down an array of Progressive social and economic legislation in the late nineteenth and early twentieth centuries, pitched political battles over the role of the court ensued.[10] In a sense, from a constitutional perspective, the struggle between the New Deal and the court was but the final chapter of the conflict between Progressivism and an activist conservative court.

We need not replay President Franklin D. Roosevelt's confrontation with the Supreme Court.[11] For our purposes, it is only necessary to point out that when the dust had settled from the New Deal, the Supreme Court had enunciated two important maxims. The first was that when it came to social and economic legislation, Congress (and the states) would be given a wide berth. (A corollary was that the president's conduct of foreign affairs would also seldom be questioned.) The other was that the court would fine-tune the microscope more when examining legislation that might impinge on individual rights.

The first maxim can be seen in cases such as *Wickard v. Filburn.*[12] It allowed stand a congressional policy prohibiting a farmer from growing wheat to feed his own livestock. According to the court, the regulation fell within Congress's power to regulate commerce, since when aggregated such activity by other farmers would substantially affect the price of grain, which Congress wanted to keep high. Before, the court had utilized a number of categories, such as "production" and "consumption," as well as whether the regulation in question had a "direct" or "indirect" effect on interstate commerce (and therefore whether it lay within the federal or state domain) to determine whether a commercial regulation was constitutional or not. Here, the court simply swept all these categories aside, saying that they were "not material for purposes of deciding the question of federal power before us." "Congress," the justices unanimously remarked, "may properly have considered that wheat consumed on the farm where grown if wholly outside the scheme of regulation would have a substantial effect in defeating and obstructing its purpose to stimulate trade therein at increased prices." And, they added, "with the wisdom, workability, or fairness of the plan of regulation we have nothing to do."

The second had its origins in the famous footnote four in the 1938 case of *United States v. Carolene Products Co.*[13] The company was challenging the constitutionality of the Filled Milk Act, a statute that regulated the sale of various types of milk. Previewing *Wickard v. Filburn*, the Supreme Court held that economic regulatory statutes need only meet a rational basis test. In what has been called the most famous footnote in constitutional law, though, Justice Harlan Fiske Stone set forth the idea that an enhanced level of scrutiny might well apply when matters of individual rights were involved:

> There may be narrower scope for operation of the presumption of constitutionality when legislation appears on its face to be within a specific prohibition of the Constitution, such as those of the first ten amendments, which are deemed equally specific when held to be embraced within the Fourteenth.
>
> It is unnecessary to consider now whether legislation which restricts those political processes which can ordinarily be expected to bring about the repeal of undesirable legislation is to be subjected to more exacting judicial scrutiny under the general prohibitions of the Fourteenth Amendment than are most other types of legislation.
>
> Nor need we enquire whether similar considerations enter into the review of statutes directed at particular religious, or national, or racial

> minorities; whether prejudice against discrete and insular minorities may be a special condition, which tends seriously to curtail the operation of those political processes ordinarily relied upon to protect minorities, and which may call for a correspondingly more searching judicial inquiry.[14] [Citations omitted.]

This enhanced scrutiny of incursions on individual rights did not matter much for several years. But then the Warren Court began to carry it into practice, most poignantly of course in *Brown v. Board of Education.*[15] That decision sparked deep, and in places violent, resistance in much of the South, resistance that was often accompanied by a good deal of constitutional posturing. An early flashpoint was Little Rock, Arkansas, where the local school board had begun steps to desegregate its schools but was overruled by Governor Orval Faubus. Given the threatened chaos in the city, the school board asked for more time to carry out its desegregation plan. This generated the case of *Cooper v. Aaron*[16] in 1958. Frustrated with Southern reaction to *Brown*, the court unanimously denied the board's request and then underscored the need for state officials to comply with desegregation orders. In so doing, they stated, for the first time explicitly, that they were the exclusive and legitimate interpreters of the Constitution. Quoting the sentence already cited from *Marbury v. Madison*, they said, "This decision declared the basic principle that the federal judiciary is supreme in the exposition of the law of the Constitution, and that principle has ever since been respected by this Court and the Country as a permanent and indispensable feature of our constitutional system."

As Kramer says, "this was, of course, just bluster and puff. As we have seen, *Marbury* said no such thing, and judicial supremacy was not cheerfully embraced in the years after *Marbury* was decided."[17] Nevertheless, despite some grumbling about this claim at the time, somewhat surprisingly, within a short period it gained nearly universal assent.

In part, this was because a national consensus was forming in favor of civil rights, and the Supreme Court was being applauded for taking the lead in that area. Being opposed to Southern segregationists seemed synonymous with siding with the court; conversely, opposing the court put one in league with some very unpleasant company. Importantly, too, the liberal intellectual consensus favored the work of the Warren Court, and most of that of the Burger Court, and went to some lengths to justify it.[18] To be sure, specific decisions engendered opposition. But the opposition now turned to trying to secure control of the court via the appointment process rather than arguing that the court was not after all the exclusive interpreter of the Constitution.

In 1986, for example, Ronald Reagan's Attorney General Edwin Meese made a speech in which he sounded a Lincolnesque theme. Decisions by the Supreme Court, he said, "do not establish a 'Supreme Law of the Land' that is binding on all persons and parts of government, henceforth and forevermore."[19] Meese faced a firestorm of criticism and soon backed down. A few years later, Democratic Senator Patrick Leahy of Vermont, who has taken strong exception to a number of decisions taken by the contemporary court, felt compelled nonetheless to fall in line with the current orthodoxy: "As a member of the bar of the Court, as a U.S. Senator, as an American, I, of course, respect the decisions of the Supreme Court as . . . the ultimate interpretation of our Constitution, whether I agree or disagree."[20]

Thus during the years of the Rehnquist Court a broad consensus reigned across the political spectrum and among the country's legal elite that the Supreme Court had no challengers when it came to constitutional interpretation. It was a role, too, in which the justices seemed to bask. Yet for the Rehnquist Court that was not all there was to the story.

While the second prong of the New Deal court's constitutional settlement continued to enjoy hardy endorsement, although the individuals upon whom special attention was lavished might have changed, the first prong began to lose its power. Prominent conservatives developed an argument that the court should be more energetic in setting limits on federal power,[21] and in time this attitude showed up in the newer justices. The activism that accompanied the court's solicitude for individual rights was now matched by an activism connected to "restoring" the constitutional restrictions on federal power. Here is Larry Kramer again, writing in 2004:

> The consequence has been a substantial change in Supreme Court practice, as the Rehnquist Court has carried the theory of judicial power developed by its predecessors to its logical conclusion. Treating claims of interpretive authority by nonjudicial officials as erroneous and illogical, the Court has moved to resolve the disjunction between theory and practice by changing the practice. Hence, while reaffirming its supremacy in the domain of individual rights, the present Court has gone beyond the activism of the Warren and Burger Courts by simultaneously discarding or construing the doctrines and principles that served after 1937 to limit the Court's authority in other areas.[22]

In short, when *Boerne* came to the court, the justices had grown accustomed to deference from all political actors and all segments of the American public when it came to interpreting the Constitution. Any other position was seen as heretical. Furthermore, they now considered this writ to cover the entire Constitution. They and they alone, according to their view, were empowered to referee the boundaries of institutional power, including their own, as well as deliberate about the reach of individual rights.

## FEDERALISM

Federalism is a central part of the American constitutional structure, dividing political power between a national government and the states. However, no separate part of the Constitution is devoted to federalism; instead it is written into the document at any number of places. Two facts stand out about the nature of this design. First, federalism was adopted because there was no other practical choice. The states existed and no one thought they would be abolished. The vexing questions were how the new national government would be structured and how it would relate to the states. Second, at the time there simply was no theory of federalism to which the Founding Fathers could refer.[23] Scattered historical examples of multilayered government existed, to be sure, and they had some general experiences to draw on (such as the relation each colony had enjoyed with London and the unhappy life they had had under the Articles of Confederation), but nothing even resembling an overarching theory existed. Consequently, what resulted was a series of untidy patchwork elements, often dictated by necessary political compromises. Edward Purcell observes that "the Constitution neither gave the federal structure any single proper shape as an operating system of government nor mandated any particular and timeless balance among its components."[24] Of necessity, therefore, the operation of the system has had to develop from experience.

When it comes to how best to maintain federalism as a central part of constitutional practice in the United States, constitutional theorists have offered two contrasting models. On the one hand, there have always been those who have contended that the Supreme Court must assume the role of policing the division of powers between the two levels. Inevitably, the two levels of government will challenge each other's authority, and some entity must act as an umpire if chaos is not to ensue. One central prop for this argument comes from a wide-ranging discussion at the time of the founding: how can the states be kept from undermining the union itself? Jettisoning a proposal to give Congress a veto over state laws, the second paragraph of Article VI, the supremacy clause, was inserted: "This Constitution, and the Laws of the United States which shall be made in Pursuance thereof; and all Treaties made, or which shall be made, under the Authority of the United States, shall be the supreme Law of the Land;

and the Judges in every State shall be bound thereby, any Thing in the Constitution or Laws of any State to the Contrary notwithstanding." As the highest court in the land, from which appeals from state supreme courts may be had, the Supreme Court clearly has the power under this provision to overturn state laws that overstep a state's authority. Thus if the Supreme Court is to control the states whenever they run afoul of federal prerogatives, it would seem only logical that it should also see that the federal government adheres to its own designated sphere.[25] Buttressing this stance, as noted in the previous section, as the Constitution has come to be seen more and more as a legal document, it is natural to turn to the court to determine its reading.

The alternative view is that the political safeguards built into the Constitution are quite enough to contain federal power.[26] The first point to be made here is popular sovereignty. That is, the American people as a whole have allocated certain powers to the state governments and certain powers to the national government. Within the broad limits set forth in the Constitution, therefore, they should be free to utilize whatever level of government they wish for the addressing of public concerns. Since state governments, as representatives of the political communities that compose the various states, are held in high esteem by the people, the people will not allow the states to be swallowed by the national government.[27] Second, the states are themselves represented in the national legislature. Originally, of course, the Senate represented state governments directly. Even with the adoption of the Seventeenth Amendment and direct election of senators, the political communities that make up the states have direct representation in the upper chamber.[28] Going further, the legislatures of the states are charged with the responsibility of drawing the district lines for members of the House of Representatives. Thus state governments wield enormous influence over who sits in the House. Too, as a practical matter state and local governments are very effective lobbyists in Washington. Justice Harry Blackmun once pointed to their success in securing federal funds and exempting themselves from many federal regulations as proof of this proposition.[29] Third, states heavily influence the selection of the president. To begin, state legislatures determine how electors are to be chosen. Although these officers are now elected in every state, how they are elected is at the behest of the legislature. For example, some states have experimented with electing them by congressional district (with two chosen statewide). Or, if a state so chose it could alter the winner-take-all rule. Perhaps more important, early in the process states choose the dates for their presidential primaries, clearly helping favor some candidates over others. Taken together, in sum, all these factors ensure that Congress simply will not enact a law that treads too heavily on state power.

After the Civil War, the Supreme Court embraced the first of these frameworks, and for its interpretive task developed the doctrine of dual federalism. According to this theory, the Constitution creates two sovereignties, and each one is supreme within its domain. To the extent possible, each should be hermetically sealed off against the other. Moreover, within each one's province, certain restrictions apply, restrictions that constitutionally limit what policies can be pursued by each. Between roughly the last decade of the nineteenth century and the first three and a half decades of the twentieth, dual federalism was married to legal theories closely bound to classical economics. The result was that the federal government was hemmed in by a highly restricted view of the commerce clause (drawing a sharp distinction, for example, between "commerce" and "production") and the states by a sweeping property-based reading (giving, that is, a high priority to "economic liberty") of the due process clause of the Fourteenth Amendment.

The New Deal court abolished dual federalism and simultaneously, in effect if not in overt doctrine, moved toward the political safeguards approach to federalism. The landmark case was *United States v. Darby Lumber Co.* in 1941,[30] which upheld federal minimum wage and maximum hours legislation (the Fair Labor Standards Act of 1938). The act's enforcement mechanism was to ban the shipment in interstate commerce of any goods manufactured in violation of the regulations set forth in the law. Darby Lumber Company challenged the statute's constitutionality on two main grounds. The first was that the law exceeded Congress's power under the commerce clause, that the motive here was to regulate production (something denied to the federal government by previous cases) not commerce. In response, the court explicitly abolished the "production" and "commerce" distinction,[31] granting Congress wide latitude under the commerce clause to draft whatever regulations it saw fit: "Whatever their motive and purpose, regulations of commerce which do not infringe some constitutional prohibition are within the plenary power conferred on Congress by the Commerce Clause." In time, this refusal to look into motives would allow Congress to use the commerce clause to enact laws covering a wide variety of activities.[32] The second argument was that the law violated the Tenth Amendment, which provides that "the powers not delegated to the United States by the Constitution, nor prohibited by it to the States, are reserved to the States respectively, or to the people." The court pushed this argument aside and in effect virtually gutted the amendment: "The amendment states but a truism that all is retained which has not been surrendered. There is nothing in the history of its adoption to suggest that it was more than declaratory of the relationship between the national and state governments as it had been established by the Constitution before the amendment or that its purpose was other than to allay fears that the new national government might seek to exercise powers not granted, and that the states might not be able to exercise fully their reserved powers."

In the ensuing years, the ever-increasing growth of a national economy and the involvement of the country in first World War II then the Cold War strengthened the role of the national government. In the meantime, the turmoil over civil rights delegitimized arguments for state power. The fact that Southern partisans tried to hide behind a smoke screen of "states' rights" made it hard for any respectable constitutional theorist to advocate a reinvigorated federalism. Robert Schapiro concludes that "the concept of federalism, with its redolence of arguments for states' rights, became tarred for a generation by its association with racism."[33] Who wanted to put on the same uniform as George Wallace?[34]

Thus to most of the legal and political intelligentsia of the period federalism seemed both outmoded and toxic. However, William Rehnquist was never convinced of either. To him, federalism was a hallmark of the American constitution and in need of vigorous reassertion. Having served as a law clerk to Justice Robert Jackson, a lawyer and Republican Party activist in Arizona, and then a staff attorney in Richard Nixon's Justice Department, he got a chance to shape constitutional jurisprudence when the president named him to the Supreme Court in 1971.

Very shortly, Rehnquist began staking out his position on federalism, beginning with a thorough and carefully argued dissent in *Fry v. United States* in 1975.[35] At issue was the Economic Stabilization Act of 1970, which controlled wages throughout the economy, including those of people working for state and local governments. The court's majority upheld the act as a valid exercise of the commerce power. Rehnquist contended that even if the commerce power basis of the act was granted, the Tenth Amendment standing alone and the original understanding of federalism illustrated by the Tenth and Eleventh Amendments insulated traditional state governmental functions from federal regulation of this type. It was not until some years later, though, after he became chief justice in 1986 and was joined by several Reagan appointees, that he was able to win over a majority of his colleagues. When he did so, the result was what Erwin Cherminsky has called a "federalism revolution."[36] By 1997, when *City of Boerne v. Flores* reached the court, the revolution was in full swing.[37]

Before *Boerne*, four areas of constitutional law made up this revolution: the commerce clause, the Tenth Amendment, the Eleventh Amendment, and the "clear statement" rule.

After the court's decision in *Wickard*, there were no real constitutional limits on Congress's use of the commerce clause. This can be seen especially in *Heart of Atlanta Motel v. United States*, which upheld the Civil Rights Act of 1964's ban on discrimination against interstate African American travelers in restaurants and hotels.[38] Then in 1995, in *United States v. Lopez*,[39] the court caught many analysts by surprise when it unexpectedly invalidated a congressional statute that was based on the commerce power. In 1990, Congress had enacted the Gun-Free School Zones Act, which barred the possession of a firearm within one thousand feet of a school. Congress paid little mind to justifying the act, merely routinely citing the commerce clause. Writing for a five-person majority, Rehnquist began with the broadest of strokes: "We start with first principles. The Constitution creates a Federal Government of enumerated powers." After reviewing the history of commerce clause holdings, he laid out a list of acceptable categories for congressional regulation. Then he declared that this law fitted none of them and was in fact merely a criminal statute masquerading as a commercial regulation. When brought into court, the government had contended that people possessing guns near schools contributes to violent crime and that that has a substantial effect on interstate commerce. Rehnquist brushed that argument aside, however, countering that accepting that postulate would transform "congressional authority under the Commerce Clause [into] a general police power of the sort retained by the States." The effect would be to demolish "the distinction between what is truly national and what is truly local." It was the first time since the New Deal court had broadened the meaning of the commerce clause that a federal law had been struck down for exceeding its bounds.

The Tenth Amendment found its rejuvenation in 1992 in *New York v. United States*.[40] The law at issue here was the Low-Level Radioactive Waste Policy Amendments Act of 1985. Through a complex set of rules, it required states to take title to certain radioactive wastes generated within their borders if other mechanisms failed to lead to proper disposal of the material. Justice O'Connor wrote the opinion for a 6–3 majority. She vacillated a bit about whether Congress had power under the commerce clause to adopt the act. But more to the point, in line with the now chief's dissent in *Fry*, she said that the question is whether the Tenth Amendment posed a barrier to the federal government basically conscripting a state government to implement a federal policy. It does, she held, and therefore the federal government may not "commandeer" a state to carry out one of its own policies. In effect, it overturned *Darby's* "truism" interpretation of the Tenth Amendment.

The Eleventh Amendment was adopted in 1795 in response to the Supreme Court case of *Chilsolm v. Georgia*, which had allowed a suit in federal court against Georgia brought by a citizen of another state.[41] It reads, "The Judicial power of the United States shall not be construed to extend to any suit in law or equity, commenced or prosecuted against one of the United States by Citizens of another State, or by Citizens or Subjects of any Foreign State." At issue in *Seminole Tribe of Florida v. Florida*,[42] brought to the court in 1996, was a provision of the Indian Gaming Regulatory Act of 1988. The law commanded that Native American tribes and states negotiate "in good faith" to establish regulations regarding casinos on reservations.[43] If the negotiations could not be concluded satisfactorily, the tribes were given authority to bring a suit in federal court. Accordingly, when discussions broke down between the Seminole Tribe and Florida officials, the tribe brought a suit. The state urged, however, that the suit was prohibited by the Eleventh Amendment.

Reading beyond the text, Rehnquist, writing for five justices, held first that the amendment stands for a "presupposition" composed of two parts: "first, that each State is a sovereign entity in our federal system; and second that 'it is inherent in the nature of sovereignty not to be amenable to the suit of an individual without its consent.'"[44] Only two provisions might give Congress the power to abrogate the enhanced immunity Rehnquist found in the Eleventh Amendment: section 5 of the Fourteenth Amendment and the commerce clause. The act under review did not invoke section 5; thus, it could be put to one side and only the commerce clause considered. A 1989 case[45] had held that Congress indeed had power under the commerce clause to abrogate state immunity from suits. However, the court now overruled that case and denied that the commerce clause granted such authority.

The clear statement rule does not ordinarily result in the invalidation of a federal statute; instead, it limits its reach. This came about early on during the federalism revolution in the 1991 case of *Gregory v. Ashcroft*.[46] Congress had made discrimination on the basis of age (people over forty) in employment illegal in the Age Discrimination in Employment Act (ADEA) of 1967. The court had held in 1985 in *Garcia v. San Antonio Metropolitan Transit Authority*[47] that the federal government could regulate the terms of employment offered by state governments, even when those employees worked in core areas of state government. In the ADEA, though, there was no clear statement about how far its provisions would reach when it came to state employees; in fact, there was an exception granted to "policy making" positions in the states. A clause in the Missouri constitution mandated that judges retire at age seventy, a fact that led a group of them to complain that this requirement violated the ADEA.

In line with what Rehnquist was to say in *Seminole*, Justice O'Connor here granted that section 5 might be a broader source of authority to extend the ADEA to state employees of whatever type.[48] However, Congress had not rested its power to enact the ADEA on section 5 but had instead relied on the commerce clause. Without a clear statement that the law was to reach employees such as judges (it was ambiguous, she said, whether they were "policy makers"), protecting the representative character of state government must trump the extension of the law. The rule therefore would be that if Congress wants to regulate some state activity it must declare that intention in an unambiguous fashion. The reason this demand limits federal power is that, given the practicalities of legislative politics, inserting such sweeping stipulations into legislation is often difficult. Thus, if the courts take it as an automatic rule of construction that the absence of a clear statement will impede the reach of federal acts, federal power will often be circumscribed.

Taken together, these cases signified a marked and substantial shift in the federalism jurisprudence of the Supreme Court in the 1990s. If Cherminsky's designating this a "revolution" seems to be overstating the matter a bit, it is not by much. In fact, buttressing his claim, many of these decisional lines would be extended further after 1997.[49] However, for our purposes the important point is that the Rehnquist Court's federalism revolution was in full swing when *City of Boerne v. Flores* was placed on the docket in the fall of 1996.

## CONCLUSION

The court's theory of separation of powers—granting itself the exclusive role in constitutional interpretation—and a renewed emphasis on federalism dovetail nicely. Both put the court at the center of constitutional politics and denigrate the role of Congress and the president. On the one hand, the elected branches are denied any role in divining the meaning of the Constitution; on the other, the range of public policies they may pursue and how they may pursue them are sharply limited. And it was this combined view, the court as constitutional oracle and a rigid judicial federalism, that prevailed when arguments began over the constitutionality of RFRA.

CHAPTER 5

# THE FEDERAL DISTRICT COURT AND THE COURT OF APPEALS

WHEN MARCI HAMILTON, WHO HAD BEEN ENGAGED to represent the city, rose for her oral argument at the Supreme Court, she began by saying, "This case is not about religious liberty. This case is about Federal power."[1] She was right, of course, and it had been so since the city had challenged the constitutionality of the Religious Freedom Restoration Act (RFRA) before Judge Bunton and he had set aside all other issues. To be sure, religious liberty issues occasionally surfaced in the arguments of opposing counsel, but only in the context of whether Congress had adduced enough evidence to justify a remedial statute based on section 5. It was, simply put, separation of powers and federalism that were now determinative.

RFRA's constitutionality had actually surfaced in a case arising in Hawaii before Bunton made his ruling.[2] The district court there had upheld the measure, and its thinking will be summarized in what follows. As required by statute, Bunton notified the Department of Justice (DOJ) that the constitutionality of a federal statute had been challenged.[3] The DOJ immediately intervened to support the archdiocese. Then when Bunton ruled that the measure was unconstitutional, it attracted national attention. Concerned interest groups hurried to New Orleans (where the Court of Appeals for the Fifth Circuit sits) to file amicus curiae briefs, largely again on the side of the archdiocese. Because of the importance of the case, it was given an expedited route of appeal from the district court to the court of appeals. On January 23, 1996, a three-judge panel of the Fifth Circuit—Justices Patrick E. Higginbotham, Emilio M. Garza, and Fortunado P. Benavides—ruled that RFRA was constitutional. A request by the city to have the case heard en banc was denied, setting up an appeal to the Supreme Court.

Before embarking on an analysis of how the Hawaii District Court, Judge Bunton, and the Federal Court of Appeals formulated their decisions, it will be helpful to lay out the framework of the act, review several of the precedents that were deemed to be especially relevant, and enter a note on what is called the "one way ratchet" theory.

## THE FRAMEWORK OF THE ACT

Congress began by making five "findings:"[4]

1) The framers of the Constitution, recognizing free exercise of religion as an unalienable right, secured its protection in the First Amendment to the Constitution;
2) Laws "neutral" toward religion may burden religious exercise as surely as laws intended to interfere with religious exercise;
3) Governments should not substantially burden religious exercise without compelling justification;
4) In *Employment Division v. Smith*, the Supreme Court virtually eliminated the requirement that the government justify burdens on religious exercise imposed by laws neutral toward religion; and
5) The compelling interest test as set forth in prior federal court rulings is a workable test for striking sensible balances between religious liberty and competing prior governmental interests.

The purpose of the act was simple: "to restore the compelling interest test . . . and to guarantee its application in all cases where free exercise of religion is substantially burdened." Then came the core of the act: "Government shall not substantially burden a person's exercise of religion even if the burden results from a rule of general applicability," unless "it demonstrates that application of the burden to the person" meets the strict scrutiny test. "Government" was defined to include all governments within the United States.

Of special note is that there was a threshold of "substantial" burden on religious exercise. This was, of course, a term that would have to be defined by the courts in individual cases. Noteworthy also is the fact that even though Congress referred to the "compelling interest test," it had included the need for government to have employed the "least restrictive means" to reach that interest. It is somewhat unclear, as the compelling interest test developed after *Sherbert v. Verner*, whether it contained a least restrictive means component or not. In other contexts (such as freedom of expression and equal protection cases), the court had made clear when strict scrutiny was used that it required both a compelling governmental interest and the use of the least restrictive means. Now Congress was folding compelling interest into strict scrutiny in all free exercise cases (where, again, the substantial burden threshold was breached).

Finally, a section was added mandating that nothing in the act could be read to interfere with the establishment clause.

## PRECEDENTS

One older case that had an indirect but nonetheless relevant bearing on RFRA was *United States v. Klein*.[5] During the Civil War, Congress had authorized the seizing of property held by Southerners who had aided the Confederacy. Upon the granting of a presidential pardon and the taking of (and abiding by) an oath of loyalty, these persons could file a claim to receive the proceeds from the sale of their property. In 1869 the Court of Claims ruled that Klein, representing a deceased former sympathizer's estate, was entitled to moneys from the sale of some seized cotton. The following year Congress passed a law saying that the acceptance of a pardon was evidence of active involvement in the Confederate cause and that this made these people ineligible to receive such proceeds. Accordingly, the treasury blocked Klein's payments. In the ensuing case, the Supreme Court ruled that Congress had violated the separation of powers by attempting to impose a rule of decision on the judiciary in a particular case and that the 1870 act was therefore unconstitutional.

Two cases from 1879 provide something of a mixed bag regarding this case. In 1875 Congress enacted a law, pursuant to both section 2 of the Thirteenth and section 5 of the Fourteenth Amendment, that attempted to make criminal trials in the Southern states conform to standards of due process. One provision forbade states from excluding people from jury service "on account of race, color, or previous condition of servitude" and another allowed the transfer of certain cases from state to federal courts. *Strauder v. West Virginia* and *Ex Parte Virginia* involved challenges to the constitutionality of this law.[6]

*Strauder* involved an appeal by an African American man convicted of murder. West Virginia law prohibited blacks from serving on juries. Further, his request to have his case heard in federal court was denied by the West Virginia Supreme Court. The US Supreme Court held, first, that West Virginia's statute was a violation of the Fourteenth Amendment and therefore unconstitutional. However, in doing so it penned a lengthy discussion regarding the fact that, in its view, the amendment was designed only to protect African Americans. The door was left slightly ajar for the possible inclusion of others' rights, but the tenor of the decision was to restrict the rights it guaranteed to the newly freed slaves. However, when it came to discuss the power of Congress to enact the provision removing certain trials to federal court, the justices (a 7–2 majority) spoke in more expansive terms: "There is express authority to protect the rights and immunities referred to in the Fourteenth Amendment, and to enforce observance of them by appropriate congressional legislation." And a bit further on, "The act put in the form of a statute what has been substantially ordained by the constitutional amendment. It was a step towards enforcing the constitutional provisions. [It] was an advanced step, fully warranted, we think, by the fifth section of the Fourteenth Amendment."

In *Ex Parte Virginia* a state trial judge had refused to seat black jurors and was arrested and held in custody for violating the 1875 law. He, and the state, petitioned for *habeas corpus* on several grounds, one of which was that Congress had acted beyond its section 5 powers. The court, however, upheld congressional authority. After stating that the purpose of the Thirteenth and Fourteenth Amendments was to "raise the colored race from that condition of inferiority and servitude in which most of them had previously stood into perfect equality of civil rights with all other persons within the jurisdiction of the States," it turned to the structural question. Both these amendments "were intended to be what they really are—limitations of the power of the States and enlargements of the power of Congress." As for the enforcement provisions specifically, it said this:

> It is not said the *judicial power* of the general government shall extend to enforcing the prohibitions and to protecting the rights and immunities guaranteed. It is not said that branch of the government shall be authorized to declare void any action of a State in violation of the prohibitions. It is the power of Congress which has been enlarged, Congress is authorized to *enforce* the prohibitions by appropriate legislation. Some legislation is contemplated to make the amendments fully effective. Whatever legislation is appropriate—that is, adapted to carry out the objects the amendments have in view . . . is brought within the domain of congressional power.

Thus these two cases seem to stand for the proposition that Congress's power is broad but that its field is restricted. It has sweeping enforcement powers to secure the civil rights of African Americans but seemingly little else. Thus they offered both comfort and difficulties for both sides.

A group of cases known collectively as the *Civil Rights Cases* of 1883[7] involved another section of the same 1875 act. This portion of the act had required "that all persons within the jurisdiction of the United States shall be entitled to the full and equal enjoyment of the accommodations, advantages, facilities, and privileges of inns, public conveyances on land or water, theatres, and other places of public amusement, subject only to the conditions and limitations established by law and applicable alike to citizens of every race and color, regardless of any previous condition of servitude."

The court struck down this provision as unconstitutional. The problem, as the court saw it, was that this part of the law struck at private action, not something done by a state or its officials. The Fourteenth Amendment only referred to action by states, not individuals.[8] The rights guaranteed by the amendment "are secured by way of prohibition against State laws and State proceedings" that deny those rights. Congress could not reach, therefore, into the realm of private action unsanctioned by state law. However, the wording of the decision went even further. It speaks of Congress's power to "correct" state legislation. It seems to say that Congress must wait for a state to violate the substantive provisions of the amendment before it can act under section 5. Thus it cannot pass preemptive legislation, only that which is remedial. Thus, while the direct holding of the *Civil Rights Cases* would seem to offer little that was directly pertinent to *Boerne*, in that RFRA was aimed at state action only, the way the court elaborated its holding would, if followed, mean a rather restricted reading of section 5 power in all instances.

Far and away the most important precedent was *Katzenbach v. Morgan*.[9] To understand that case, though, it is necessary to go back, first, to 1959 and the case of *Lassiter v. Northampton Election Board*.[10] North Carolina required that all persons registering to vote demonstrate that they could "read and write any section of the Constitution of North Carolina in the English language." Although many Southern states had used literacy requirements to disenfranchise African Americans, there was no evidence that this had happened here. Instead, this case presented a facial challenge under the equal protection clause of the Fourteenth Amendment. The court acknowledged the unsavory (and unconstitutional because discriminatory) use of literacy tests in some states but noted that notwithstanding such abuse the ability to read and write English might well be considered a reasonable qualification to the exercise of the franchise. Thus, if uniformly administered, literacy tests were constitutional.

Then, second, a brief explanation of *South Carolina v. Katzenbach*[11] from 1966 will solidify the background for *Morgan*. The Voting Rights Act of 1965 (VRA) swept away many of the barriers Southern states had habitually used to bar African Americans from registering to vote. Authority for the statute rested mainly on section 2 of the Fifteenth Amendment, which, recall, is almost identical to section 5 of the Fourteenth. South Carolina argued that the power of Congress was confined to remedying defects in voting rights on a case-by-case basis, not prophylactically. The Supreme Court threw out this contention, noting that Congress had compiled "voluminous" evidence regarding the denial of the right to vote in certain states. In the process, it gave a very broad reading to section 2 of the Fifteenth Amendment and also, by implication at least, to section 5 of the Fourteenth Amendment. According to the court,

> The basic test to be applied in a case involving section 2 of the Fifteenth Amendment is the same as in all cases covering the express powers of Congress with relation to the reserved powers of the States. Chief Justice Marshall laid down the classic formulation, 50 years before the Fifteenth Amendment was ratified: "Let the end be legitimate, let it be within the scope of the constitution, and all means which are appropriate, which are plainly adapted to that end which are not prohibited, but consist with the letter and spirit of the constitution, are constitutional."
>
> The Court has subsequently echoed his language in describing each of the Civil War Amendments "Whatever legislation is appropriate, that is, adapted to carry out the objects the amendments have in view, whatever tends to enforce submission to the prohibitions they contain, . . . if not prohibited, is brought within the domain of congressional power."[12]

Thus Congress had ample power under section 2 of the Fifteenth Amendment to enact the VRA.

*Morgan*, decided the same year as *South Carolina v. Katzenbach*, actually dealt with another provision of the same law. New York had long had a requirement that a prospective voter had to be proficient in English. The general provisions of the VRA made the possession of a sixth-grade education a proxy for literacy.[13] However, it also said that that education could be obtained in Spanish in "American-flag" schools in Puerto Rico. New York argued that the *Lassiter* decision's certification of an English literacy requirement meant that Congress had overreached its authority. We now move onto section 5 turf, because Congress was basing this part of the law on the Fourteenth Amendment's equal protection clause. Could Congress, that is, provide people who had completed the sixth grade in Spanish in Puerto Rico more rights than the Supreme Court said were necessary?

The court began by holding that the same test applied here as for section 2: "The *McCulloch v. Maryland* standard [the first quote above] is the measure of what constitutes 'appropriate legislation' under section 5 of the Fourteenth Amendment. Correctly viewed, section 5 is a positive grant of legislative power authorizing Congress to exercise its discretion in determining whether and what legislation is needed to secure the guarantees of the Fourteenth Amendment."[14] This part of the law can be considered "appropriate legislation" for two reasons. First, Congress could have weighed how best to provide citizens of Puerto Rican ethnicity access to public services, and then decided that granting them the right to vote was the most efficient and just method for doing that. "It is not for us to review the congressional resolution of these factors. It is enough that we be able to perceive a basis upon which the Congress might resolve the conflict as it did."[15] Second, Congress might have equally concluded that granting literate Spanish-speaking citizens educated in American-flag schools was a way of enforcing the equal protection clause itself.[16]

## THE "ONE WAY RATCHET" THEORY

When it comes to the rights of the citizenry vis-à-vis government, the usual problem is that the legislature has passed a law or the executive has acted in some way that infringes on an individual's liberty. The individual then goes to the courts asking them to block the action in question. In this way, the courts have always been viewed as one of the major bulwarks against governmental tyranny. And, of course, in doing this they must balance the liberties of the citizenry against various needs of the government.

Suppose in the process of deciding civil liberties cases, the courts develop certain doctrines that seek to strike a balance between liberties and governmental needs. Suppose, further, that the legislative branch decides that individual liberty needs more protection than that given by the court's doctrines. The "one way ratchet" theory holds that they may do so by statute.[17] The legislative branch, that is, may not cut back on the protection the courts have provided to individual liberty, but it may expand it. The goal of government is to secure and protect liberty, and there is nothing wrong, in this view, with that protection being enhanced by the legislature. Indeed it is a praiseworthy sign of a healthy polity that it chooses to do so.

## *BELGARD V. HAWAII*

Belgard was an inmate in the Hawaii state prison. He belonged to a Native American faith, some of whose practices were denied to him by the prison authorities. The case had a somewhat complicated procedural history, but in the end the question of RFRA's constitutionality had to be addressed before a trial on the merits could proceed. It had to be clear, that is, which standard of review would apply.[18]

Regarding the constitutional question, the state's first argument was that RFRA superseded Congress's power under section 5 because it treaded onto the judiciary's powers. The district court turned to *Morgan* and, citing both rationales already noted, found this argument wanting. A second argument adduced by the state was that prior to *Morgan* the Supreme Court had not ruled directly on the question of whether English literacy tests violated the equal protection clause whereas RFRA was trying to overturn a clear ruling by the court on the applicability of the compelling interest test. The district judge, however, found this argument also "unpersuasive." The Supreme Court had ruled, he said, on English literacy tests and the Fourteenth Amendment in *Lassiter*. Thus the essential point was "that *Morgan* gave Congress wide latitude to interpret the Constitution and expand a fundamental right pursuant to section 5 of the Fourteenth Amendment in an area where the Supreme Court had already spoken and afforded that right a narrower scope." Finally, Hawaii argued that a distinction should be drawn between Congress's power to enforce prohibitions found in the Fourteenth Amendment itself and those that were incorporated via the due process clause. Thus *Morgan* was a weak precedent since it dealt with equal protection, whereas RFRA involved the First Amendment. The district court, though, found insufficient support for that proposition. It referred to the case of *Hutto v. Finney*[19]as precedent, a case that upheld Congress's awarding of attorney fees in civil rights suits challenging the Eighth Amendment's cruel and unusual punishment clause. The Eighth Amendment was incorporated against the states in the same way as the First Amendment.

Citing Congress's explicit statement that RFRA should apply to prisoners' religious claims, the court concluded,

> *Morgan* held that Congress acted within its enforcement authority under section 5 of the Fourteenth Amendment when . . . it limited prior Supreme Court doctrine in order to expand a right guaranteed by the Fourteenth Amendment. Here, the basis for Congress's limitation on—or restoration of—judicial doctrine is plainer and, absent a particularized demonstration to the contrary as to a specific application not before this Court, no less sound. Accordingly, the Court finds that Congress was equally within the bounds of its enforcement powers under the Fourteenth Amendment when it enacted the RFRA to restore the pre-*Smith* boundaries of freedom of free exercise of religion under the First Amendment.

### JUDGE BUNTON'S OPINION

Given the rather detailed analysis advanced by the Hawaiian court, Judge Bunton's opinion is remarkably brief.

He began with the standard quote from *Marbury v. Madison* that it "is emphatically the province and duty of the judicial department to say what the law is." He then offers two more quotations, one from *Baker v. Carr* and another from *United States v. Nixon* that stress the role of the courts in constitutional interpretation.[20] In the case before him now, the Congress was seeking to overturn a Supreme Court precedent, and while "the Court is cognizant of Congress' authority under Section 5 of the Fourteenth Amendment, yet [it] is convinced of Congress' violation of the doctrine of Separation of Powers by intruding on the power and duty of the judiciary."

He admitted to being cautious in this holding, though, as there had not yet been much case law on RFRA. Nonetheless, he dismissed the Hawaii court ruling in a footnote, which is worth quoting in its entirety:

> This Court seriously questions the District Court of Hawaii's interpretation of RFRA's legitimacy through Section 5 of the Fourteen Amendment. RFRA only mentions the First Amendment as the empowering provision to change the burden of proof standard to compelling interest. "Typically, the Court looks to the language of an Act or its legislative history for guidance on which power Congress understood itself to be invoking, and for factual support of its legal determination as to whether the power was invoked properly. As applied to federal law, Congress simply did not enter into such an inquiry regarding RFRA." Furthermore, because the First Amendment is not an enumerated power of Congress, but merely a limitation, *Katzenbach v. Morgan* and its progeny are inapplicable. The First Amendment to the Constitution does not empower Congress to regulate all federal law in order to achieve religious liberty, unless it is done pursuant to an enumerated power.[21]

He then held the act unconstitutional and requested that the fifth circuit grant an expedited appeal.

### THE COURT OF APPEALS

By the time the case was argued at the court of appeals, both sides had added well-known legal scholars to their teams: Douglas Laycock, the University of Texas professor who had been instrumental in helping draft and defend RFRA, had already been asked by Thomas Drought to help the archdiocese in the district court. Professor Marci Hamilton, a law professor at Yeshiva University who had written widely on church-state matters, was engaged by Lowell Denton to aid the city. The Department of Justice also turned to some of its top legal talent. Furthermore, the court allowed a number of amici briefs, most of which supported RFRA's constitutionality.

On the day of oral argument, the courtroom was packed.[22] Along with other Boerne people, Marie Burgon came in her wheelchair. Lowell Denton handled the oral argument for the city and Laycock for the archdiocese. Patricia Millett represented the federal government. Justice Higginbotham was more involved in the colloquy than his two colleagues and asked all three several questions. At the end, Laycock and Denton both felt good about their chances.

Given his interest in the case, Higginbotham was chosen to write the opinion.[23] He began by summarizing the many references to section 5 made by the act's proponents during the hearings, including those in David Ackerman's legal analysis for the Congressional Research Service. He acknowledged that some scholars had expressed doubts about Congress's section 5 authority in this field but pointed out that both the House and Senate Reports on the bill explicitly referred to section 5. He then took aim at Bunton's footnote: "There is no question that Congress drew on its power under Section 5 in enacting RFRA. The district court's doubt that it did is without basis."

Higginbotham also included a note putting the familiar *Marbury* quote in context:

> That the Executive and Legislative branches also have both the right and duty to interpret the constitution casts no shadows upon Justice Marshall's claim of ultimate authority to decide. The judicial trump card can be played only in a case or controversy. The power to decide the law is an incident of judicial power to decide cases. There is no more. A power of review not rooted in a case or controversy would impermissibly draw to Article III the interpretive role of the Executive and Legislative branches of government. So it is that the familiar recitation that Congressional legislation comes to us with a presumption of constitutionality is a steely realism and not merely a protocol of manners or an empty formalism.

Turning to whether Congress had authority under section 5 to adopt RFRA, the city mounted four arguments. The first was that Congress had acted beyond the power granted by section 5, the second that the law violated separation of powers. These were by far the most important contentions. The third and fourth—that RFRA violated the establishment clause and the Tenth Amendment—appear merely tacked on.

Taking up the scope of section 5 power, Higginbotham began by citing the case of *City of Rome v. United States*, which held that all three post–Civil War amendments "were specifically designed as an expansion of federal power and an intrusion on state sovereignty."[24] He next surveyed the history of cases dealing with section 5, holding that a flexible view of Congress's power had been a consistent feature of these holdings. Moreover, in elaborating on similar grants of power to Congress in the Thirteenth, Fifteenth, Eighteenth, Twenty-Third, Twenty-Fourth, and Twenty-Sixth Amendments, the Supreme Court had taken a comparably broad view. In conclusion, "This continued adherence to the principle that Congress may explicate textually located rights and obligations pursuant to Section 5 persuades us that the three-part test from *Morgan* remains the benchmark." That three-part test asks (1) whether the law in question is one that enforces the Fourteenth Amendment, (2) whether it is clearly tied to that objective, and (3) whether it is consistent with "the letter and spirit of the constitution."[25]

As for the first, the court rejected out of hand any hierarchy of rights protected by the Fourteenth Amendment. The rights incorporated through the due process clause, that is, stand on an equal footing with the equal protection clause. Congress, therefore, had as much power to reach the free exercise clause as it would have had that clause been stated within the text of the Fourteenth Amendment. From the legislative history, it is unmistakable that Congress was seeking to enforce a right guaranteed by the free exercise clause. Thus the first test is met.

Turning to the second, what precisely was Congress attempting to remedy through RFRA? The Justice Department offered three purposes: deterring free exercise violations, "prohibiting laws that have the effect of impeding free exercise," and protecting the religious liberty of minority religions.

Post-*Smith* it was necessary for free exercise claimants to show that the law in question was targeted at them. Consequently facially neutral laws would only fall if the courts looked behind the law itself to the motives of those who adopted it. Congress could well view this as misguided and a test that will lead to less protection for religious liberty than what it deemed desirable. Thus strict scrutiny is a good way to "smoke out" illegitimate laws that are neutral on their face:[26] "These considerations, analogous to those underlying the Voting Rights Act Amendments of 1982, convince us that RFRA serves the remedial goal of identifying budding or disguised constitutional violations that would otherwise survive judicial scrutiny under *Smith*."

Akin to that problem, Congress had solid grounds for worrying about laws that have the effect of interfering with free exercise, not only those with the intent to do so. In the area of racial discrimination, for example, the effect of a law has been considered by Congress when it has adopted policies regarding voting rights. In 1980, in the *City of Rome* case already cited, the Supreme Court had ruled that while the Constitution may require a racially discriminatory intention for an electoral system to be held invalid, Congress has the power to make a system with a discriminatory effect equally suspect. Therefore there is no reason to limit Congress's parallel power when it comes to free exercise. The justices admitted that adopting this approach can often put the courts in the uncomfortable position of having to weigh how much of a burden given policies are to an individual's free exercise, "but this begs the question of congressional power. That some generally applicable laws must yield their unwitting grasp of religious practices is the price Congress has chosen to pay to achieve its desired level of accommodation."

Finally, *Smith* left religious minorities to the fate of the normal democratic process, and Justice Scalia admitted that that would disadvantage them. Congress had listened to testimony regarding such groups as the Hmong, Jews, Mormons, and the Amish. From this evidence, it could well conclude that these and other minorities need the protection of enhanced scrutiny of laws that trespass on their free exercise rights.

Higginbotham concluded that taken together, "These justifications fit within the remedial power of Congress under Section 5."

Now for the third part of the *Morgan* test. Is RFRA in step with "the letter and spirit of the constitution"? Conceivably, there were three barriers: the separation of powers, the establishment clause, and the Tenth Amendment. Since these are the same arguments as numbers two through four of the general objections raised by the city, they can be considered in that vein.

Separation of powers, as previously noted, is by far the most serious of these arguments. It was here that the attorneys for the two sides drew the most dramatic contrasts. According to the city, to uphold RFRA would amount to overturning *Marbury v. Madison*. In contrast, the government argued that RFRA was merely an example of the one way ratchet, that Congress was expanding individual rights through a statute.

Higginbotham said that the contention that Congress was creating a statutory right was "incomplete." Rather, Congress was building on Supreme Court precedents regarding its powers under section 5. To be sure, Congress is demanding that the courts apply a standard of review that the judiciary had rejected. However, the matter should not be read as a conflict between the legislative and judicial branches. Instead, "whether the courts must obey RFRA's command to do so [apply strict scrutiny in cases where religion is substantially burdened] turns only on the independent issue of the power of Congress."

It would be a mistake to assume that *Smith* prescribed "not only how little the Government *must* accommodate religion but also how much it *may* accommodate it" (emphasis in original). In fact, *Smith* said explicitly that exceptions to generally applicable laws were constitutional; it was only that they had to be specified by the legislature. RFRA is a general exemption adopted by the legislature: "That RFRA speaks in broad generalities where other legislatively mandated religious exemptions . . . address specific conduct is of no moment. Congress may paint with a broad or narrow brush."

As Congress did when it enacted the Voting Rights Act of 1965 and modified *Lassiter*, it is here supplementing the courts, not taking their power of judicial review away: "In short, the judiciary's duty is to say what the law is, but that duty is not exclusive. The district court's holding that RFRA usurps the judiciary's power under *Marbury v. Madison* to interpret the Constitution is incorrect."

One other argument regarding separation of powers deserves at least a mention. When RFRA ordered that the compelling interest test be applied by the courts was it demanding that the judges do something they have said they could not do? In *Smith* Scalia had recoiled from the idea that judges should be put in the position of having to "weigh the social importance of all laws against the centrality of all religious beliefs." Higginbotham thought, though, that members of the court had not thereby said that they could not apply the compelling interest test; after all, they do in other areas of the law. He felt that there was an important distinction between the test being applied as a constitutional matter and as a result of a statutory command. If Congress disagreed with how courts applied it in the former situation, the only recourse would be a constitutional amendment (or, he did not mention, waiting for the court to change its mind). In contrast, in the latter, Congress can simply alter the statute to strike a different balance. This argument seems to skate over a number of complications, and it does not seem central to the holding. Nonetheless, it does get a nod.

In sum, the judges concluded that RFRA did not breach the separation of powers.

On its surface, the establishment clause argument seems pointless; the act itself said that nothing could be done under its aegis that would violate the establishment clause. Nevertheless, the city drew on two aspects of the three-part *Lemon* test to mount an establishment clause challenge.[27] Specifically, they argued that the law had no secular purpose and that its primary effect was to advance religion. The court brushed aside the first postulate by simply saying that RFRA's "remedial justifications belie the City's contention that Congress acted with a sectarian purpose." This is a curious choice of words. There is a distinction between a "sectarian" purpose and a "religious" one. It would seem that a bit more analysis is called for here. As for the "advancing religion" argument, the refutation is clearer. A 1987 case involving Congress granting an exemption from equal opportunity demands in employment law to religious institutions contained the following observation: "A law is not unconstitutional simply because it *allows* churches to advance religion, which is their very purpose. For a law to have forbidden 'effects' under *Lemon*, it must be fair to say that the *government itself* has advanced religion through its own activities and influence."[28] RFRA entailed no direct governmental activity in advancing religion and therefore did not run afoul of this part of the *Lemon* test.

As we said in the previous chapter, the Rehnquist Court was in the midst of reinvigorating limits on federal power, including the breathing of new life into the Tenth Amendment. The city pointed to *United States v. Lopez* from the year before as a reason the Tenth Amendment might be applicable here. However, Higginbotham responded that that case involved a statute enacted under the commerce clause and that the Supreme Court had previously held that Congress's powers under the Civil War amendments exceeded those granted by Article I. Treading cautiously, though, he added a note that he did not wish to suggest that the Tenth Amendment was without effect. However, how far RFRA might be able to go without running headlong into the Tenth Amendment would have to be decided on a case-by-case basis. For the moment, RFRA's general provisions do not transgress the amendment.

Section 5, consequently, Higginbotham concluded, contained ample authority for Congress to enact RFRA. In addition, it did not take away the judiciary's power to say what the constitution means. The case was now ready for appeal to the Supreme Court.

CHAPTER 6

# THE SUPREME COURT DECISION

WHEN THE CASE WAS ACCEPTED BY THE Supreme Court, it garnered national attention. As one indicator of the importance of the case, amici briefs began to pour into the court. Altogether, 27 of these were submitted, 19 on the archdiocese and the federal government's side and 7 in support of the city (with one taking neither side).[1] The most important of the amici parties, given the large stakes for federalism, was a group of states, led by Ohio. That state's attorney general, in fact, was allowed to participate in oral argument. Thus both parties had the support of governmental entities. Clearly, the direct interests of the parties—building a new church versus historical preservation—had been swallowed by much larger issues.

Both legal teams spent a great deal of time preparing their briefs. In some ways, the United States had become the main party to the case, as the central issue was the constitutionality of an important federal statute. In fact, there was a slight division between the archdiocese and the Department of Justice before the case came up. Satisfied with the court of appeals' decision, the department would rather the case not have gone to the Supreme Court at all.[2] The archdiocese's legal team, however, felt it would be helpful to have the high court endorse the court of appeals' decision. Laycock felt confident that since six appellate courts had upheld the constitutionality of the statute, the Supreme Court was likely to do so also.[3] Winning at this level would then immunize RFRA against further challenges. On the city's side, Denton felt that they had a strong case. He decided to turn oral argument over to Hamilton, though, since she had been a clerk to Justice Sandra Day O'Connor.[4] This gave her a "badge" at the bar of the Supreme Court that he did not have. The written brief, nonetheless, was a joint product.

Oral argument was set for February 19, 1997. A number of people from Boerne public life, along again with Marie Burgon, went to Washington, and back in the town interest was high. The *Star* and the *Recorder* both reported the case in detail.

We will look first at how each side developed its argument in their written briefs. Then we will summarize how the oral argument went. After that, we will turn to a detailed analysis and critique of Justice Anthony Kennedy's opinion, along with the concurrences and dissents.

## THE WRITTEN BRIEFS

Taking Boerne's brief first, since the city was the petitioner, Hamilton and Denton opened with an attempt to put a favorable twist on the facts:[5] "This case is about a request to tear down a beautiful stone church, whose times and memories are graven into the souls of a city . . . Boerne's historic preservation law represents years of effort on the part of the City and evidences the citizens' commitment to their community's heritage." As for legal issues, RFRA was depicted as a "brazen attempt to take over free exercise law[, which] knows no parallel in congressional history and violates the separation of powers, federalism principles, and the Establishment Clause."

While federalism and the establishment clause got due coverage in the brief, it was separation of powers that accounted for most of the paragraphs and that brought forth the most unequivocal arguments. The attorneys began by asserting, quoting James Madison from *The Federalist* for support, that the purpose of separation of powers is to prevent tyranny. Then, turning to the venerable *Marbury v. Madison* quote about the role of the "judicial department," they argued that RFRA was an attempt to take over this "core judicial function."

The alleged reason was that Congress was trying to alter the court's free exercise doctrines. The city quoted at some length Scalia's *Smith* summary of previous free exercise case law. Stressing that the court had never applied the compelling interest test outside the unemployment compensation field, the brief painted a picture of how sweeping RFRA would be if allowed to stand. Further, they emphasized that the compelling interest test applied by the courts had only once even hinted at a least restrictive means requirement,[6] much less used it as a basis for overturning a governmental policy. This, too, meant that Congress was trying to invalidate judicial doctrine.

Some notes were added on Congress's "hostile" reaction to *Smith*. Calling the court's opinion in *Smith* "thoughtful," the brief goes on to say that RFRA "is nothing less than a competing interpretation of the

Free Exercise Clause. In the Free Exercise context, it turns day to night." Its scope is unparalleled. It reaches "every government" and "every law" "every time." In enacting RFRA, "Congress has co-opted the Court's interpretive role. As a direct result, the courts have been relegated in free exercise cases to the role of interpreting Congress's inaccurate assessment of the Constitution, rather than their constitutionally appointed role of interpreting the Constitution itself." Adding to this stroking of the justices' egos, it said a bit later, "RFRA is nothing short of a hostile takeover of this Court's constitutionally appointed role in free exercise cases."[7]

At this point, the brief took up the section 5 question. It began by citing the well-worn three-pronged test from *McCulloch v. Maryland*: that to receive constitutional blessing a statute must "be within the scope of the constitution," that it must be "plainly adapted to that end," and that it must conform to the "letter and spirit of the constitution." While some attention was given to the first and third of these, it was the second that the brief writers realized was crucial.

It was crucial because of the Voting Rights Act (VRA) cases. For RFRA to be an acceptable extension of the VRA cases, one has to rely on either the "remedial power theory" or the "substantive power theory." Both, however, in their view, fail.

In this reading of remedial power, the holdings in *Katzenbach v. Morgan* and *City of Rome v. United States* stood for the proposition that Congress could act to expand Supreme Court doctrine only when two conditions are met. First, Congress must utilize the same standard as the court. Second, Congress must employ, and claim to employ, its superior fact-finding abilities. Thus RFRA cannot be said to be "remedial" in any meaningful way: "Neither *Morgan* nor *City of Rome* provides precedent that supports the extraordinary exercise of power found in RFRA. Even in the Court's most expansive Section 5 cases, the remedial power has been limited to the exercise of superior factfinding skills in the context of applying the Court's designated standard for constitutional violations. This Section 5 doctrine in no way creates a haven for RFRA's bald rejection of the Court's interpretation of the Free Exercise Clause of the First Amendment in all cases." Clearly, RFRA is moving outside established judicial doctrine, declared in *Smith* and restated in *Church of Lukumi Babalu Aye v. City of Hialeah*, [8]and the legislative history of the act is "only sporadically dotted with a limited number of anecdotal reports of religious suppression."

What they called the "substantive power theory" we discussed in the last chapter as the "one way ratchet" theory. In brief, Congress may add to rights announced by the court but not subtract from them. The attorneys here stress, though, that the court has never itself said that this theory is valid. Some cases can be read as giving it some credibility, but it has never won explicit judicial endorsement.[9] Even so, for the city's position the court's holdings were ambiguous enough to be worrisome. Consequently, they resorted to broader arguments designed to appeal to judicial authority: "The substantive power theory hands Congress a power at odds with the separation of powers, and it permits Congress to yoke the states to its policy predilections in violation of the federalism constraints inherent in Section 5." Then, later on, the brief adds, "The substantive power theory deserves to be definitively interred by this Court at this time."

The most important of the amici briefs was the one authored by the attorney general and the state solicitor of Ohio and supported by 12 other states.[10] This is largely because Jeffrey Sutton, the Ohio solicitor general, was given the opportunity to participate in oral argument. Clearly, the court felt it important that the interests of state governments be formally represented.

Although the brief touched on several areas of state concern—education, criminal law, and general police powers—the major emphasis was on prison administration. Several paragraphs were devoted to reciting the alleged difficulties RFRA had wrought in the running of the nation's prisons. They called attention, first, to the increase in the sheer number of lawsuits states had had to defend (sixty were then currently pending in Ohio, for example). Second, they listed several instances in which "violent inmate gangs, racist organizations, drug distributors and like minded groups [shrouded] illicit activity under cover of 'religious' belief." Even when these efforts are stymied by prison officials, valuable time is consumed in contesting them. Third, RFRA had led to state-funded chaplains having to change the way they do business, in that they had been called upon to help sort out legitimate from illegitimate religious claims, resulting in a diminution of religious services available to inmates, as inmate trust often broke down.

Constitutionally, Ohio's officials repeated many of the section 5 arguments covered in the city's brief. However, they added two important amplifications: a more historically based analysis of the meaning of *enforce* in the text of the Fourteenth Amendment and an unallayed attack on RFRA's federalism implications.

Three lines of argument were advanced to support the proposition that the scope of congressional power under section 5 should be interpreted narrowly. First, Ohio's officials turned to dictionaries to locate the meaning of the word *enforce*, saying that both "old and new dictionaries confirm that the verb 'enforce' is a confining one." (However, these definitions do not seem as limited as the brief wishes to make them out to be. For instance, the one quoted from 1869 says, "To put force upon, to force, to constrain, to compel; as to enforce obedience to commands.") The dictionary definitions were reinforced, in this reading, by other enforcement clauses in the Constitution. That these clauses should be read narrowly can be inferred from the fact that when the framers wished to give Congress broad authority they used the term *regulate.*[11] Accordingly, "the power 'to enforce . . . the provisions of this article' means the power to make the States follow these provisions, not the power to define the rights themselves or to regulate under them generally. Unless anchored to a violation of the Fourteenth Amendment, in short, Congress has no authority under section five."

The second support for a restricted reading of the reach of section 5 came from a reference to the debates that accompanied the amendment's proposal in Congress in 1866. This is important because, as we shall see momentarily, Justice Kennedy invoked this matter in his opinion. According to the states' brief there are two noteworthy features of the post–Civil War debate. The first is that "Congress had an opportunity to approve a proposed amendment that would have supported (or at least begun to support) the interpretation advanced here [by RFRA's supporters]." Representative John Bingham, on whom more information follows, offered this wording for the proposed amendment: "The Congress shall have power to make all laws which shall be necessary and proper to secure to the citizens of each State all privileges and immunities of citizens in the several States, and to all persons in the several States equal protection in the rights of life, liberty, and property." This wording was rejected, however, and the current edition, with Congress's power limited to enforcing the amendment's prohibitions put in its stead. The second is that whatever ambiguity exists about the intentions of the members of Congress who approved the Fourteenth Amendment regarding whether it incorporated the Bill of Rights, no one believed it gave Congress authority to make its own interpretations of the first eight amendments. (We will discuss the role of these debates in more detail later.)

The third leg of the argument for a circumscribed gloss on section 5 turns to the Supreme Court's interpretation. A couple of quotations from *Ex Parte Virginia* and *Strauder v. West Virginia* are laid out that suggest that Congress's power under section 5 was subject to significant limits. The *Civil Rights Cases* are cited as further proof that the power is "remedial" only in scope. (Recall, though, that the *Civil Rights Cases* dealt with a federal statute that regulated private conduct, not state action.) Finally, all the VRA cases are read in the narrowest of fashions, and they all, in this view, "establish that Congress must take the Constitution as it finds it."

The conclusion, then, is as follows: "All things considered, the text of section five, the history behind the provision and the case law construing it establish this: Before Congress may invoke its enforcement authority under section five, there must be a prior or ongoing constitutional wrong. And, while the egregiousness of the wrong may extend Congress's remedial discretion [an admission made necessary by the VRA cases], a constitutional wrong is—and always has been—a preliminary requirement." Some effort is then given over to showing that there were no "prior" or "ongoing" violations for Congress to remedy in this instance.

The brief acknowledges up front that there is "no doubt the Fourteenth Amendment took power from the States and gave it to the federal government." Nevertheless, it denied that in so doing it repealed "the Tenth Amendment or the principles of federalism for which it stands."

The basic argument is in essence a slippery slope exercise. If RFRA withstands judicial challenge, there will be nothing to "prevent Congress from passing legislation regulating all encounters between state law enforcement and the citizenry in the name of protecting Fourth and Fifth Amendment values." Or, to keep Congress from using the Fifth Amendment's takings clause to block local land use policies. Or, to stop it from nationalizing criminal punishments using the Eighth Amendment. Or, to block an attempt to federalize "education, marriage and family laws in the name of protecting privacy and other substantive due process guarantees." Congress might even decree that all state laws must be "substantially rational," converting "section five from an enforcement provision into a general police power."

Yet this approach rests upon a mechanistic view of the Constitution. It posits that Congress and the state governments are two entirely separate entities and often hostile to each other. By this view, one or the other is constantly trying to cut down or interfere with the power of the other. But the political reality, of course, is quite different. Both represent the people, and as federalism is a central American political value, Congress is hardly likely to go on a state-bashing rampage. Moreover, the states are strong lobbyists in Washington and defend their interests regularly. Naturally, various political interests will find themselves more or less favored depending on which level of government makes certain decisions. But one could easily argue that here the people's representatives in Congress listened to the voices of state government officials (especially prison officials) and made a (near unanimous) decision.

Nevertheless, the state governments assembled here felt that federalism was at risk: "In the end, because all legislation in one way or another addresses the zero-sum conflict between the security interests of the collective citizenry and the liberty interests of the individual, there is almost nothing Congress could not do under this version of section five power. Quite simply, Congress's authority under the provision does not extend this far. The court of appeals' contrary ruling should be reversed."

The briefs for the archdiocese and the United States were filed several weeks after those of the city and the states. Thus they had a chance to address directly some of the issues raised in those entreaties.

Taking that of the archdiocese first,[12] it began, expectedly, with a slightly different take on the facts: "This case involves the right of a religious community to worship together, and the right of excluded individuals to attend the Roman Catholic Mass, in St. Peter Church in Boerne, Texas . . . The City has refused every request for a permit to enlarge the church building to make it adequate to the parish's needs . . . [A]fter the adverse ruling in the trial court, the church began celebrating Mass in an ill-suited secular auditorium."

The central constitutional point of the brief was that RFRA was hardly unique. It fit well within the framework of previous congressional enactments that enforced section 5 and the parallel enforcement provisions of other amendments as well as the court decisions that had upheld them. Bolstering this conclusion was the fact that every appellate court that had faced the applicability of RFRA to state and local governments had upheld its constitutionality.[13]

The constitutional argument began on a broader plane: that an act of Congress is entitled to significant deference by the court, especially when Congress devoted as much attention to constitutional issues as it did when it considered RFRA. Then, in an attempt to show how much RFRA was in accord with previous pieces of legislation and the judicial precedents upholding them, the discussion turned to Congress's power under section 5. Several cases were cited that purported to show that the enforcement clauses of the various amendments have been held to grant power that is coterminous with the necessary and proper clause. Following that was a discussion of how RFRA complements the constitutional protections against public policies that by purposeful design impose burdensome effects on liberty. A close tie-in was suggested to the handling of similar policies that prevent such discrimination on racial or gender grounds.

Yet the core of the argument here was a lengthy and detailed discussion of prior enforcement legislation. Importantly, the first section of this discussion dealt with the original VRA, its amendments, and the cases upholding these measures. Six different statutory provisions were reviewed, stressing how broad the authority granted to Congress by the court had been in each instance. Next, the brief delineated five portions of the Civil Rights Act of 1964 and its amendments that overrode previous Supreme Court rulings. To add icing onto these elaborations, one provision of the Civil Rights Attorneys Fees Awards Act, two segments of the Civil Rights Act of 1866 and its amendments, one example from the Civil Rights Act of 1871, and two portions of the National Prohibition Act and its amendments were also listed. In each of these instances the court had granted a generous reading to Congress's constitutionally sanctioned enforcement powers.

Several lessons were said to be easily drawn from this chronicle. First, they show that congressional enforcement power can reach beyond judicial interpretation of a constitutional amendment. Moreover, they stretch for more than a century and are "deeply embedded in our law." And then in a bit of a slippery-slope argument of its own, the brief alleged that all these laws' protections "would be cast in doubt if the judgment below were reversed; there cannot be a reversal without a drastic shrinkage of the enforcement power." In case the justices needed reminding, the VRA and the Civil Rights Act of 1964 and its various amendments were extremely sensitive points of public and political concern.

Returning to the constitutional points raised by these two measures, the brief observed that both these statutes are quite broad, especially compared to RFRA: "Unlike RFRA, these statutes do not merely require occasional exemptions from state policies that remain generally enforceable; rather, these statutes fundamentally change voting and employment systems." Therefore, they "intrude far more deeply than RFRA into the core processes of state and local government."

Two other conclusions stand out. First, cataloging this experience shows that it is not true, as Ohio argued, that Congress can only use section 5 to overcome "a prior or ongoing constitutional wrong." Many of these statutes established a legal regime that was independent of any previous constitutional wrong having been committed. Second, the city's distinction between "remedial" and "substantive" uses of the enforcement power is untenable. RFRA is remedial, as are the listed statutory provisions, in the sense that it provided a statutory right without a prior judicial holding regarding the specific right. It may well be substantive in the sense that it does not require "proof of deliberate or overt discrimination," but then many of the other statues discussed previously are equally so.

Nevertheless, the brief acknowledged that there are limits to the enforcement power. Because, however, "Congress has rarely tested the limits of the enforcement power, . . . the Court has had few occasions to squarely consider them." A lengthy discussion ensued covering some possible ways Congress might exceed its enforcement powers, but most were hypothetical, and the court opinions cited are mostly only tangential to this question. RFRA, though, does not transgress any conceivable limit, and in any event presents only a narrow question: "Can Congress dispense with proof of deliberate or overt discrimination? That is the only question presented here, and the answer is clearly yes. No use of the enforcement power is better settled than this. Reaffirming this settled rule does not dictate any answer to the myriad of other questions not presented."

Two relatively straightforward points followed, although the first was the subject of controversy later. The first was that Congress had indeed produced adequate evidence to justify RFRA. A recitation of several components of the legislative process was then offered to demonstrate this. Further, the brief contended that the fact-finding that Congress did regarding RFRA was as thorough as that done when the VRA and some of the amendments to the Civil Rights Act of 1964 were being considered. The court, as we shall see momentarily, however, did not concur. The second was that Congress's power to enforce religious liberty—flowing from the incorporation of the Bill of Rights via the due process clause—is on a par with its power to enforce the equal protection clause. This was probably mentioned because the city had raised this question in its brief.

An important and somewhat lengthy section followed, examining the original understanding of the enforcement power. The analysis offered here contrasts sharply both with that from Ohio's brief and with that adopted by Justice Kennedy in his opinion. It is important, first of all, the brief's authors contended, to separate the intentions of the framers of the amendment from later judicial interpretations. The latter are useful as precedent, certainly, but they do not provide a window onto the thoughts of the members of Congress who wrote the amendment.

The brief took the view that the first incantation of an enforcement clause came when Congress considered whether the Civil Rights Act of 1866 could be justified by the Thirteenth Amendment. This is somewhat problematic, as I will discuss in the critique of Justice Kennedy's opinion. Nevertheless, the brief is accurate in its assertion that Congress debated its enforcement power on several occasions during Reconstruction. And their conclusion seems to accord better with the facts than that of Ohio: "Congress acted on the view that the enforcement power should and did have limits, and that it should not and did not confer a general power to substitute federal law for state law." But one cannot jump to the conclusion that all federal action was therefore banned: "Many prophylactic rules to achieve the purposes of the Amendments fall far short of general power to substitute federal law for state law." Even many of those who were initially opposed to the Civil Rights Act of 1871 (also known as the Ku Klux Klan Act) because they felt it extended federal power too far, as it created federal criminal and tort offenses for several acts, nonetheless ended up voting for it when it was only slightly modified. These men therefore "believed that the enforcement power should not be allowed to grow into a general legislative power, but they plainly did not believe that it was confined to the judicially enforceable meaning of the Amendments." RFRA therefore is perfectly in line with this original understanding. It does not create a federal tort law, and state governments are free to pursue whatever policy they wish; it is only that they must show a compelling interest if the policy significantly burdens someone's religious exercise.

It is important, too, as the brief explained, to keep the context of the amendment's adoption in mind (a point to be stressed even more shortly). The Supreme Court with which the Reconstruction Congress was familiar had handed down *Dred Scott*. How much confidence could they have in that type of court? Many statements can be collected to support the view that members of Congress, consequently, took a broad view of the enforcement powers.[14]

Moreover, the brief argued that it seems clear also that most of the amendment's framers believed they were incorporating the Bill of Rights against the states. Floor leaders in both the House and Senate referred to incorporation and hailed section 5 as a vehicle for ensuring that the states complied with the Bill of Rights. If correct, RFRA can hardly be said to lie outside the bounds of the enforcement clause.

Finally, the brief added discussions of three additional matters: whether RFRA encroached on the judicial power to interpret the law, whether RFRA violated the establishment clause, and whether RFRA infringed on the separation of powers. Regarding the first, the brief writers had to exercise care, for during the congressional debates there was much talk of striking a fatal blow at *Smith*. They skirted this by denying that Congress was attempting to challenge the court: "It is undisputed that *Smith* remains the law of the Constitution." To emphasize the point, they noted that in the case the archdiocese had filed they alleged a violation of RFRA *and* a violation of the free exercise clause "as interpreted in *Smith*." What Congress was doing, and said many times, was creating a new statutory right.

Concerning the establishment clause, the archdiocese first pointed out the irony of the raising of an establishment clause challenge to a law supported by almost all America's religious bodies. They also made much of the fact that the city had ignored the *Amos* decision, and had thereby confused "the advancement of religious liberty with the advancement of religion." If Congress has the power to grant specific exemptions, as *Smith* said they would, then how is it that a general exemption is invalid?[15]

As for separation of powers, the brief opened this part of the argument by stressing that the separation of powers is not an end but rather a means to the enhancement of liberty. That being the case, all three branches have a responsibility to protect the citizens' liberties. When Congress convened after the Civil War it faced a serious problem regarding liberty. The Southern states were likely to use any means at hand to restrict the liberties of the newly freed slaves (discussed below). Federal power was the only conceivable answer, and the chances that federal power would be deployed to the desired end were enhanced if two institutions had enforcement power. When the enforcement powers of the courts were coupled together with the enforcement powers of Congress there was a better chance of protecting the newly freed slaves than if either stood alone. So it is now: religious liberty is best protected when both institutions bring their special strengths to the task.

In most respects the brief for the United States reiterated the points made in that for the archdiocese.[16] However, there were some different emphases, and some matters covered that were barely if at all mentioned in the respondent brief. Among the latter were paragraphs devoted to the role of the Fourteenth Amendment in specifically protecting religious minorities, the link between section 5 and the necessary and proper clause, and federalism. In addition, the government brought some additional details to bear on the overall argument for constitutionality.

The brief began, not surprisingly, with a note on the need for judicial deference to congressional legislation. Moving to the specific constitutional arguments, the brief started by emphasizing in the strongest terms that the court should not reconsider *Morgan*. Should the court do so, not only would RFRA be very difficult to defend, but the continued enforcement of the VRA would also receive a body blow. The brief sought, therefore, all at once, to retain *Morgan*, use it as a springboard to defend RFRA, and appeal to the justices' sense of their own authority. After summarizing the court's opinion in the case, they concluded, "Thus, *Morgan* held that Congress has independent authority to identify and invalidate specific governmental practices when it determines as a factual matter that they violate Section 1 of the Fourteenth Amendment under the standards announced by this Court."

They next took a swing at the city's invitation to the court to "inter" the "substantive power theory":

> It is unclear to which aspect of *Morgan* petitioner objects, because the language from *Morgan* the petitioner attacks appears only in a footnote that precedes the Court's articulation of both rationales. If petitioner is challenging *Morgan's* holding that Congress may prohibit a specific state action or law because Congress independently has determined that it actually violates the Fourteenth Amendment, this case presents no occasion to revisit that question. Through RFRA, Congress did not determine that any specific state or local law constituted an invidious discrimination against religion.
>
> If, instead, petitioner challenges *Morgan's* holding that Congress's enforcement power includes the authority to increase the security of Fourteenth Amendment guarantees by adding a statutory layer of protection beyond the floor set by the Constitution, petitioner's argument should be rejected as inconsistent with Section 5's plain language and legislative history, as well as with principles of *stare decisis*.

For the "plain language" argument, the briefs turned to dictionaries. In contrast to Ohio's brief, though, they found a reference in a standard 1865 dictionary to "enforcing a law" that meant "to invigorate," "to strengthen," "to give force to," and "to cause to have force and effect." Moreover, they chided the Ohio brief writers for selecting the tenth definition in the *Oxford English Dictionary*, whereas the first one is "to put force or strength into."

The legislative history that they unearthed seconded the archdiocese's brief, underlining the comments of the principal backers of the Civil War amendments that supported independent authority for Congress in the enforcement clauses. Because these men could not trust the Southern states to abide by the amendments, they wished to confer enforcement power on as many governmental organs as possible: "The Civil War Amendments thus made Congress an independent guarantor of constitutional liberties." The importance of following *Morgan* and similar precedential cases is that Congress has relied on these rulings to write subsequent legislation (with a lengthy statutory list provided).

RFRA also meets the test of "appropriate legislation" under section 5. The framework the court has established to judge this is the three-part *Morgan* test: the measure has to enforce a right that is stipulated in the Fourteenth Amendment; the law must be "plainly adapted" to accomplish that purpose; and the statute must not run afoul of any other constitutional limitation.[17] RFRA meets all three.

When discussing the first of these, the brief broke some new ground. After making the point that both the due process clause and the equal protection clause are on the same footing as far as section 5 is concerned, it brought up the matter of religious rights after the Civil War. Southern states had harassed both African American churches and Northern pastors who had ventured below the Mason-Dixon Line.[18] Thus religion had a role at the inception of the amendment. A bit further on, the brief elaborated another concern about equal protection: religious minorities are often also racial or ethnic minorities. Consequently, minimizing religious discrimination, as RFRA does, will aid in the country's efforts to combat racial and ethnic discrimination. But even if religious minorities are not coincident with racial or ethnic minorities, they deserve protection on their own. Congress has determined, by compiling a more than sufficient factual record, that such groups need a generalized protection since they are unlikely to prevail in the ordinary give and take of legislative politics. Section 5 is an adequate vehicle through which Congress can provide these prophylactic rules.

In the main, the brief tracked the arguments regarding separation of powers that had been developed in the archdiocese's submission. It did devote more time to the establishment clause question and advocated utilizing the three-pronged *Lemon* test for this matter. According to the brief, RFRA easily passed each hurdle. First, despite its religious subject matter, it had a secular purpose: "to advance uniformly the civil rights of all religious adherents; Congress played no favorites." In addition, the "substantial burden" requirement meant that "Congress acted only 'to alleviate significant governmental interference' with religious autonomy and exercise." *Amos* was cited for the proposition that the establishment clause does not require that an exemption granted to a religious body must also be granted to secular organizations. Second, RFRA has an acceptable primary effect. Referring to *Amos* again, the brief contended that RFRA did not directly advance religion, which meant that "religious practitioners will not be any better off than before coming into contact with the State." Third, RFRA avoided excessive entanglement between church and state: "Religious exemptions, as a whole, decrease governmental involvement with religion." Furthermore, the values enshrined in the establishment clause stand a better chance of flowering when there is a uniform exemption in place than when religious groups must mount a political effort to secure them individually.

The final section of the brief waltzed straight into the crucial area of federalism. With the trend of decisions discussed in an earlier chapter, RFRA stood on precarious footing here. A majority of the justices were known to be skeptical of any action by the federal government that might diminish the discretionary power of the states. In an attempt to counter any leanings in this direction, the brief tried to ground RFRA in the precedents of the court itself rather than theories of federalism. Its introductory paragraph to this section concluded with the sentence "Indeed RFRA is more responsive to federalism concerns than other Section 5 legislation sustained by this Court." It then turned to three bundles of cases to demonstrate that point.

First, there was the matter of the Tenth Amendment. The brief reminded the court that it had "repeatedly" turned down Tenth Amendment challenges to laws enacted under section 5 and had in the process endorsed an expansive reading of congressional powers under it. As examples, quotations from *Gregory v. Ashcroft*[19]and *EEOC v. Wyoming*[20] were put on the table. In the former, the court had said that the normal principles of federalism "are attenuated when Congress acts pursuant to its powers to enforce the Civil War Amendments," while in the latter it referred specifically to the Tenth Amendment when it held that "when properly exercising its power under Section 5, Congress is not limited by the same Tenth Amendment constraints that circumscribe the exercise of its Commerce Clause powers." While, from a practical point of view, the court had begun a shift in its federalism jurisprudence, the hope was that the justices would still find precedential value in these sentences.

Second, the brief argued that RFRA does not specify which policies states must follow. Instead, it merely establishes a test (and one only triggered by the "substantial burden" requirement), and it is a test with which the courts are intimately familiar. It does not guarantee that religious plaintiffs will win all their cases; it simply puts a measuring rod in place. We can still expect to see policy "variation and experimentation among States in light of their unique interests, history, and circumstances."

Third, there was the troublesome case of *New York v. United States*, which, recall, had invalidated a federal statute demanding that states either create policies to deal with radioactive waste or take title to it. The brief, though, argued that there were three important distinctions between the statute in question in that case and RFRA.

First, that law had been based on the commerce clause whereas RFRA rested on section 5, which gives Congress a direct authority to regulate state actions. Second, RFRA, unlike the radioactive waste law, does not "commandeer" state decision making. States are not required to do or not do anything. They must simply adapt their policies to be mindful of a certain standard of judicial review, just as they must under the VRA and the laws outlawing employment discrimination. Finally, no problem of opaque political accountability is raised by RFRA, as it seemed to be in *New York*. Making both the states and the federal government subject to RFRA ensures that Congress is not merely passing on the cost of a public policy to the states.

## ORAL ARGUMENT

It is always unclear how much importance should be assigned to the oral arguments before the court. The dictates of time necessarily force the attorneys to either capsule their entire argument or focus on a few critical points. At the same time, the court's rule that allows the justices to interrupt the advocates in order to pose questions, which does not lengthen the time available to the attorney, can cut short even the best-prepared presentations. Nonetheless, the need for brevity does let the observer see what the attorney thinks is his or her most persuasive propositions. Moreover, the questions the justices ask provide something of a window into their thinking and something of a predictor, although an imperfect one, of their votes. The exercise is not without importance, then, for in many cases, as former Chief Justice Charles Evans Hughes said, it allows the court "to be able to more quickly separate the wheat from the chaff."[21]

Marci Hamilton led off, and the first matter she had to deal with was how to pronounce the city's name.[22] Her main approach was to convince the court that Congress had clearly overstepped its appropriate constitutional role and that in so doing they were all but insulting the justices themselves. The case, she said "is about the ability of the United States Constitution to restrain Congress . . . [RFRA], which was passed in an emotional and heated response to this Court's determination in *Employment Division v. Smith*, is a brazen attempt to reinterpret the Free Exercise Clause and to impose that reinterpretation on the courts."

Almost immediately, Justice O'Connor interrupted to ask how she would distinguish RFRA from the VRA cases. Hamilton replied that the wording of section 5 limited Congress to enforcing explicit constitutional guarantees. Justice Rehnquist added that he thought *Morgan* went further than that. Her response was that in that instance Congress had built a better factual record. But Justice O'Connor was having none of that, saying that it was unsatisfactory "to think that all you'd get from your argument is at best a notion that we would say Congress had to do a better job of making facts." Hamilton fought back by stressing the term *appropriate* in section 5. Then she uttered a term that was to take a central role in Justice Kennedy's opinion. "There must be," she said, "some kind of proportional fit between the means and the end to be appropriate."

Justice Souter wanted to return to the VRA cases. Hamilton tried to distinguish them by saying that in RFRA Congress's purpose was to inject a higher level of scrutiny into certain cases than the court had ruled proper. Souter then said that by that light Congress's failure was that it was too candid. When Hamilton replied that it was not candor but purpose, he retorted that it was then "candor in expressing the purpose." But Hamilton's rebuttal was that there must be some evidence of state malfeasance for Congress to act under section 5 and that none existed here. Still not satisfied, Souter said that by that contention it was then just a matter of timing. O'Connor then raised the question of whether Congress could prohibit "any law that disproportionately affects religious minorities." Hamilton admitted that would be possible but argued that was not what RFRA did. Rehnquist then asked whether she was arguing for a narrow reading of *Morgan*, and she replied that indeed she was.

Justice Scalia then led Hamilton along another path, one she found more agreeable: discussing whether incorporated liberties have the same standing as those mentioned in the amendment itself and the targeted populations of those latter liberties. Scalia stressed that the equal protection clause was about African Americans and that applying the Bill of Rights against the states was accomplished only by judicial fiat. A back-and-forth on the original intentions of the amendment's drafters led them to agree that section 5 should not be construed as giving Congress authority over the Bill of Rights; in fact it was "staggering," they concurred, to take that position.

Justice Ginsburg interjected that the history of the Fourteenth Amendment is cloudier than Scalia suggested. Justice Breyer was clearly put off by characterizing a congressional effort to protect the due process liberties—the incorporated portions of the Bill of Rights—as a "staggering" modification of the Fourteenth Amendment. Hamilton backtracked a bit, saying that the term *staggering* related to the term *appropriate*. Nonetheless, she stuck to the point that "it would seem like they [Congress] should have most expansive power that they could have under the meaning of the Fourteenth Amendment with respect to racial discrimination." Souter wanted to be sure he understood the distinction she was attempting to draw: "Your argument is that with respect to the protection of rights incorporated under the incorporation theory there can be no substantive expansion." She agreed. Further, when pressed she said that even in the equality rights area *Morgan* should be the "upper limit" of congressional authority under section 5.

In the final few minutes of her time, the discussion turned to separation of powers. Kennedy asked if it were a separation of powers argument that the court should proceed on a case-by-case basis in the free exercise area rather than apply a general standard. Hamilton stressed again that Congress should not be able to enact a wide-ranging general standard and that RFRA was therefore equally invalid in its application to federal law as well as state law. The dialogue returned briefly to fact-finding, with Hamilton pointing to the contrast with the Civil Rights Act of 1964, upheld in *Heart of Atlanta Motel*, for which Congress had compiled a solid record of facts.

Jeffrey Sutton was up next. Although he touched on several of the same points as Hamilton, he always emphasized the federalism dimension, and in so doing occasionally diverged from Hamilton's positions. For example, he denied that rights guaranteed by the equal protection clause should be differentiated from those growing out of the due process clause. In his view, they stood on an equal footing and section 5 should be read narrowly in both instances. He also ventured to offer a slightly different twist on the establishment clause. States, he felt, should be free to "overprotect" free exercise without running afoul of the establishment clause. Of course, he admitted that there was a ceiling on how far states could go in granting exemptions to generally applicable laws without violating the establishment clause, but in general he preferred that states be given maximum discretion. In fact, he said states could enact their own RFRAs (and would do so if RFRA were struck down) and that to do so would be constitutionally appropriate.

He pressed the factual record argument with special vigor. Congress had not compiled any list of state violations of free exercise rights and would not have been able to do so had they tried. Had they been able to do so, RFRA could perhaps have been justified, but as it was it could not stand. Congress could, of course, he admitted, submit a piece of legislation without the necessary factual record, but it was taking a chance that the Supreme Court would invalidate their work in the absence of such a record. Of course, the court might conclude on its own that there were enough violations to warrant the legislation in question, but that was up to the court: "If they [Congress] want to take their chances, be completely silent as to why they're doing something, they can take a risk, and it then becomes your job, regrettably, to figure out whether there are underlying violations." Again, Justice Kennedy gave a hint about the direction of his thinking: "And in that respect, is there some requirement that the degree of intrusion on the States must be roughly balanced by the severity of the problem they're trying to correct? Is that the calculus we use?" Sutton quickly approved: "Justice Kennedy, that is precisely it."

When it was Douglas Laycock's turn, he opened with an appeal to precedent: "This case is controlled by an unbroken tradition of practice and judicial decision that begins with the Civil War amendments themselves. From the Civil Rights Act of 1866 to RFRA in 1993, Congress has always understood that it has the power to make constitutional rights effective in practice and to go beyond the floor set by this Court." Rehnquist interrupted this historical narrative to say that "some of the early cases on which *Katzenbach* relied are not to that effect," naming *Ex Parte Virginia*. Laycock replied that the while the issue in that case was different from that raised here, the standard used supported broad enforcement power resting in Congress. Justice O'Connor then pressed Laycock about the power of Congress to overturn a Supreme Court ruling. Trying to avoid a focus on that term, he said once again that "overturn is shorthand, but yes, to achieve a different result on similar facts under the statute than we would achieve under the Constitution itself, that's correct, but that's no different from the Voting Rights Act or from Title VII."

A brief exchange involving prisoners' rights with Justice O'Connor followed, but a follow-up question from Scalia led to a more important issue. Scalia raised the pre-*Smith Goldman* case, in which the court had denied a Jewish Air Force officer's free exercise claim to wear a yarmulke while on duty in spite of military regulations that banned it. The court had said that the compelling interest text did not apply to the military. Would RFRA compel the court to revisit that case, he asked? Laycock asserted that his feeling had always been that the court created a "military exception" in *Goldman*, in which case, yes, the case would now have to be governed by a different standard (which could, of course, produce the same result, just on a heightened basis of review); however, if as Scalia seemed to be saying, they had applied the compelling interest test and found the government's argument convincing, then, no, it would not be changed.

This latter point was vital, because it underscored the range of judicial independence that would survive RFRA. The court would retain the discretion to interpret the statute as they saw fit, applying their long-used canons of statutory interpretation. Kennedy seemed to agree. He said, "Well, compelling interest has an institutional, a juridical meaning based on our past cases, and I assume under ordinary principles of statutory construction that that is what Congress intended." Laycock agreed, and Scalia chimed in with, "So Congress really hasn't tied our hands very much." When Rehnquist tried to add a qualifier that they would have to abide by Congress's reading of compelling interest, Laycock attempted to smooth that over by reiterating that "you still get the final word on what the statute means."

Justice Stevens interjected to say, "I'm not even sure what compelling interest means in the peyote case itself, because the Court was divided on that issue. I'm not sure this is quite as clear a concept as everyone assumes." Laycock pounced on that statement, saying that that very fact shows how much discretion would stay in the hands of the court post-RFRA. "The power of interpreting compelling interests remains in this Court."

Justice Ginsburg pursued another line of questioning: if RFRA stood, would there ever be any litigation pursued directly under the free exercise clause, since RFRA set a higher standard than the amendment itself? A bit of sparring left this matter dangling. Then Justice Kennedy wanted to move to the question of whether RFRA created a special preference for religious groups and whether this might lead to establishment clause problems. Without referring to the case at hand, he raised the matter of zoning. Laycock tried to focus on the fact that the substantial burden requirement would act as an important threshold. Kennedy was unsatisfied, saying that "an establishment violation is measured by whether there is a preference." Laycock's reply cited *Amos* (stressing it was "nine–zero") for the proposition that ordinary exemptions do not create establishment clause problems.

Mentioning the establishment clause brought another question to Scalia's mind. Could Congress enforce the establishment clause through section 5? To be consistent, Laycock had to agree that it could. Putting forth an *in extremis* argument, Scalia asked whether Congress could then pass an act prohibiting states from granting tax exemptions to churches. Laycock conceded that it was possible. This led O'Connor to ask about abortion. Could Congress enact a law stipulating that all laws regulating abortion were to be "subject only to the rational basis test, no more"? Or, in mirror fashion, could it enact a law commanding that the strict scrutiny test must be applied in abortion cases? Laycock, admitting his "client obviously has a problem with the abortion decisions," argued that Congress could do the second but not the first. The reason was, although he did not use the term at this time, the "one way ratchet." He tried to press the point that when Congress acts to elevate individual rights it is not countermanding the court.

In the final few minutes of Laycock's time, the VRA cases resurfaced. Justice Souter gave him the opening, and Laycock drew a parallel between RFRA and the 1982 amendments to the VRA. The legislative record of that enactment contains few facts but is filled instead with denunciations of the Supreme Court's decision in *City of Mobile v. Bolden* and many explanations of why motive is hard to prove. Congress stated explicitly that the reason for the 1982 amendments was that the court had applied the wrong test and they were setting out to rectify that. If that statute is constitutional, then RFRA surely is.

As Solicitor General, Walter Dellinger appeared for the government. While the other three attorneys were all interrupted, Dellinger's presentation was all but derailed by interjections from the justices. Some of their remarks, in fact, wandered into rather tangential concerns. It seemed, counter to Chief Justice Hughes's claims, it was the justices themselves who were bringing up the chaff.

Dellinger began by attempting to reinforce Laycock's point about the way RFRA fit into already-established constitutional principles: "This case," he said, "does not require the Court to break new ground in upholding the statute, because the act prevents what everyone would agree is an actual violation of the Constitution as noted by this Court." Before he could go further, he got sidetracked. Kennedy asked if Boerne's denial of the permit was a violation of RFRA. He replied by simply stating that the government was only in court to defend the constitutionality of RFRA and that the trial court had not ruled on whether the substantial burden threshold had been met or not. Kennedy then got off into charitable deductions from the federal income tax, asking if Congress could abolish them. If it did so, would that put a substantial burden on churches? After a good bit of wrangling over peripheral matters, such as whether taxation was a burden, he tried to make the point that relieving a burden is not necessarily a benefit, legally at least.

Justice Stevens got back on the constitutional path by asking whether, as in the VRA, there was a "long, well-documented history of violations" that would justify the act: "should we assume as a predicate for our decision that there is a comparable violation of religious rights that's prevalent throughout the country?" Short answer: "No." Congress, Dellinger argued, has adequate power under section 5 to act prophylactically. Indeed, the court itself has sometimes acted prophylactically, as in *Miranda v. Arizona*,[23] when by requiring certain police procedures it hoped to prevent abuses.

Asked by Justice Breyer what type of violations Congress was endeavoring to prevent, he said, first, it was a matter of keeping the state from treating one denomination differently from others. Breyer's retort was that under *Smith* that did not violate the Constitution. Dellinger begged to differ but felt the main point was the normal difficulty in proving such targeting, in contrast to how easily it had been shown in *Church of Lukumi Babalu Aye v. Hialeah*. But effect is as important as motive. He cited the case of a religiously devout Nebraska student who did not want to live in university housing because of the alcohol, drug use, and casual sex that went on there. His request to live off campus was denied by the university. Congress has a right to worry about small religious groups and their adherents, and providing a statutory right to have their cases treated under the strict scrutiny test is a reasonable way to go about it.

For some reason, Justice O'Connor wanted to return to the tax issue, especially regarding the role of business or businesslike enterprises operated by religious organizations. A somewhat rambling—and in truth rather unenlightening—interchange followed.

Trying to return to one of his main points, Dellinger said that it could not be doubted that the piecemeal legislative granting of exemptions was too haphazard and inevitably biased against minority religions. A couple of justices offered the success of the Native American Church in removing peyote from the list of banned drugs as a comeback (with Justice Souter commenting that perhaps they had help from nonchurch members). Justice Ginsburg put Sutton's point to Dellinger. The states agree with RFRA's aims and will in fact pursue them diligently if left alone. What they object to is Congress making the decision for them. Dellinger responded by saying that an eight-hundred-page record testified to the lack of state respect for free exercise, adding for emphasis, that "the Lukumi had to come all the way to this Court before they got a single person to vote for them."

## THE DECISION OF THE SUPREME COURT

The justices voted 6–3 to strike down RFRA. The voting, however, followed no predictable pattern. Most obviously, liberals and conservatives split. But neither was there any particular gathering of justices who generally share various interpretive and methodological proclivities on one side or the other. The majority consisted of the chief justice, William Rehnquist, alongside Justices Anthony Kennedy, John Paul Stevens, Clarence Thomas, Ruth Bader Ginsburg, and Antonin Scalia. The dissenting side consisted of Justices Sandra Day O'Connor, Stephen Breyer, and David Souter, although they did not necessarily vote to uphold RFRA's constitutionality. Kennedy was selected to write the opinion, which Rehnquist, Stevens, Thomas, and Ginsburg joined in its entirety.[24] Stevens filed a short concurrence in which he added an establishment clause rationale to that offered by Kennedy. Scalia refused to join a portion of Kennedy's opinion dealing with the history of the Fourteenth Amendment and wrote a concurrence. He did not explain his reservations about this section of Kennedy's effort, though; instead, he devoted his pages to a lengthy refutation of Justice O'Connor's dissent. O'Connor's dissent, with the lone exception of one paragraph, was joined by Justice Breyer, who also filed his own dissent. Finally, Justice Souter also wrote a dissenting opinion.

### KENNEDY'S OPINION FOR THE COURT

As usual, the first section of the opinion recited the basic facts of the case and the second gave the details of RFRA's passage. There is a brief hint in this latter portion that the justices may have taken umbrage at the tone of the congressional criticism of *Smith*. After discussing that case, he said, "These points of constitutional interpretation were debated by Members of Congress in hearings and debates. Many criticized the Court's reasoning, and this disagreement resulted in the passage of RFRA."

In section 3 the analysis begins. The opening sentences, though, set the tone: "Under our Constitution, the Federal Government is one of enumerated powers. The judicial authority to determine the constitutionality of laws, in cases and controversies, is based on the premise that the 'powers of the legislature are defined and limited; and that those limits may not be mistaken, or forgotten, the constitution is written.'"[25]

We next get a taste of the strategy justices often use. Before they declare their holding, they lay out some generalities that could point the other way. It is much like the person who says, "You make a good point, but . . ." He concedes, for example, that "all must acknowledge that section 5 is 'a positive grant of legislative power' to Congress"[26] and, further, that "legislation which deters or remedies constitutional violations can fall within the sweep of Congress' enforcement power even if in the process it prohibits conduct which is not itself unconstitutional and intrudes into 'legislative spheres of autonomy reserved to the States.'"[27] He then cites a string of VRA cases to demonstrate how generous the court has been with Congress.

Then we get the "but": "It is also true, however, that '[a]s broad as the congressional enforcement power is, it is not unlimited.'"[28] We then get a summary of the holding, with the detailed rationale to follow. Congress only has the power to enforce the Fourteenth Amendment, and that power is solely remedial. This does not give Congress the power to determine the substance of the rights the Fourteenth Amendment confers: "Congress does not enforce a constitutional right by changing what the right is." The next paragraph contains the terms that have come largely to define the case: "While the line between measures that remedy or prevent unconstitutional actions and measures that make a substantive change in the governing law is not easy to discern, and Congress must have wide latitude in determining where it lies, the distinction exists and must be observed. There must be a congruence and proportionality between the injury to be prevented or remedied and the means adopted to that end. Lacking such a connection, legislation may become substantive in operation and effect."

He begins his explication of the reasons behind this proposition with a discussion of the history of the Fourteenth Amendment, which, he says, "confirms the remedial, rather than substantive, nature of the Enforcement Clause." Kennedy begins his story on January 1866 when the Joint Committee on Reconstruction presented its initial draft of the Fourteenth Amendment, which he quotes (as did Sutton's brief, as noted previously): "The Congress shall have power to make all laws which shall be necessary and proper to secure to the citizens of each State all privileges and immunities of citizens in the several States, and to all persons in the several States equal protection in the rights of life, liberty, and property." According to Kennedy's telling, this proposal "encountered immediate opposition . . . from across the political spectrum." He supports this conclusion with a list of quotations from various members of Congress who worried that this wording would grant too much power to Congress. These objections forced the joint committee to reconsider. Their revised draft, presented in April of 1866, closely paralleled what was eventually adopted. The substantive features of the new amendment were to be "self-executing" (i.e., enforceable in court) and Congress's power under section 5 "was no longer plenary but remedial." It could only be invoked when states transgressed the declarations of section 1.

Kennedy buttresses this reading of section 5 with a reference to the debates over the Ku Klux Klan Act, which occurred in 1871. Two members of the House of Representatives and two scholars are cited for the position that this debate shows that section 5 was designed to have a limited reach.

Up to this point, the discussion focused on section 5's federalism dimension, but Kennedy also contended that his reading of the Fourteenth Amendment is in line with the traditional understanding of separation of powers. His conclusion is that, "as enacted, the Fourteenth Amendment confers substantive rights against the States, which, like the provisions of the Bill of Rights, are self-executing. The power to interpret the Constitution in a case or controversy remains in the Judiciary."

The problem with this version of history is that it is attenuated, selective, and in some cases, just plain wrong. The Fourteenth Amendment was part and parcel of the history of Reconstruction, and one cannot simply begin its life with the report of the Joint Committee on Reconstruction.

This is not the place to offer a comprehensive rebuttal to this history, but some correction is essential.

The historical record of the political maneuverings that resulted in the Fourteenth Amendment's adoption is voluminous. For years, historians relied chiefly on the ample record of official documents, such as committee reports and congressional debates. Recently, though, their reach has expanded to include sources such as letters, speeches given outside Congress, and newspaper articles. Mountains of these documents exist also. What this means, though, is that a diligent researcher, if he or she wants to push a particular thesis, can find quotations supporting almost any position. To try to understand what the framers of the amendment meant, it is important to step back and examine the context in which they worked, to contemplate the goals they were seeking to accomplish and the ideas they carried around in their heads.[29]

When Congress convened in late 1865, the Thirteenth Amendment ending slavery in the United States had just been ratified. However, most recognized that there were still important tasks ahead and that they would need to wrestle with several dilemmas.

The problem that overrode all others was that the Southern states showed no signs of accepting anything but the most limited interpretation of their defeat on the battlefield. For example, they immediately chose prominent former Confederate officials to serve in public office. The Georgia legislature even selected Alexander H. Stephens, the vice president of the Confederacy, as its senator. On top of this, the population remained hostile to Union sympathizers in their midst and people who came from the North. Furthermore, the report of General Carl Schurz, sent to the South by President Johnson to survey the situation, reported a widespread belief that things would soon return to "normal," with the structure of Southern society little disturbed.[30] Some Southerners were even talking about presenting the bill for the emancipated slaves to the federal government. State laws, too, sought to stifle freedom of expression, as they had before the Civil War. But it was their treatment of the newly freed slaves that upset the congressional majority the most. All the defeated states enacted a legal regime labeled "Black Codes," which all but returned slavery under another guise. Thus, in the view of the congressional Republicans, who held a majority in both houses, state governments in the South could not be trusted to abide by the outcome of the war and given any chance would furthermore deprive the freed slaves of even the most basic civil rights and liberties. This view was underscored by a race riot in Memphis, in which public officials had clearly sided with the white perpetrators of violence. Bringing these recalcitrants to heel, therefore, was seen as an essential first step in making the expenditure of the blood and treasure of war worthwhile. Nevertheless, congressional Republicans retained a favorable view of American federalism. The states were still viewed in light of the Jeffersonian tradition that touted the benefits of small, self-governing republics; but they wanted to make all those republics respectful of the rights of all their citizens. How to remake the Southern states in the image of Northern states without going too far in eroding the legitimate powers of the states was, therefore, the central issue they faced.

This matter was overlaid with the conflict with President Andrew Johnson. The president had at first signaled a willingness to work with the Republicans in Congress and gave speeches in the immediate aftermath of the war praising the end of slavery. Soon, however, he was advocating policies that would return the Southern states, even with their largely prewar personnel and policies, to the fold quickly. Furthermore, from an institutional perspective he insisted that Reconstruction policy should be lodged in the executive alone.

Another institutional, and practical, question was staring congressional Republicans in the face. With the end of slavery, the three-fifths clause had been abrogated. The resulting increase in the South's population would, therefore, magnify its number of seats in the House. Republicans believed that the "slave power" had dominated and disfigured American politics before the war, and now these same elites would return with even more enhanced power. They could well combine with Northern Democrats to dominate Congress in the future, an appalling prospect.[31]

On another institutional front, they mistrusted the Supreme Court. After all, it had issued the infamous *Dred Scott* decision, and Southerners continued to sit on it. Nevertheless, the American tradition of reverence for the law was still strong enough to mitigate any direct assault on the integrity of the judiciary.

Finally, they faced the dilemma of whether the newly freed slaves should be enfranchised. Racial beliefs, which varied among the Republicans, intertwined with practical considerations, such as the fact that almost all the freedmen were illiterate, to cause a significant difference of opinion on this question. Yet giving blacks the right to vote would be one way of checking the power of the Southern elite. Nevertheless, there was opposition to this move even among many of the Northern states, most of whom outside New England did not allow blacks to vote. (Eventually, though, a consensus emerged that enfranchisement was both moral and practical, resulting in the Fifteenth Amendment. However, it proved largely ineffective until the VRA was passed nearly a century later.)

The first congressional attempt to control Reconstruction was the Freedmen's Bureau Bill, a rather modest measure that Johnson promptly vetoed. In his message he argued that he alone had complete control over Reconstruction. Incensed, Republican leaders began drafting what became the Civil Rights Act of 1866. As Garrett Epps has said, "the story of the Civil Rights Bill forms an important part of the background of the Fourteenth Amendment."[32] The measure's supporters thought the enforcement clause of the Thirteenth Amendment provided ample authority for Congress to enact the bill. Some Republicans, including John Bingham, an acknowledged constitutional law expert, worried that this was inadequate and that another amendment was needed. Nevertheless, the bill passed, but Johnson vetoed it on March 27. With political tensions rising, for the first time in American history, on April 6 Congress overrode a presidential veto of an important piece of legislation.

While the Civil Rights Act was being debated in February and March of 1866, discussions about an amendment to the Constitution were under way. One matter that later became hotly contested even through the mid-twentieth century seems settled by modern scholarship.[33] The drafters of the amendment thought that they were incorporating the Bill of Rights against the states.[34] It appears it is more likely they thought the privileges and immunities clause rather than the due process clause was the mechanism for doing so, but the fact of intended incorporation (or at the very least a list of fundamental liberties that would include most of the Bill of Rights) seems certain. In fact, freedom of expression and freedom of religion were mentioned explicitly.

Any number of proposals were put on the table, and it would take us far afield to list them here. Robert Dale Owen, son of the famous English reformer and a respected social reformer, journalist, and former member of Congress, seems to have provided the framework for what eventually became the Fourteenth Amendment.[35] The important point is that all of them included a congressional enforcement provision. In fact, this was seen as the main goal. Bingham said on February 28, 1866, that the whole purpose of the amendment was "to arm the Congress of the United States, by the consent of the people of the United States, with the power to enforce the bill of rights as it stands in the Constitution today."[36] To be sure, the provisions of the substantive sections of the amendment would be actionable in the courts. Representative Giles W. Hotchkiss was a major proponent of this view, arguing that it was necessary to insulate the amendment against a return of the Democratic Party to power in Congress.[37] Still, the aim of the amendment was to overcome any doubts about the power of Congress to enforce the Bill of Rights against the states.

When a draft emerged from the Joint Committee on Reconstruction in April of 1866, it did indeed encounter the opposition Justice Kennedy quoted. But that opposition centered on the newly added equal protection provision, not on whether Congress could enforce the provisions of the Bill of Rights against the states. Earl Maltz sums up this debate in the following words: "They [the opponents of Bingham's draft] found no fault with the grant of authority to secure privileges and immunities. Instead, their criticisms were aimed at the equal protection component of the proposal."[38]

In short, Kennedy's assertions are overdrawn at best and misleading at worst. Looking at the historical record, it seems beyond dispute that the amendment's drafters and backers thought they were providing a dual track enforcement mechanism to make the states adhere to the provisions of the Bill of Rights. There is great irony that in *Boerne* one of those institutions checked the ability of the other to do so. Rather than complementing each other, one prohibited the other from acting.

A similar point is to be made regarding Kennedy's analysis of the debate on the Ku Klux Klan Act. True, there was an emphasis on the limits of congressional power. But the issue in the debate was over how far Congress could go in regulating private conduct when that conduct was done in collusion with state officials. There was little discussion of Congress's power to regulate state public policy itself. Thus it is hardly relevant to the question at hand in RFRA.

Returning to the opinion, despite its historical shortcomings, Kennedy offered this overview mostly as background. He was on sounder, though not entirely solid, ground when he turned to the early judicial interpretations of the Fourteenth Amendment. He first adduced the *Civil Rights Cases* to show how limited the court has historically taken section 5 to be. However, these cases, as noted in the last chapter, dealt with attempted federal regulation of private action, not state policy. In fact, that was seen as the central defect of the statutes in question. The wording he quotes even makes that clear. Then three other cases from 1875, 1883, and 1903, which repeat similar wording, are cited. Then he sweeps rather broadly in a concluding sentence: "Although the specific holdings of these early cases might have been superseded or modified, their treatment of Congress section 5 power as corrective or preventive, not definitional, has not been questioned." Not questioned perhaps because not raised. One of the two cases he cited as superseding or modifying the three earlier cases, *Heart of Atlanta Motel*, rejected any consideration of section 5 in favor of a ruling on the commerce clause. In the other, *United States v. Guest*,[39] the court explicitly removed the section 5 issue: "We emphasize that [the federal statute] by its clear language incorporates no more than the Equal Protection Clause itself; the statute does not purport to give substantive, as opposed to remedial, implementation to any rights secured by that clause. Since we therefore deal here only with the bare terms of the Equal Protection Clause itself, nothing said in this opinion goes to the question of what kinds of other and broader legislation Congress might constitutionally enact under section 5 of the Fourteenth Amendment to implement that Clause *or any other provision of the Amendment*" (emphasis added).

Kennedy next turned to the VRA cases. His review focused on the factual record that Congress had compiled in each of these cases. But then he had to address the two rationales of *Morgan*. "There is," he admitted, "language in our opinion in *Katzenbach v. Morgan* which could be interpreted as acknowledging a power in Congress to enact legislation that expands the rights contained in section 1 of the Fourteenth Amendment." He quickly added, though, that "this is not a necessary interpretation . . . or even the best one." He then summarizes the two rationales, treating them as equally valid, and concludes that both "rested on unconstitutional discrimination by New York and Congress' reasonable attempt to combat it."

Can RFRA therefore be considered enforcement legislation as defined in section 5? The archdiocese and the federal government have insisted that "if Congress can prohibit laws with discriminatory effect in order to prevent racial discrimination in violation of the Equal Protection Clause, then it can do the same . . . to promote religious liberty." But he will not allow them to go this far: "While preventive rules are sometimes appropriate remedial measures, there must be a congruence between the means used and the ends to be achieved. The appropriateness of remedial measures must be considered in light of the evil presented. Strong measures appropriate to address one harm may be an unwarranted response to another, lesser one."

He then says that Congress's thin evidence to support RFRA stands in stark contrast to the record found in the VRA. He refers to a number of instances in the former record (even, ironically, citing two general sentences from Douglas Laycock's congressional testimony, ripped, it must be said, entirely out of context) to validate the lack of detail on which RFRA could be based. Because he adhered to the need for a showing of discriminatory purpose, a la *Smith*, he was able to dismiss much of the record that focused on effects. From these highly selective quotations, he concludes that "it is difficult to maintain that they [the state statutes and rulings mentioned in the hearings] are examples of legislation enacted or enforced due to animus or hostility to the burdened religious practices or that they indicate some widespread pattern of religious discrimination in this country." Consequently, "Congress' concern was with the incidental burdens imposed, not the object or purpose of the legislation."

Even so, the gaps in the legislative record were "not RFRA's most serious shortcoming." Instead, the biggest problem was that RFRA "cannot be considered remedial, preventive legislation, if those terms are to have any meaning." It is completely "out of proportion" to any "remedial or preventive" objective. Rather, it was an attempt to usher in "a substantive change in constitutional protections." Conceivably, a congressional statute preventing state enactments in certain areas might be valid if "there is reason to believe that many of the laws affected by the congressional enactment have a significant likelihood of being unconstitutional." RFRA, in contrast, was much broader. It applied to every federal and state statute, was retroactive, and had no termination date. He then shows how much more limited the VRA and its amendments were. They confined their reach to specified geographical areas; they had termination dates; and they addressed clearly documented wrongs that were plainly unconstitutional. Allowing future courts a bit of wiggle room, he follows this assertion with the comment that while none of these is necessary for a statute to be judicially sanctioned, some type of limitation is needed "to ensure Congress' means are proportionate to ends legitimate under section 5."

In light of these principles, "the stringent test RFRA demands of state laws reflects a lack of proportionality or congruence between the means adopted and the legitimate end to be achieved." The strict scrutiny test is too high a barrier for states to have to climb over in every instance. But even if in practice the courts were to retreat to something approaching intermediate scrutiny in practice, RFRA would still be a "considerable congressional intrusion into the States' traditional prerogatives and general authority to regulate for the health and welfare of their citizens."

The rest of the opinion is a bit of window-dressing. He discusses, first, the costs RFRA would impose on the states as they would be forced to defend themselves repeatedly in court. Then he addresses a bit of a constitutional civics lesson to Congress: "Our national experience teaches that the Constitution is preserved best when each part of the Government respects both the Constitution and the proper actions and determinations of the other branches." Inasmuch as the court had already laid out the appropriate interpretation of the free exercise clause, it was illegitimate for the Congress to pass a law "designed to control cases and controversies, such as the one before us."

The final paragraph nods, as court opinions often do, to the deference that is due Congress but restates the *Marbury*-inspired axiom that it is for the court to "determine if Congress has exceeded its authority under the Constitution." In this instance, that judgment is that "RFRA contradicts vital principles necessary to maintain the separation of powers and the federal balance."

### The Concurring and Dissenting Opinions

Justice Stevens penned a brief stand-alone concurrence in which he argued that RFRA's constitutional defect was that it violated the establishment clause. RFRA provided a legal shield for churches that was unavailable to secular institutions: "This preference for religion, as opposed to irreligion, is forbidden by the First Amendment."

Justice Scalia's concurrence, which Justice Stevens joined, is devoted to answering the points advanced in Justice O'Connor's dissent. Thus it makes more sense to examine her dissent first. She believed that the court should have used this case to reconsider the holding in *Smith*. She continued to think that it was improper to discard the compelling interest test then without the question even being briefed. If the court corrected this misstep, then it could consider RFRA purely as a constitutional matter. (Of course, if *Smith* were reversed, there would be little need for RFRA, save that it added the least restrictive means requirement to the judicially stated version of the compelling interest test.)

O'Connor indicated that she agreed with Kennedy's analysis regarding the scope and limits of section 5, deriving her view from the history recited in the court opinion. She expressed her clear support for applying the "congruence and proportionality" criterion to any attempt by Congress to alter the court's reading of the Constitution. Her problem was that the court applied this framework to RFRA assuming that the holding in *Smith* is the correct interpretation of the free exercise clause. In her view, that case "is gravely at odds with our earlier free exercise precedents." To find the proper interpretation of the free exercise clause, it is necessary to turn to its early history.

The remainder of the opinion is a lengthy vindication of her stance that the colonial and early national experience with religious liberty shows that religious exemptions from generally applicable laws was meant to be the default position. They were to be granted, in short, unless there was some strong reason to require universal adherence to a given law. She surveys a large number of documents, contemporary statements by leading figures of the day, and secondary historical writings to demonstrate that "at the time the Bill of Rights was ratified, it was accepted that government should, when possible, accommodate religious practice." Today, the compelling interest test is a logical descendant of this position. Thus the court should return to the appropriate framework for free exercise jurisprudence by overruling *Smith* at its earliest opportunity. This case would have been the ideal time to do that, she felt.

Scalia was clearly offended by this attack on his *Smith* opinion. With his usual verve, he launched into a broadside against the "historical evidence" (quotation marks his) offered by O'Connor. He adduced historical quotations and notes of his own that would make the historical evidence lean his way. His most telling point is that many of the early advocates of religious liberty, and most of the statutes and state constitutional provisions, contain something like a "peace" and "order" caveat. To Scalia, this signifies a preference for generally applicable laws. From a legal perspective, it is important, he felt, to note that none of the material O'Connor quoted indicated that exemptions were required. But, of course, the compelling interest test does not say that they are "required," only that they must be granted unless the government has a very good reason to deny them.

In truth, the historical evidence can be read either way. Nevertheless, none of the people who drafted and commented on these early efforts at codifying religious liberty had any conception of either modern religious diversity or the scope of the modern state. Therefore this controversy over original meaning proves only that the historical record is mixed and that, in any event, it is of limited utility for settling today's issues.

Justice Breyer had some qualms about Justice O'Connor's complete embrace of Justice Kennedy's rendition of Fourteenth Amendment history and meaning. Other than that, he joined O'Connor's dissent and also thought the case afforded an opportunity to have *Smith* reargued.

Finally, Justice Souter offered the view that O'Connor's essay had raised substantial doubts about the correctness of *Smith*. He was not, however, prepared to reject that holding without further argument. Thus, until there was a full and vigorous reexamination of the *Smith* rule, it was, in his view, inappropriate to decide on the constitutionality of RFRA.

Thus, for students of Supreme Court decision making, the case presents a fertile field for speculation. We have reliably conservative members of the court, such as Rehnquist and Thomas, being joined by a duo of members from the liberal wing, Ginsburg and Stevens. Stevens then also joins an opinion by Scalia, normally the most strident of the conservatives.

Justice Kennedy himself presents something of a puzzle here. Usually, his most deeply held value is thought to be individual liberty.[40] In this instance, though, he opts for governmental power, state governmental power anyway, over individual liberty. Rehnquist and Thomas are easier to pigeonhole, as their vote conforms to their usual deep skepticism of federal power vis-à-vis the states.

Interestingly, too, the dissents did not directly challenge the holding of the court. They merely wanted another issue considered before the constitutionality of RFRA was decided. From an institutional perspective, the case presents a bit of an anomaly. The court was in essence claiming power to deny Congress the power to increase judicial power.

If there is perhaps an overriding explanation to be had, what seems to run throughout is the justices' possible resentment at Congress treading on their turf. True, in this case to uphold RFRA would have placed more power in the hands of the judiciary, in that they would have had more discretion to decide individual cases. Yet to uphold the principle of enhanced congressional power under section 5 would have opened the door to Congress perhaps using that power to offer alternative constitutional interpretations in other domains of constitutional law. And that would have undermined the outsized pronouncement of judicial supremacy, since 1958 an article of faith among almost all Supreme Court justices, made in *Cooper v. Aaron*.

Whatever the constitutional merits of the court's opinion, America's religious leaders and a parade of members of Congress were outraged. We turn now to consider how they reacted.

CHAPTER 7

# POLITICAL REACTION

REACTION TO THE SUPREME COURT'S DECISION FROM those who had supported RFRA was predictably harsh. Rev. Oliver Thomas of the National Council of Churches said he believed that "every religious person will be hurt by this decision."[1] The Baptist Joint Committee on Public Affairs issued a statement contending that the Supreme Court has "nullified . . . the most important piece of legislation affecting our religious liberty since the First Amendment itself . . . Our 'First Freedom' is no longer first, it is barely a freedom at all."[2] Rev. Barry Lynn of Americans United for Separation of Church and State added, "Religious minorities are out of luck until there's a change in the makeup of the Court . . . You'd think the Congress had decided to revoke the First Amendment by statute."[3] Rabbi David Saperstein of the Religious Action Center for Reform Judaism was equally strident: "Are Americans going to remain free to practice their religion protected from undue government interference? Today, Americans will once again find that their free exercise of religion will be subject to government regulation, even when no significant government interest in the infringement of religion is involved."[4] In another interview, he asserted that the decision will "go down in history . . . among the worst mistakes this court has ever made,"[5] and in still another he compared it to the *Dred Scott* case.[6]

Secular groups expressed similar dismay. Steven R. Shapiro, the National Legal Director for the American Civil Liberties Union (ACLU), had this to say: "This is a disappointing ruling that further erodes the constitutional protection for our free exercise of religion. In our view, this law was well within Congress' authority to enforce the Constitution. Unfortunately, the Court's decision today has once again lowered the threshold at which the government can take away our religious freedom."[7] A lead editorial in *The New York Times* sounded special disappointment that the court had not taken this opportunity to revisit *Smith*:

What is troubling is not what the Court did but what it did not do, which was to reconsider its contentious 1990 ruling.

Whether the Court's ruling has severely damaged Congress' ability to redress civil rights violations as some fear, remains to be seen. But it is abundantly clear that by striking down the Restoration Act without reviewing its earlier decision and reaffirming religion's First Amendment protections, the Court has left religious observance alarmingly vulnerable.[8]

## State RFRAs

The first legal and policy reaction was passage of several state RFRAs.[9] The first of these had actually been passed in 1993 in Connecticut, but the major action on this front came after *Boerne*. In 1998 Florida, Illinois, and Rhode Island enacted RFRAs. Alabama, Arizona, South Carolina, and Texas joined these three states in 1999. Then in 2000 Idaho, New Mexico, and Oklahoma passed their versions. By 2009 five other states had also adopted RFRAs: Pennsylvania (2002), Missouri (2004), Virginia (2007), Utah (2008), and Tennessee (2009). Attempts to pass RFRAs in other states, most notably California and New York, failed, however.

Although the provisions of these laws vary, the thrust in all is to restore the strict scrutiny test when an individual or religious institution claims a state policy violates free exercise. It is not clear, though, how much impact these statutes have actually had. Christopher Lund's careful study shows that they are not used much in actual litigation and that even when they are the plaintiffs often lose.[10] Nevertheless, as even Lund admits, it is impossible to know how much influence these laws have, because lawyers urge many parties to settle out of court, and the presence of a RFRA in a state undoubtedly shapes the outcome of those settlements.

In the end, though, this is a haphazard approach both because not every state has a RFRA and because of the unevenness of the protections those on the books offer.

## The Religious Liberty Protection Act

As with religious and civil rights leaders, members of Congress did not react passively. On the day of the decision, Senator Ted Kennedy urged his colleagues to come up with a revised law that would pass muster with the justices. "We cannot," he said, "take no from the Supreme Court as the final answer."[11] In less than three weeks the House Subcommittee on the Constitution (whose parent body was the Judiciary Committee) opened hearings on the question of how Congress should react to *Boerne*.

Charles Canady, a Republican from Florida and chair of the subcommittee, laid out the important issues in his opening statement:

> Before we begin, I would like to make two observations. First, there have been questions raised as to whether RFRA is a valid exercise of Congress' authority with respect to Federal laws. The *Boerne* decision struck down RFRA as being outside the scope of Congress' enforcement authority under section 5 of the 14th amendment. The 14th Amendment allows Congress to protect individual rights against state infringements. It would appear, therefore, that RFRA is still valid as to the Federal Government . . .
>
> Second, and most importantly, the Court's holding regarding the role of Congress in interpreting the Constitution and protecting individual liberties raised troubling questions concerning the relationship between the judiciary and the elected representatives of the people in the Legislative branch.[12]

Rep. Jerold Nadler, a Democrat from New York, followed with a tirade against the decision, then concluded on a hopeful note: "Just as a broad and diverse coalition of religious and civil liberties groups, with bipartisan cooperation in the Congress, succeeded in passing the Religious Freedom Restoration Act, I am confident that we will succeed in restoring once more the freedom of religion this Court has so cavalierly stripped from our citizens."[13]

Indeed, the coalition of which Nadler spoke was already working to come up with a way to respond to *Boerne*. In an effort to give life to these efforts, committees in both the House and Senate followed up on the initial hearings with several others.[14] At the outset, there was near unanimity in the need to search for a rebuttal to the court. However, Nadler's optimism proved premature, as the coalition that had worked together over RFRA frayed before what became known as the Religious Liberty Protection Act (RLPA) could be passed. The source of the fissure was a concern voiced ever more loudly by groups backing gays and lesbians that the act might be used to challenge state and local civil rights laws banning discrimination in employment and housing on the basis of sexual orientation. Their concern was heightened by the statements of some conservative Christian groups that when it passed they intended to use RLPA for that very purpose. In time, the major civil rights organizations and most major liberal religious groups withdrew their support from the new bill. Although it passed the House, but not before a protracted fight over this issue, it was stillborn in the Senate. In the end, only a scaled-back version of RLPA, the Religious Land Use and Institutionalized Persons Act of 2000, could be placed on the statute books.[15]

Because *Boerne* had gone from a religious liberty case to one concerning the deeper issue of constitutional interpretation, it provoked a number of reactions. Mark Chopko, the general counsel for the United States Conference of Catholic Bishops, told the House subcommittee that "what the Court did was write a decision about power and the allocation of constitutional power, not a decision about religious liberty."[16] Some who saw the case as part of a recent pattern of judicial imperialism felt that a stern and draconian response was called for (although Chopko himself was more restrained). For instance, one of the more strident suggestions was that Congress should debate impeaching a justice or two; another was to take up a measure expanding the size of the court. Even if, the argument went, neither actually passed, the debate itself might have a curative effect on the contemporary court, with the analogy drawn to Franklin D. Roosevelt's "court packing" plan of 1937. Other irate witnesses told the House committee that they should either repass RFRA or offer a resolution telling the court how angry Congress was at the turn of events. Calmer heads pointed out that none of these was likely to pass and that even if they did it would only anger the court; besides, they would do nothing to advance religious liberty.

Some of those concerned mainly with protecting religious liberty thought that a constitutional amendment would be the surest route to that end. While if it passed it would certainly set the strict scrutiny test on an uncontestable foundation, the "if" was one of its two problems. Proposing and ratifying a constitutional amendment is a difficult and problematic enterprise at best, and few felt it was realistic to try at this point. Some took the view that it was a possible last resort but that other approaches should be tried first. The other problem with the amendment path was that in a way it would concede the separation of powers argument. That is, if Congress is to claim a role in interpreting the Constitution as currently written, then proposing a constitutional amendment would amount to granting that it was lacking that power. For both practical and theoretical reasons, therefore, this approach was abandoned early on.

The legal experts to whom the congressional committees turned—most important again was Douglas Laycock—thought that the best strategy was to pass a new statute keeping the substance of RFRA but making its constitutional underfootings more secure. This could be done in one of three ways: searching for alternative constitutional provisions on which to base congressional power to legislate to protect free exercise; constructing a more comprehensive evidentiary record with an eye on section 5; or some combination of these two. As the committee's consultants set about drafting RPLA, they discussed three alternative constitutional bases: the treaty power, the commerce clause, and the spending power.

## THE TREATY POWER

Article II, Section 2 of the Constitution gives to the president the "power, by and with the advice and consent of the Senate, to make treaties, provided two thirds of the Senators concur." In an important case from 1920, *Missouri v. Holland*,[17] the Supreme Court ruled that a treaty overrides a state law, even if that state law lies within the scope of power granted to the states. In 1966 a branch of the United Nations had drafted the International Covenant on Civil and Political Rights.[18] The United States belatedly ratified the covenant in 1992 but added important reservations. One of them was that it was not to be self-executing, meaning that no American citizen could file a suit claiming its protection. What if Congress should now grant them that authority?

Laycock told the House committee that if Congress were to find that the "United States is out of compliance [with the treaty], *and* . . . Congress *chooses* to bring the United States into compliance, Congress may pass implementing legislation to achieve compliance."[19] The covenant stipulates that everyone has the right "to have or to adopt a religion or belief of his choice." Further, he has the right "to manifest his religion or belief in worship, observance, practice and teaching," but this right can be limited when "necessary to protect public safety, order, health, or morals or the fundamental rights and freedoms of others." Should this language be utilized, as Laycock urged should this route be taken, it would not provide as much protection for religious exercise as strict scrutiny, but the law would be safe from being voided by the judiciary, unless the court were prepared to overrule *Missouri v. Holland*.

However logical this course might have been, it ran onto political shoals. Religious conservatives, along with other conservatives, have in recent years taken a rather insular view of constitutional law and are suspicious of foreign and international documents and precedents.[20] Members of Congress wished to keep the coalition backing the bill as large as possible and feared raising any matter that might be controversial. Consequently, when there was a break in the hearings, they sent a congressional staffer to Laycock and the others asking them to put this recommendation aside. It was not mentioned again.

### THE COMMERCE CLAUSE

To be clear, no one thought use of the commerce clause implied that religious bodies and institutions are commercial institutions. Rather, the idea was that their activities pull them into the realm of commerce and that that fact could be used as a pillar on which to base RLPA. Still, though, many were discomfited, and some found the idea most distasteful.

Nevertheless, from a constitutional standpoint there were good reasons for thinking that the clause might win approval from the courts, which after all was the whole idea. The commerce clause (Article I, Section 8) grants Congress the power "to regulate commerce with foreign nations, and among the several States, and with the Indian tribes." To see why this clause might be a valid legal foundation for a federal law placing limitations on state and local governments, a bit of constitutional history is helpful.

Although in the early days of the Republic the Supreme Court had read the commerce clause rather broadly, giving a wide scope to congressional power, beginning in the late nineteenth century the court took a much more restricted view. For example, it read the word *commerce* very narrowly, placing many activities (such as manufacturing) outside the reach of congressional regulatory power.[21] Further, it adopted a crabbed view of the word *regulate*, holding that it could not be used to prohibit the movement of certain goods in interstate commerce.[22] Starting in 1937, however, the court moved away from this stance; by 1941, it had turned 180 degrees.[23]

Of special note in this regard is the case of *Wickard v. Filburn*.[24] Recall from Chapter 4 that in an attempt to raise the price of wheat, Congress had passed a law restricting the acreage that could be devoted to wheat production and provided an administrative mechanism for allocating that acreage among farmers. Mr. Filburn used his allotted acreage to grow wheat for the market but then also planted some additional land in wheat for feeding to his own livestock. His argument was that this self-consumption was not really "commerce" and therefore lay beyond the reach of congressional regulation. The Supreme Court thought otherwise and developed two important doctrines that continue to shape commerce clause jurisprudence. One is the "aggregation principle" and the other the "substantial effects" doctrine. True, the justices said, Mr. Filburn's activities would not seem to be commerce in the ordinary sense of the term. However, if you add together what everyone such as Mr. Filburn could do if allowed (aggregate it, that is), then it would have a substantial effect on the price of wheat (since less would be bought in the market). This would then undermine if not cancel out the goal of Congress's policy.

In 1964, the Supreme Court broadened the reading of the commerce clause even further. At issue was the Civil Rights Act of 1964, which forbade racial discrimination in hotels and restaurants. While the act was being considered, there was some discussion of basing it on section 5; however, there was a fear that the Civil Rights Cases of 1883 might make the court skittish about upholding it. Thus the decision was made to rest the law on the commerce clause. Accordingly, several government officials were called upon to offer evidence regarding the harm to the free flow of interstate commerce that was being engendered by racial discrimination in accommodations and food service. The court quickly upheld the act in two cases, one concerning a motel and the other a restaurant.[25] It was sufficient to bring the motel within the orbit of interstate commerce when it advertised on interstate highways, and likewise the restaurant when it bought food from interstate vendors. The important point for our purposes is that everyone knew this was an antidiscrimination statute and that the "commerce" element was only a legal hook. In short, if Congress said it was a regulation of commerce, the court would not look behind that assertion to uncover any other motives.

After that, Congress used the commerce clause as the basis for a wide variety of legislation, with the sanction of the court. This trend continued until 1995 when the case of *United States v. Lopez* was decided.[26] Congress had enacted the Gun-Free School Zones Act of 1990, forbidding the possession of a gun near a school. Legislators had made the usual nod to commerce, citing the role of education in interstate commerce. The court, however, overturned the act, saying that it was a criminal statute masquerading as a commercial regulation. Nevertheless, the court did reaffirm both the aggregation principle and the substantial effects doctrine. As the hearings on RLPA proceeded, some legal experts voiced concern that this case was a signal that the court would apply a more exacting standard than in the past when Congress used the commerce clause for purposes lying at the margins of commercial regulations.

Thus, to strengthen the contention that religious activities have a substantial effect on interstate commerce, a variety of evidence was put in the record.[27] Figures for the revenue of churches were provided, along with estimates for capital construction projects. The value of property held by churches was also included. Along with this data, one had to add the revenues and expenditures of religiously affiliated hospitals; elementary and secondary schools, colleges, universities, and seminaries; and broadcasting outlets. Then there was the large national market for dietary products consumed by Jews and Muslims. Furthermore, there was the sale of various religious items (robes, communion wafers, altar cloths, and the like) and the revenues of religious bookstores and publishers. Finally, the growing business of attracting religious conventions was noteworthy. In short, the sums involved from all these activities ran into the billions, and most of it moved in interstate channels.

### The Spending Clause

The spending clause (Article I, Section 8) empowers Congress to spend public monies to "provide for the common defense and general welfare of the United States." Under this clause, Congress provides a great deal of money to state and local governments, and it is not unusual that various conditions are attached to these allocations. Why, therefore, could Congress not attach a blanket condition that state and local governments had to accede to RLPA if they took the grant?

In fact, there was ample precedent for doing this. Three important federal statutes, for instance, contain general prohibitions: Title VI of the Civil Rights Act of 1964 (banning discrimination on the basis of race, color, or national origin in all programs receiving federal financial assistance), Title IX of the Education Amendments of 1972 (prohibiting gender discrimination in educational programs receiving federal financial assistance), and the Equal Access Act of 1984 (requiring all secondary schools that receive federal financial assistance to allow any valid student group equal use of facilities).

There was one potential complication, however: how one read the Supreme Court's 1987 decision in *South Dakota v. Dole.*[28] Congress had required that states receiving federal funds for highway construction (all fifty) raise their legal drinking age to 21. When this statute was challenged, the court saw no problem with Congress pursuing "broad policy objectives by conditioning receipt of federal moneys upon compliance by the recipient with federal statutory and administrative directives." Furthermore, "the power of Congress to authorize expenditures of public moneys for public purposes is not limited to direct grants of legislative power found in the Constitution." However, the court did hold that there were three limitations on this sweeping power. First, the conditions had to be geared toward achieving "the general welfare." Second, the stipulations must be clearly stated. Third, "conditions on federal grants might be illegitimate if they are unrelated 'to the federal interest in particular national projects or programs.'"[29]The first and second of these posed no real problem; it was the third that might lead to difficulty when it came to RPLA. Religious discrimination, that is, might well be far from the central objectives of "particular national projects or programs."

There was another problem with using the spending clause. It would easily bring within its purview prisons, schools, hospitals, and almost every other state institution. However, its applicability to land use was more uncertain. That is, land use decisions are ordinarily made by local zoning or landmarking bodies (as in Boerne), and these institutions do not operate programs that receive federal funds. Unless, therefore, one were prepared (and few seemed willing to go this far) to argue that a state's acceptance of federal moneys for any program obligated all its institutions and instrumentalities to abide by the conditions, land use would lie outside the strictures RPLA would be able to place via the spending clause.

Given this shortcoming of the spending clause, the land use part of the act would have to rely on either the commerce power or section 5. Conceivably, the commerce clause could validate making local bodies abide by strict scrutiny (in that land use often involves construction or accessory use activities that touch interstate commerce), but that was uncertain. It would be better to marshal evidence for another shot at relying on section 5.

## Evidence to Justify Using Section 5

Proponents of RLPA brought forth a good bit of evidence that attempted to show that there was widespread religious discrimination being practiced by state and local governments not only in land use but also in a wide variety of areas. Laycock stressed to the members exactly what they were trying to accomplish here: "The question is not whether the witnesses believe that there are many violations and not whether the Supreme Court believes that there many violations. The question is whether Congress believes that there is a substantial likelihood of many violations and whether Congress' reasons for believing that are rational."[30]

Turning to the hotly contested area of land use, there were actually three separate issues: the denial of building permits, what accessory uses churches could make of their property, and landmarking. As for the first of these, the House subcommittee was presented with three statistical studies and a large parcel of anecdotes. The most wide-ranging statistical study was one conducted by Brigham Young University.[31] Their researchers compiled a list of all court cases over a number of years that pitted a church against a zoning board. One limitation of the study, therefore, was that instances where there was no case were not included. Even so, the results pointed to some disturbing trends. They found that small denominations taken together account for only 9 percent of the population but that they were involved in fully 49 percent of all zoning court cases. If nondenominational churches are included, the figure rose to 68 percent. Likewise, Jews make up only 2 percent of the population, but synagogues were parties to 20 percent of the cases. The other studies came from the Presbyterian Church (U.S.A.), studying its own congregations, and a Chicago land use attorney. The former pointed out problems faced even by a mainline denomination while the latter concluded that in Chicago itself and a number of suburbs it was almost impossible to build a new church, while secular assembly places readily obtained building permits. Testimony regarding individual cases came from Mormons in Forest Hills, Tennessee; an Orthodox Jewish community in Los Angeles (along with their counterparts elsewhere); Muslims in Starkville, Mississippi; Pentecostals in Rockford, Illinois; Baptists in Northlake, Illinois; and a spate of others.

When it came to accessory use, pastors from Richmond, Virginia, Washington, DC, and St. Petersburg, Florida, all testified how city officials had attempted to block their efforts to feed the homeless. In addition, the Brigham Young study had also looked at accessory cases and found a similar pattern.

It is interesting, especially in light of *Boerne*, that landmarking received the least attention of the three land use issues. To be sure, a study showing that churches in New York City were 42 times more likely to be landmarked than other buildings was cited. And a church in Ypsilanti, Michigan, detailed its woes in trying to tear down an old dilapidated building. Other than that, however, the matter elicited little attention.

In view of the concerns expressed by Senator Simpson when RFRA was being considered and the issues raised by the amici brief from the Ohio Department of Corrections in *Boerne*, it is no surprise that the matter of how far the scope of free exercise for prisoners should reach was controversial this time around as well. Prison administrators from several states offered examples of prisoners making outrageous claims based on religion, or in some cases engaging in violent behavior when religious privileges had been granted. While RFRA had been in force, they claimed, they had had to spend an excessive amount of time dealing with prisoner demands, most of which were frivolous and designed more often than not merely to harass prison staff.

An Ohio official stated that there had been 254 prisoner suits based on RFRA when it was in force: "The cases included such bizarre claims as demands for recognition of the right to burn bibles [*sic*], the right to possess and distribute racist literature, the right to engage in animal sacrifice and the right to group martial arts classes . . . RFRA cases were particularly time consuming due to the law's application whenever prison security regulations 'substantially burdened' any and all religious practices. Consequently, corrections officials had to spend an inordinate amount of time on discovery and trial related matters."[32] A New York state official added that RLPA would provide an ideal tool to jailhouse lawyers seeking only to wage "an all-out war on the system."[33] For systematic evidence, they brought up a survey conducted by the Florida attorney general's office of prison leaders in all fifty states regarding RFRA.[34] Their conclusion was that it had had a quite significant effect on the ability of prison officials to maintain order and discipline. They urged, therefore, that if Congress had to enact RLPA prisons be exempted.

Advocates for prisoner rights denied that RFRA had burdened prison operations as much as the administrators claimed. They pointed out that Congress had passed the Prison Litigation Reform Act of 1995, a statute that had made it more difficult for prisoners to file frivolous suits. Furthermore, they called attention to a statement from Federal Bureau of Prisons that "although compliance with the additional requirements of RFRA certainly places limited additional administrative burdens on Bureau of Prisons staff, these burdens have been manageable."[35] In addition, they cited a study from the Texas attorney general's office that found that of 2,200 prisoner cases the office handled while RFRA was in force, only 60 involved RFRA.[36] Finally, a law professor's analysis of RFRA cases filed by prisoners during the first three years of the law's life found that courts seldom ruled in favor of prisoners.[37]

To buttress the conclusions of these studies, individual prisoner rights advocates from various traditions—Protestant, Catholic, Jewish, and Muslim—testified how RFRA had helped them negotiate religious rights for prisoners of their faiths. To them, the claims that prison administration was seriously hampered by RFRA were seriously overblown.

Beyond land use and prison issues, witnesses brought a variety of other matters before the committee. The compulsory autopsy issue was raised once again, while others spoke about matters as diverse as the need for confidentiality in pastoral communications, Jewish high school basketball players not being permitted to wear yarmulkes, antiproselytizing ordinances, Muslim police officers and firemen not being allowed beards over a certain length, and the denial of exemptions from public school activities and curricula.

## THE DEATH OF RLPA

In addition to prison officials there were some who opposed RLPA from the outset. Representatives of local government bodies argued that the act would fetter their ability to formulate useful public policies. Possible examples included licensing and regulating child care facilities, securing buffer zones around residential areas, or preventing cruelty to animals.

Advocates for the prevention of child abuse seconded these concerns for their area, fearing it would be harder to remove children from abusive homes if RLPA were enacted. The Home School Legal Defense Association, whose leader had actually helped draft RFRA, also expressed displeasure with the bill. Their objection centered on using the commerce clause to underpin the act. It was not only an insult to religion to view it as a commercial activity, they said, but on practical grounds, individuals and smaller churches would not likely be able to avail themselves of a law resting on this basis.[38]

Several constitutional scholars also voiced objections to or reservations about the bill. Marci Hamilton felt the whole effort was illegitimate.[39] It was an attempt to do by statute what should require a constitutional amendment. The Supreme Court had spoken and Congress was exceeding its power in trying to overturn a constitutional decision. Neither the commerce clause nor the spending clause was, in her view, adequate to the task of supporting the bill; in particular, to use them in this way would be making an end run around the enumerated powers, thereby distorting the very essence of Article I. When it came to section 5, she reiterated what she had said in her *Boerne* brief: that for that to work Congress would "need fairly persuasive evidence that there is a national practice of discrimination which amounts to targeting of particular religions."[40] This was, of course, an impossible bar.

Christopher Eisgruber and Lawrence Sager came at the matter from a rather different constitutional angle, but on specifics they largely agreed with Hamilton.[41] Agreeing with Stevens's *Boerne* dissent, their central point was that RLPA would create two categories of citizens, the religious and the nonreligious, and would grant special privileges to the former. This was not only unfair; it would violate the establishment clause. As for the commerce clause, spending clause, and section 5, their doubts largely paralleled Hamilton's. Several other law professors voiced doubts about various parts of the bill, even though most of them supported the effort to deal with *Boerne* through legislation.

Even though the first hearing on how Congress should respond to the court began soon after the decision was handed down, the complexities of drafting the new act, the need to get various people and groups on board, and the usual press of the congressional agenda moved RLPA off the front burner for nearly two years. It was not until May of 1999 that the House Subcommittee on the Constitution was ready to submit its bill to its parent, the House Judiciary Committee.

However, a controversy over civil rights would soon derail RLPA. Gay and lesbian groups had spent years campaigning for laws to protect them against discrimination in housing and employment. These efforts were finally bearing fruit. As RLPA moved out of the House subcommittee, leaders of these groups expressed in ever more worrying voices the view that landlords and employers would use RLPA as an enhanced defense against claims of discrimination. Their sense of alarm began in 1998 when the subcommittee heard from a California woman who owned a few apartments. A devout conservative Christian, she did not wish to rent to unmarried people. She had been fined by the state for engaging in marital status discrimination and lost in court.[42] Nonetheless, situations such as this could possibly become commonplace under RLPA, gay and lesbian groups felt, and might succeed in some places. For example, in 1999 the Court of Appeals for the Ninth Circuit ruled that a state's protection of marital status was not a compelling interest.[43] Moreover, their fears were hardly allayed when spokespersons for the Christian right indicated that they intended to use RLPA in exactly that fashion.

They began an intense lobbying campaign to have their liberal allies peel off from the coalition backing the bill unless they could secure a "carve out" for civil rights laws. As a result, in time cracks in the coalition began to form. Liberal civil rights groups wavered; several members of Congress began to express doubts about the breadth of the bill; and the Clinton Justice Department became more reticent. As but one example, Senator Kennedy seemed to be backing away from his earlier support for new legislation: "While we consider ways to strengthen the religious liberties of all Americans, we must also be careful not to undermine existing laws carefully designed to protect other civil rights and civil liberties. Our efforts to strengthen religious liberty should not become a setback in the Nation's ongoing struggle to provide equal opportunity and equal justice for all our citizens."[44] Supporters of the measure tried to address these arguments. They contended that it was unlikely anyone except a religious institution would be able to use the law as any kind of legal shield. Further, the suggestions made by civil rights groups were all hypothetical, and plenty of other court decisions cast doubt on the precedent power of the ninth circuit ruling. Moreover, traditional protections afforded to racial minorities and women would certainly be found to be compelling interests. It was only marital status in housing and sexual orientation in both housing and employment that might afford any possible free exercise grounds. Here, Marc Stern of the American Jewish Congress took up an important gauntlet. While his group strongly favored civil rights laws protecting gays and lesbians, many from other religious traditions took the opposite view and had, in their eyes, legitimate reasons for doing so.

Was it not one purpose of the free exercise clause to ensure that public debate on important moral issues was not cut off prematurely? Furthermore, the very success of gay and lesbian groups in securing civil rights legislation showed their increasing power and hence the ability to win the day.

There was an even stronger argument to drive home. Here were powerful interest groups demanding an exception to a generally applicable law. Was not this the very type of legislative logrolling *Smith* had unleashed and RLPA was designed to overcome? If this carve out were granted, others would undoubtedly press their own cases. Were that to happen, the whole point of RLPA would be negated.

Nevertheless, the controversy and the politicking continued unabated and increased in intensity. In early May of 1999 the ACLU became the first group to formally desert the coalition, framing a message to Congress accordingly: "The ACLU regrets that we have no choice but to ask you to refrain from supporting RLPA. We are no longer part of the coalition supporting RLPA because we could not ignore the potentially severe consequences that RLPA may have on state and local civil rights laws."[45]

On June 23, 1999, a badly divided House Judiciary Committee reported the bill to the House floor. The accompanying report reflected the ongoing debate:

> Some discussion in the Committee process was motivated by a concern that [RLPA] will "trump" certain civil rights laws. [RLPA's] purpose is to protect religious liberty, one of the most fundamental of "civil rights." The question should not be [RLPA's] effect on "civil rights," but how to resolve the inevitable conflicts between the exercise of one civil right, in this case religious liberty, and other civil rights. [RLPA] imposes a standard of review, not an outcome, and cases are litigated on real facts before the court. Thus it is difficult in some hypothetical cases to predict with certainty which interests will prevail. One thing, however, is certain: without [RLPA], the free exercise claimant, burdened by a law of general application, will very nearly always lose.[46]

Even the subcommittee, which had been so unanimous in support of reenacting a RFRA-like statute, had become infected with the debate. On the House floor, Representative Nadler, showing some sympathy for the civil rights lobby, offered an amendment to the bill.[47] Although somewhat complicated, in essence it restricted the range of individuals and entities that could claim an RLPA defense. Canady spoke against the amendment, insisting that this was the very type of exception and carve out that would make a mockery of RLPA's attempt to be a general statute.

Nadler's amendment failed 190–234. When the question was called on the unamended bill it won by a 306–118 count.

The coalition became even more wobbly throughout the summer, however. Reflecting this, additional senators publicly expressed their reservations. On July 14, the day before the House vote, the NAACP announced that it was joining the opposition. By the end of September, not only had secular groups such as People for the American Way switched sides, but many religious groups had done so as well. These included the Religious Action Center for Reform Judaism, the Anti-Defamation League, the National Council of Jewish Women, the National Council of Churches, the Presbyterian Church (U.S.A.), the United Church of Christ, and Americans United for Separation of Church and State.[48]

By early October it was obvious to Senate leaders that the bill had no chance in the upper house, and it thus died a quiet death by never being brought up for a vote.

## THE RELIGIOUS LAND USE AND INSTITUTIONALIZED PERSONS ACT (RLUIPA)

Before long, however, civil rights groups and religious leaders were meeting in an effort to reach some kind of compromise. The result of their efforts was a bill focusing on two main areas of contention, land use and prisoner rights. For constitutional support, all three bases—the commerce clause, the spending clause, and section 5—were to be utilized. Religious leaders and their backers in Congress were disappointed, but political realities dictated that this was the best they could do. It still took nearly a year, though, to work out the details and set a date for a congressional vote.

On July 27, 2000, the scaled-back bill was brought to the floor of both houses of Congress. Letters endorsing the bill from the Coalition for the Free Exercise of Religion (the remaining groups that had initially backed RLPA), the Leadership Conference on Civil Rights, and the Department of Justice were read into the record and a show of unity was the order of the day. In the House, both Canady and Nadler voiced support for the bill. Canady noted that "while this bill does not fill the gap in the legal protection available to people of faith in every circumstance, it will provide critical protection in two important areas where the right to religious exercise is frequently infringed." Nadler added that RLPA "had some people concerned with some civil rights implications. Those concerns have been allayed."[49] Over in the Senate, Senator Orrin Hatch, a backer of RLPA to the end, said, "It is no secret that I would have preferred a broader bill than the one before us today. Recognizing, however, the hurdles facing passage of such a bill, supporters have correctly, in my view, agreed to move forward on this more limited, albeit critical, effort."[50] After that, he and Senator Kennedy entered a lengthy joint statement into the record that was clearly designed to guide, and has guided, judicial interpretation of the act. When the question was called, the bill passed both houses unanimously. It was still uncertain, however, whether the Supreme Court would find this renewed effort to compel the judiciary to use the strict scrutiny standard in these two areas constitutional. Plenty of constitutional scholars doubted it.

*Cutter v. Wilkinson*, decided in 2005, answered at least part of that question.[51] Three Ohio inmates—adherents of the Church of Jesus Christ Christian, Asatru, and the Wiccan faith—filed a suit under RLUIPA alleging that prison authorities had denied them the right to practice certain aspects of their religion. Prison administrators acknowledged the denials, and for the record conceded that all three were legitimate religions and that the inmates were sincere in their beliefs. Their justifications were that the faiths in question contained white supremacist doctrines that had led to violent conflict within the prison and that members of all three had been involved in several murders and prison escapes.

The district judge turned the case over to a magistrate judge to determine if the state "must meet RLUIPA's higher standard of justifying security-based restrictions on religion, or only the lower, pre-RLUIPA standard."[52] Thus, for the time being at least, the substantive merits of the prisoners' claims were not at issue, only the constitutionality of RLUIPA.

The magistrate began by noting that the spending clause basis for RLUIPA was more appropriate here and that if the law were valid on one ground it would be unnecessary to consider the others. Thus he set aside the commerce clause question entirely. Regarding transferring money to states, Congress was to be given wide latitude, even when it used money for purposes that lay outside its other Article I powers. However, there were four limitations, one more than *Dole* required: the funds had to be for the "general welfare;" the conditions had to be clear; the expenditure had to bear some relationship to "national projects or programs"; and the program could not violate any other constitutional provision.

The first two of these caused little trouble. Regarding the third, he drew a connection between religion and various rehabilitative programs that Ohio prisons offered. Consequently, this objection was met. The only remaining barrier, then, was that RLUIPA might run afoul of another constitutional demand. Ohio offered three: the Tenth Amendment, the Eleventh Amendment, and the establishment clause.

The Tenth Amendment is hard to use as a basis on which to challenge an unambiguous Article I power, and the magistrate did not spend much time on it here. The Eleventh Amendment issue was potentially more troubling for RLUIPA, though. Quoting again, the Eleventh Amendment says that "the judicial power of the United States shall not be construed to extend to any suit in law or equity, commenced or prosecuted against any one of the United States by citizens of another State, or by citizens or subjects of any foreign state." As discussed earlier, as part of its increased attention to federalism the Supreme Court had recently given new life to this amendment.[53] In a series of cases it had blocked Congress's ability to grant individuals and other entities (such as Indian tribes) the right to bring suits against states for violating a federal law. Ohio claimed that that was precisely what RLUIPA authorized and that these precedents should mean it is invalid. However, the magistrate saw a difference. Most of the previous cases had involved statutes enacted under the commerce clause, regulating the states as employers, for example. The spending clause was different in that the state had voluntarily taken the money. Therefore, they had in effect waived any immunity one might read into the Eleventh Amendment.

Turning to the establishment clause, the state's position was that by requiring it to give preference to religion over nonreligion, or possibly one religion over another since it was unlikely every single one could be accommodated, RLUIPA forced the state to engage in an establishment of religion. For guidance, the magistrate turned to the three-pronged *Lemon* test.[54] Under that framework, to be valid a law had to (1) have a secular purpose, (2) have as its primary effect neither the advancing nor inhibiting of religion, and (3) involve no "excessive entanglement" between government and religion. Ohio zeroed in on the second of these stipulations, contending that RLUIPA led to state endorsement of religion.

The magistrate relied on the 1987 case, *Corporation of the Presiding Bishop of the Church of Jesus Christ of Latter-day Saints v. Amos*[55] to address this aspect of the *Lemon* test. There, the Supreme Court had held that Congress's exempting a religiously affiliated fitness center from an employment statute did not create establishment, even though it thereby gave a religious institution a privilege denied to a secular counterpart. Ohio accepted this ruling but argued that that case involved a dispute between private parties. In the instant case, in contrast, the policy posed a possible danger to third parties—namely, prison guards. Therefore, the precedent was inapplicable. However, the magistrate replied, first, that no cases supported this reading of the second prong of the *Lemon* test and, second, that there was no evidence courts would interpret RLUIPA in such a way as to create dangers for prison employees. Finding no further defects, he ruled that there was no establishment clause violation.

The district judge adopted the magistrate's opinion as his own, but the Court of Appeals for the Sixth Circuit overturned this holding.[56] The justices there began by quoting from Justice Stevens's dissent in *Boerne* where he stressed that RFRA was creating a preference for religion. For their formal analysis they too adopted the *Lemon* guidelines and found in the second prong the appropriate standard. The core of the opinion was a comparison drawn between two inmates, both of whom have white supremacist literature confiscated by prison officials. One of the inmates claims his religion teaches white supremacy while the other offers only secular reasons for his beliefs. If a court were called on to evaluate the rights of the two, the former would have, if RLUIPA is allowed to stand, a distinct advantage. Government has then become decidedly nonneutral regarding religion, which is forbidden by the establishment clause. Additionally, because of the special privileges that will be accorded prisoners claiming religious beliefs, RLUIPA will encourage insincere assertions of religious beliefs merely in order to gain benefits. This amounts to an endorsement of religion.

The Supreme Court voted unanimously to overturn the court of appeals, and Justice Ruth Bader Ginsburg was chosen to write the opinion. She steered away from the *Lemon* test entirely and turned instead to a formula developed in another early 1970s case, *Walz v. Tax Commission*.[57] The court went to some lengths in that case to essay the way the two religion clauses can come into conflict if either is pushed to an extreme. There must be, therefore, some "room for play in the joints" between the two clauses. According to Justice Ginsburg, this means the court must allow "space for legislative action neither compelled by the Free Exercise Clause nor prohibited by the Establishment Clause."[58] RLUIPA "fits within the corridor" between the two clauses. Two observations supported the fact that RLUIPA had the appropriate balance (again, at least the prison section). First, through RLUIPA the government was softening the burden of incarceration, which it itself had imposed. Naturally, the need to maintain order would trump religious rights when they were taken to an extreme, and she quoted with approval a sentence from the Hatch-Kennedy statement, which expressed confidence that the courts would grant "due deference to the experience and expertise of prison and jail administrators" when interpreting RLUIPA. Second, the act made no distinctions among religions. All were to be treated equally.

In what amounted to a coda to the opinion she stressed that this decision did not deal with the merits of these particular claims. Further, she sent a barely veiled message to the lower courts: "Should inmate requests for religious accommodations become excessive, impose unjustified burdens on other institutionalized persons, or jeopardize the functioning of an institution, the facility would be free to resist the imposition."[59] In short, this section of RLUIPA was constitutional, but the courts must be wary of outrageous claims.

As yet, the Supreme Court has not ruled directly on the land use provisions of RLUIPA. However, a number of courts of appeals have upheld the act, and the Supreme Court has not seen fit to review one of those cases.[60] Furthermore, the district courts are applying the law day in and day out, and it has become a staple of land use policy.[61]

## RFRA and the Federal Government

Before returning to Boerne to discuss how the decision was received there, we need to add a footnote to this chapter regarding the applicability of RFRA to the federal government. Recall that Representative Canady was concerned about this matter when he opened the July 1997 hearing on *Boerne*. In 2006, the Supreme Court, at least indirectly, set Canady's fears at rest in *Gonzales v. O Centro Espirita Beneficente Unial do Vegetal.*[62]

The O Centro Espirita Beneficente Uniao do Vegetal (UDV) is a small Christian Spiritist sect originating in the Brazilian Amazon, which has approximately 130 adherents in the United States. In its religious services, communion is served using a special tea known as *hoasca*. One of the plants used to make this tea contains dimethyltryptamine (DMT), which is listed as a Schedule I drug in the federal Controlled Substances Act. Federal agents had seized a shipment of imported *hoasca* and threatened to prosecute church leaders.

UDV argued that prohibiting the group from using the tea violated RFRA as applied to the federal government. The government granted that the sect was a genuine religion and that the ban would impose a substantial burden on the group's free exercise. However, it argued that it had a compelling interest at stake and that prohibiting the importation of *hoasca* was the least restrictive means of accomplishing those interests. The compelling interests asserted by the government were threefold: a desire to protect the health of the members of the sect, the need to forestall distribution of DMT to people outside the sect, and an obligation to fulfill a treaty signed by the United States in 1971. The Supreme Court surveyed the evidence that had been presented in the district court regarding the first two contentions and found it "virtually balanced." Therefore, the government had not met the compelling interest test. Furthermore, the court held that the 1971 treaty did not apply to *hoasca*.

The court did not explicitly discuss whether or not RFRA was constitutional as applied to the federal government. However, the fact that it decided the case on the merits means that it saw no constitutional defect in that aspect of the statute.

CHAPTER 8

# BACK IN BOERNE

## COMPROMISING TO BUILD A CHURCH

IN ORDER TO OFFER A COMPLETE PICTURE of what happened in Boerne, it is necessary to step back a bit before the Supreme Court decision. The ups and downs of the route to a new church finally being built begin in January of 1996, around the time of the court of appeals' decision.

Back in the fall of 1995 a couple of informal meetings were held between city and church officials, but nothing had come of it. And the war of words, sometimes rigid, sometimes sounding more flexible, continued on both sides. After the court of appeals' decision on January 23, 1996, talk of a compromise of some sort surfaced. Ron Bowman, the city manager, said on January 25 that "maybe both sides will agree enough is enough. I'd like to have the case resolved, because we have other things to do. This has been a hard struggle for both sides."[1] Nevertheless, the recriminations continued, and each side blamed the other for being inflexible.

Mayor Heath held a press conference on January 25 and said that if St. Peter's did not already possess enough land on which to build a new church, he might feel differently. He felt the city was imposing no undue burden on the church, and in any event, everyone should comply with the ordinance.[2] Fr. Cummins responded, as the church had before, contending that Heath's position was not reasonable because the unimproved land was not usable. He added that the city had rejected all the reasonable offers the church had made and that "we are not able to pray in a prayerful fashion and are suffering a terrible burden at the Rainbow Center."[3] Heath left the door ajar a bit, though, by saying that the city was willing to consider a plan to save 80 percent of the church. Meanwhile, the church offered its own plan that would involve demolition of 40 percent of the old church. When asked about the city's response to this idea, Fr. Cummins said, "They haven't said no, but they're not exactly jumping and down about it. We'll see what happens now with the latest court decision."[4] Phillip Bell, the Historic Landmark Commission (HLC) chairman, wanted to reiterate that "we never meant to deny them the right to worship. We just want to preserve its historical value."[5] For now, though, he took the position that the HLC would support whatever decision the city council took; that was to change, however, as we shall see shortly.

The city council held two closed-door sessions with Lowell Denton after the court of appeals handed down its ruling to review the legal situation. The mounting legal fees, at the moment standing around $150,000, were of growing concern to some on the council and in the community.[6] On February 12 the city council once again met in executive session, this time for half an hour, to discuss their options.[7] When they emerged two motions were put on the floor. The first was to request an *en banc* hearing by the fifth circuit (which was turned down soon thereafter). The other was to "propose to the church, that both the city and the church authorize their respective architect the authority to jointly work together to explore additional alternatives and reach a solution, to make the necessary exterior design changes to accomplish the desires of both sides, while minimizing any additional construction costs." Both carried unanimously. The immediate response from the church exuded optimism. Bob Weiss said that this motion was "a more positive statement than anything we've had in the past," adding, "What I really feel like is that we're going to work this out without going further in the court."[8] Fr. Cummins endorsed this view in the parish newsletter: "I'm very pleased that the City has made the offer. Within the next week or so the process will be set in motion."[9]

The architects did hold two lengthy meetings, but in the end these talks collapsed. In part, this was because on April 9, the city council voted unanimously to appeal the court of appeals' decision to the Supreme Court. This cast something of a pall over the negotiations. Church officials (who were for the moment in a favorable position legally) felt they had offered all they could. A "Building Update" in the April 28 bulletin declared that "since April 1994 the Parish has offered a variety of compromises. The latest one was March 1995 when we offered to lower the roof line and keep intact approximately 60% of the present church. It was rejected . . . We formally, as part of the mediation process, also made offers. All rejected. None of our offers to bring about a settlement outside of court have been accepted by the city."

By late summer, though, another set of meetings was held. They came up with a proposal to save more of the south wall (about 75 to 80 percent) than the north wall (about 45 to 50 percent). Altogether, this scheme would retain about 66 percent of the old church. The city council reviewed the drawings on August 27 and ordered a video made for public inspection (with half the cost to be borne by the church and half by the city). Heath said that it seemed this plan "gets close to the suggestion we've had all along and had on the table since October of 1994."[10] On September 15, Fr. Cummins wrote in the bulletin that he was "very encouraged by the consideration the City is giving the new drawings . . . They are as interested in ending this controversy as we are. Hopefully this proposed compromise will meet with your approval and will be acceptable to our elected representatives on the City Council."

On September 24 the city council met in executive session and emerged to announce that it had adopted a motion (later revealed to be 4–1, Don Gourley voting no) "to instruct the city's legal counsel to explore the elements of a proposed compromise with the Archdiocese of San Antonio, and to prepare a written proposed settlement agreement for consideration by the City Council." News reports indicated that many citizens were pressing for a solution, and that two city council members had told people they agreed.[11] Fr. Cummins was pleased. "Certainly," he said, "I'm very happy with the news I've heard so far."[12]

However, currents of discontent were already developing. The HLC met with the city council in executive session on September 11. Bob Vollmer from the HLC rhetorically asked a *Star* reporter a little later, "Why are we offering a compromise in the eleventh hour?"[13] By other accounts, the majority of the HLC agreed, saying they were "surprised and disappointed" that the city was seeking a compromise. Both sides began waging a campaign for and against the compromise. St. Peter's furnished cards for parishioners to sign and send to the city council. Opponents mounted a telephone barrage to the mayor and council members. On October 16 Marci Hamilton sent the council a letter urging that they not settle with the church.[14] At the October 8 council meeting Vollmer and Bell both requested another executive session with the council. Other citizens voiced their displeasure at the prospect of a compromise at the same meeting.

Ultimately, things fell completely apart. Although the attorneys met on October 1, they did not finalize an agreement. Then at its October 22 meeting the city council all but withdrew from the negotiations. Mayor Heath was delayed en route from New York, but the meeting went ahead on schedule. As soon as it opened, Dub Smothers presented a check for $12,500, the first half of a $25,000 pledge, from the St. Peter's Men's Club to help defray the city's legal expenses for an appeal to the Supreme Court. The council went into executive session with the HLC for over an hour to discuss the case. When they came back into public session they took up a spate of routine business (e.g., land annexation, a contract to manage the city tennis courts, and a compliment to city crews for the speed of sidewalk construction). Mayor Heath arrived and took over the gavel at 9:25. The council immediately went back into executive session, this time alone. No settlement documents were examined, and when they reconvened they adopted the following motion: "The city of Boerne is committed to go forward with the lawsuit to the Supreme Court represented by our attorney, Professor Marci Hamilton, until such time, if at all, the settlement is agreed by both sides." The vote was 5–0. Bell was relieved, saying that the decision "signified that there is a harmony between the council and the landmark commission."[15] It would be one of the last times he would offer that sentiment.

The church and its attorneys felt let down, and the residue of this failed attempt at compromise would make church officials wary later on when other proposals were floated. Fr. Cummins offered the parish an explanation in the November-December parish newsletter. The two central paragraphs are these:

> [Following the council's September 24 vote, the] City's attorney did indeed contact Tom Drought as instructed by the City Council and a meeting was held on October 1st in Tom Drought's office with both attorneys, the City's architect and our architect. The meeting was satisfactory and at the conclusion of the meeting the City's attorney announced that he would present to Tom Drought a proposed settlement agreement within 3 days. The City's attorney has notified Mr. Drought on three occasions that he has been delayed in preparing the settlement agreement but assured him that it was forthcoming. The proposed settlement agreement has never been received by Tom Drought.
>
> It has been rumored that the City is waiting to hear from the Church or its attorney on the settlement agreement. There is no basis for that rumor. The Church and its attorney are not in a position to do anything until the City submits the proposed settlement agreement that it undertook to prepare, at which time we will act promptly to resolve any differences that may exist and have the document into final form for acceptance by both of the parties. I must repeat that at this time there is nothing that the Church or its attorneys can do to expedite or implement the proposed settlement agreement.

With both sides taking rigid positions, all that anyone could do now was wait for the Supreme Court to rule.

As the day for oral argument approached, reporters found that conversation at the Bear Moon Bakery on Main Street, La Hacienda restaurant, and everywhere else revolved around the case.[16] At the Ash Wednesday service, Fr. Cummins asked the people of the parish to pray for the justices "as they make decisions for the good of this land."[17] The depth of the feelings of the dissenters had not diminished. They gathered at the church to pray the Rosary and add a special prayer at the end of each segment. One of them distills the flavor of them all: "Heavenly Father, as we join together in your presence and in your name, we ask for your divine guidance in our concern over the destruction of our much loved St. Peter's Church. With this unique, Holy and Sacred Shrine, we feel surrounded by the presence of our beloved ancestors. These ancestors were united heart and soul, blood and sweat, tears and determination, carrying one rock at a time up the hill to put together this undying magnificent structure."[18] They also asked for divine blessings on the attorneys representing their cause. The Men's Club and its sympathizers continued to solicit donations around town. Some people in the town, though, felt the whole dispute had gone too far. One businessman told *The New York Times*, "This has gone way, way, way further than a lot of people would have ever thought possible . . . [I]t angers me they couldn't work this out. We're talking about whether to enlarge a building." Another seconded that sentiment: "In this case, there isn't a winner no matter what happens. It's gotten beyond any kind of reason."[19]

As decision day approached, the city prepared three press releases, one for each way the court might rule. Some major flooding had hit Boerne in the days preceding the Supreme Court decision and had in fact led to the discovery of some dinosaur tracks. Mayor Heath was in a briefing on the flood when his buzzer went off. He hastened to city hall to find out how the court had ruled.[20] On June 25 the press release the city issued thanked the court for its holding but still left an opening for a compromise on the building itself: "Now that the Religious Freedom Restoration Act has been declared unconstitutional by the Supreme Court, the City stands ready and willing to work with St. Peter's Catholic Church to reach an agreement that recognizes the needs of the Church's growing congregation and the desire of the citizens of Boerne to continue to preserve the unique character and cultural heritage of our hill country community. The decision issued today helps set the parameters that can guide our negotiations with the Church."[21] Mayor Heath stressed the point to the press, saying "We're willing once again to pick up negotiations,"[22] and, "We could meet and reconcile, and I think that's still a possibility."[23] Phillip Bell felt both gratified and that the HLC had been vindicated: "We're real pleased. We'd hope the Archdiocese would abandon its plans to destroy the church, and disrupt the community." He also said that he was "not interested in a settlement." Instead, he wanted to uphold the rule of law and enforce "the city's historic preservation ordinance."[24] Whatever Heath's hope and Bell's fears, the archdiocese, for its part, indicated no plans to drop the suit. Thomas Drought was straightforward: "Where we had three legs we now have two. We are optimistic that will be sufficient to carry us to a good result in the trial court."[25] Archbishop Flores was equally adamant: "Had the Supreme Court upheld the constitutionality of RFRA it would have been helpful to St. Peter Church's efforts to obtain from the City of Boerne the necessary permission to enlarge the Church to accommodate its parishioners. For that reason we are disappointed at the result. As it is, however, litigation must proceed on the basis of the other theories relied on by the Church. We remain hopeful of ultimate victory."[26] In a letter to church members, Fr. Cummins detailed the damage he felt was being done to the parish by the continual delay. Important programs were having to be put on hold and maintenance was "in limbo." He added that if the church lost in the district court, then it would have to consider moving to another site. "We don't have the choice to fossilize parish life. A parish must answer the expressed needs of a growing Catholic Christian community."

Talk of compromise kept coming from the city council, nevertheless, and an executive session was scheduled for Monday, June 30. Neither church leaders nor the HLC felt much was to be gained from further discussions. The chairman of the church building committee said, "I'd like to see it resolved tomorrow, but it's not going to happen."[27] Meanwhile, Bell sent a confidential letter to the city council and the city's lawyers not only noting the HLC's opposition to the October efforts at compromise but urging that the city stay the course. "It is the general consensus of the Commission," he wrote, "that *any* compromise predicated on destroying even 'one rock' of the church should be withdrawn and full attention given to alternatives that suggest a stand-alone structure." "I trust your future decisions will not be weakened by intimidation," he added, and closed with a firm admonition: "Now that the City has proven to be victorious, I have adopted a 'chant' that I overheard on the streets of Boerne by a prominent senior citizen . . . 'not one rock,' 'not one rock,' 'not one rock.'"[28] Heath continued to say publicly, though, that the 80/20 plan was still on the table "and has been since 1994."[29]

On July 8, the city council met in executive session for a little over an hour. At the end, they voted 5–0 (1) to prepare for a legal fight in the district court if necessary and to engage Professor Hamilton for assistance in any forthcoming trial and (2) to issue a press release stressing their readiness to compromise. In the release, they tried to direct attention to the parish hall as the stumbling block, which city officials believed all along was an all-but-valueless building. The press release, dated July 9, is worth quoting for tone as much as content:[30]

> The City Council of the City of Boerne has discussed the Church's lawsuit with our attorneys, and we continue to stand by the previous position expressed by our Mayor. The City Council would like to settle this lawsuit to end the high cost of litigation being paid by both the Church and the City. It is the Church which sued the City, and only the Church can end this litigation. The City has always believed the Church can build the structure it needs to accommodate its growing congregation on the property it now occupies. The City wants the Church to build its new structure on that hill, too. The problem is, the Church has chosen to tear down the historic limestone church and save the parish hall, while the City ordinance requires that as much of the historic church should be saved as possible. If necessary a small portion of the parish hall may have to be removed. It's time for the Church to redirect its attention from saving the concrete tilt-wall parish hall to saving the historic limestone church itself. The City believes that the Church can build 100% of its original new church design on the site, consistent with the criteria in the Historic Preservation ordinance. The City also believes that the church's architect can build the new structure the parish desires and save virtually 100% of the historic limestone church. But in the spirit of compromise, the City is willing to accept the preservation of 80% of the historic limestone church. Stan Klein, the City's architectural consultant, believes that the compromise can actually leave the parish hall untouched. Since this suit was filed in May 1994, the City Council has had the responsibility to make the decisions of how the City would respond to the Church in this lawsuit. The City will continue to rely on the advice of its citizens as it continues to make decisions. The City wants to set aside the legal positions and arguments, and solve this problem based on architectural feasibility.

Chastened by the collapse of the last attempt at reaching a compromise, the church responded guardedly. Furthermore, they were keenly aware that the HLC was not necessarily on board with the talk of a compromise. Nonetheless, they did not want to lose an opportunity to get on with building a new church without the delay that would come with a drawn-out lawsuit. Two days later they issued their own press release:

> We were glad to read in the San Antonio *Express News* on Wednesday that the City of Boerne wishes to continue settlement negotiations. Approximately 10 months ago we read a similar article but it said that the City Council had instructed its attorney to contact our attorney and prepare the settlement documents. The contact was made but the settlement documents which were promised, never appeared.

> The Church has always sought to resolve this problem by compromise. The only reason the Church filed the suit was because the City said that no stone of the Church could be touched. In fact, we read in the newspaper a couple of weeks ago a quotation from Philip Bell, Chairman of the Historic Review Commission [*sic*], saying that he would never compromise.[31] It is difficult for us to be optimistic about compromise when the Mayor says compromise and the Chairman of the Historic Review Commission says no compromise.
>
> We are nevertheless glad to receive even this dubious suggestion of a possible compromise because we would indeed welcome compromise as a solution to the problem that has divided this community. For that reason we will not discount the Mayor's press release, or his earlier press releases, as mere political posturing.
>
> On the strength of the mayor's latest news release, I will, with the consensus of the Pastoral Council, ask our attorney to contact the City attorney, to request that he draw up settlement documents:
>
> 1. To prepare documents for the settlement previously agreed upon by both attorneys as authorized by their respective clients based on the Stan Klein and Greg Davis video concept.
> 2. If the City attorney will not prepare the documents in a timely fashion or for other reasons, the Church is willing to prepare the documents.
>
> In the absence of an equitable solution we will continue into the District Court for a legal solution.

After some waltzing around, the two sides met on Friday, July 11. The church continued to maintain that the 65 percent plan should be the framework for a compromise. Heath chose to put things on a more general plane. In obviously carefully chosen words, he said that the church's statement was "an appropriate response to our suggestion that negotiations begin again." As for the 65 percent plan, that was "simply a visualization of a possibility."[32] The following Monday the two sides met again, but nothing concrete emerged.

At its regular meeting on July 22 the city council heard from several citizens expressing opposition to and support for the compromise talks. After the regular council meeting the HLC and the council met in executive session, where members of the HLC voiced their opposition.

Meanwhile, Judge Bunton had set September 16 for the trial date. Although still seemingly far apart, the attorneys and architects continued to meet in late July and early August. On August 5, the breakthrough was achieved. At a meeting in Tom Drought's office in San Antonio the 80/20 plan was accepted by both parties, and a seven-page

Memorandum of Understanding was drafted.[33] By August 12, a more formal Memorandum of Agreement had been put together. The city council approved it that evening and the pastoral council the following day. Fr. Cummins was elated: "I consider this a wonderful opportunity for both the city and ourselves to work together after all these years. We have spent years trying to negotiate a settlement and now we have found a solution that both of us can embrace."[34] He asked for nine days of prayer for unity and healing in the community. For his part, Heath echoed Cummins's sentiment, saying, "It is time for this issue to be resolved. We've had enough long faces and vindictiveness. We've had enough harsh words and incivility."[35] The *Hill Country Recorder* began its article with a simple "It's over."[36]

The basic component of the compromise was saving 80 percent or 71 feet of both walls of the 1923 church. In order for this to be accomplished, about 25 percent of the parish hall would have to be demolished. In addition, the church agreed to have the roof of the new structure not reach above the base of the crosses on the old church. At the same time, the church could add 100 seats to its new building, bringing the total capacity to 800. The city agreed to undertake various measures to make the construction easier, for example, closing the adjacent street and moving electrical wires and fire hydrants.

As with all compromises, not everyone was happy. Some in the church wanted to keep pushing for the 65 percent solution, while opponents, including the HLC, continued to believe that the entire 1923 church should be left as it was. In fact, the members of the HLC "felt very much left out of that last loop. We were not consulted in any way."[37]

The architects continued to consult each other on construction details, all apparently in good faith and in smooth meetings. Judge Bunton canceled the trial and asked that the agreement papers be filed with him by September 29, although he later granted an extension, which was requested by both parties.

An open fissure was now evident between the HLC and the council. The procedural fly in the ointment was that since the new building permit would technically be a new request, it would, by the terms of the ordinance, have to go the HLC first. Yet the council had already signaled its acquiescence. Ron Bowman wrote a memo to the HLC explaining the favorable view of the agreement held by the council.[38] Following the guidelines, the HLC took up the permit request at its September 25 meeting.

At that meeting, Bob Weiss presented an overview of the proposed new structure. Greg Davis and Stan Klein also attended and occasionally offered comments as Weiss explained various facets of the new building to the commission and answered questions. Concerns about the guarantee that the old church would remain structurally intact during demolition were voiced, along with queries on the mass and height of the new structure and how it would blend in with the 1923 building. Although the minutes record a largely civil conversation, it was clear that the HLC did not approve of what had been done. Plus, there were some criticisms of the city council for agreeing to a compromise before the HLC had had a chance to vote on it. After about an hour Bell called for a motion, but none was made. This led to a procedural discussion. Could a nondecision of the HLC be appealed to the city council, or was a no vote necessary? Turk told the HLC that even if their action tonight blocked the compromise it would not keep the city out of federal court.

The next day Tom Drought wrote the city council filing an appeal of the HLC action.[39] On October 1, the city council met for ten minutes in a special session. The only item on the agenda was a motion "to approve the appeal of St. Peter's Catholic Church for the issuance of a building permit/demolition permit to demolish a portion of the existing 1923 church and construct a new 12,200 square foot addition. Issuance of the actual permit would be subject to the submittal of the final construction plans and the settlement agreement, and meeting all the building code requirements for issuance." With that, the wrangling between the church and the city was over. Only the construction details and the drafting of the final legal documents remained.

In the October 12 church bulletin Fr. Cummins announced that ground breaking would hopefully be in late January or February. He also cautioned that he feared "some people will attempt to keep the parish in the past" and create "negative energy." Despite this, though, he said that he was excited about the future of St. Peter's and full of hope.

The architects continued to meet and hammer out the details of the construction plans. On December 5 Stan Klein wrote Ron Bowman saying that detailed documents would be delivered on December 8.[40] He recorded Greg Davis as being "very excited about the project and stated that the old church has really become a significant design asset to the over all project." In fact, the new design was actually bigger than the original proposal, with the new sanctuary seating 800 rather than 700, as the parish had continued its growth. Gratified, Fr. Cummins said, "We are very pleased with the design. It's turning out nicer than it was four years ago."[41]

At the city council meeting of December 16 a half-hour executive session was called, after which there was a motion "to authorize legal counsel to move forward with the final resolution with the lawsuit with the Archdiocese and sign the stipulation of dismissal." On January 6, 1998, Judge Bunton signed the dismissal order:[42] "The parties so notify the Court that they have 'settled all Matters in controversy pursuant to the terms of a Settlement and Release Agreement.' After due consideration of the Motion, the Court is highly enthusiastic that a complete settlement has been reached and therefore, will gladly grant the parties' Motion."

There was a residue of resentment, however, among the vocal opponents of tampering with the old church as well as among the HLC. Dub Smothers continued to take out ads in the local papers critical of the leadership at St. Peter's. The HLC was dismayed at the turn of events, Bell saying its members were "all pretty angry. This whole thing could have been settled years ago and saved the city and the church hundreds of thousands of dollars in legal fees, but they refused to consider taking out the parish hall."[43] In addition to supporting Smothers' ads, the Men's Club urged the city council to name the newly purchased community center for Don Gourley, who before his recent untimely death had been the person on the council who had been most steadfast in pushing for the city to appeal to the Supreme Court.

Most eyes turned to the actual construction project, however. Bids were opened on January 30 and work began in February. Costs had now risen to around $3 million. The church had previously raised about $1 million, which it still had in the bank. Another campaign to raise an additional million in future pledges was launched in April of 1998 and succeeded in gathering promises for the total. Half the $2 million debt, therefore, could be retired by the funds generated by that campaign. As the interior of the old church was to be used for children's services and various small gatherings, many of the furnishings were no longer needed. They were donated to a church in Mexico. Stained glass windows were obtained from a turn-of-the-century church in Philadelphia. The rocks from the 20 percent of the old church that was demolished were used to make a new staircase. The windows in the old church were restored to their original condition, with wood frames. An enthusiastic Fr. Cummins told the *Star*, "We've had nothing but compliments about the new church. Even those who opposed demolition of most of the 1923 church have had nothing but good things to say about the new church."[44]

It was to be dedicated on October 17, 1999, with a week of festivities, including an invitation to Boerne citizens to take tours, to follow.

The program for the dedication carried a letter from Archbishop Flores to the members of the church, saying in part, "May each of you and all who come after you, find this place to be, indeed, a 'House of Prayer,' a place of peace and reflection, enabling you to go forth refreshed to make real God's justice and peace."[45] On the dedication Sunday 1,200 people showed up to join Flores, Cummins, and area priests in a two-hour Mass. This meant 400 people had to stand. Flores brought forth a hardy round of laughter when he stood and said, "We already have to build an even bigger church because so many people are standing." More seriously, he said, "I feel like yelling—shouting 'Praise be to God,' 'Glory be,' and "Praise to the Lord.'"[46]

When Fr. Cummins came forward to receive the keys from the archbishop, he received a standing ovation. "We are grateful," he said, "that God has blessed us with this wonderful place, and it truly will become for us a house of prayer." David Boerner, the president of the pastoral council said the church was "the most wonderful church I've ever seen. I love the baptismal font and the full-sized crucifix. During the difficult times several years ago, I felt some apprehension, especially for Fr. Tony. But it turned out wonderful."

Experts seemed to concur with Boerner's assessment, for the church garnered three design awards. These came from the San Antonio Masonry Construction Association, *Ministry and Liturgy* magazine, and the Interfaith Forum on Religion, Art, and Architecture at Andover Theological Seminary. Ironically, perhaps, the last of these was presented on the day President Clinton signed RLUIPA into law.[47]

Boerne has continued to grow, as more people have moved out from San Antonio. Between 2000 and 2010 the town increased from 6,178 to 10,471 souls, a 70 percent increase. The county grew from 23,743 to 33,410 during the decade, a 41 percent increase. To accommodate these new residents, housing developments have sprung up in almost every direction. The historic district, though, still maintains its integrity and is undoubtedly a major draw for both tourists and new residents alike. The downtown has a number of tourist-type shops and restaurants; yet there are still plenty of ordinary local businesses there. The town has built a new public library and named it for Mayor Heath. As with many small towns that are wrestling with growth, there are problems, from crowded schools to streets that need constant repair. Still, though, it maintains a small-town atmosphere, and that has to be credited in part at least to the viability of the historic district.

St. Peter's has continued to reflect the growth of the community. It is a vibrant parish with a wide variety of programs for people of all ages, and it plays a major part in the life of the community. Fr. Cummins still tends the flock.

However, there is as yet no plaque outside the church, as Fr. Robert Drinan prophesized there would be, designating it as a landmark in the history of church-state jurisprudence.

CHAPTER 9

# CONCLUSION

FROM THE PERSPECTIVE OF BOERNE IT SEEMS that much of the controversy was a waste. A version of the 80/20 plan, not terribly different from what was ultimately adopted, had been floated early in the negotiations. The city spent around $265,000 in legal fees defending its position. The church's legal costs have not been made public, but they must have been substantial. In addition, there was a good bit of ill will generated, both within the parish and among people in the community. As one observer said, "there were very few people who didn't take one side or the other. It was disruptive to families. There are wounds in families that still have not healed."[1]

Nevertheless, there was something important at stake. It is hard not to be sympathetic to all sides. To the descendants of those who had built the 1923 church with their own hands, the building was far more than mere stones and mortar. Their feelings ran deeply and are worthy of respect. At the same time, Fr. Cummins was certainly correct in his view that the church's facilities needed to reflect contemporary needs. The church is not, as Msgr. Stuebben said, a museum. St. Peter's was and is a parish, not a building. But then it is easy to see the point of those in Boerne who wanted to preserve the architectural integrity of the historic district. Communities are affected by their physical environments, and the needs of the community have to be weighed against those of property owners, even religious institutions. The members of the Historic Landmark Commission (HLC) bore no animosity to the church or any other property owners and were admirable people. They took their responsibility for retaining the character of Boerne seriously, remembering that once a building is gone it cannot be replaced. As for the city council, the demands they faced were those of pragmatic elected public officials. They backed the HLC but always felt a compromise would be in everyone's interest, even after winning the court case. Members of St. Peter's were their constituents also, it should be remembered. In short, there are legitimate positions on every side. Back in 1994, an editorial in the *Star* made that same point, then added what turned out to be an accurate prediction:

> It's hard to pick a winner in this situation. The losers could be many. A church divided is never a winner. Lawsuits between a church and the local government can do nothing positive for this community.
>
> Whatever the outcome, the result will become part of the local history and the stories will be repeated for generations to come. Even after the dust settles, many good people will never forget.[2]

On a somewhat lighter note, perhaps David Richelieu, a columnist for the *San Antonio Express-News*, pointed to the best way that such conflicts can be avoided in the future: "This case . . . should teach the Catholic Church to stop building attractive churches that may become cherished by the public as local landmarks. Judging from most newer churches, that's already the rule."[3]

From the perspective of free exercise jurisprudence, though, the sense of wasted time, energy, and effort is both clear and palpable. The whole series of events—RFRA, *Boerne*, RLUIPA, and *Cutter*—were all unnecessary. The compelling interest test had proved a workable standard, and the court had managed to find ways to sidestep it when need be (military uniforms, prison administration, and internal governmental operations, for example). Everyone seemed satisfied with the test, even when it was applied in a way some people disagreed with. Had Justice Scalia not insisted on writing a brash opinion in *Smith*, this whole 15-year episode could have been avoided. There would have been no RFRA, no *Boerne*, no RLUIPA, and no *Cutter*.

The experience with RFRA, *Boerne*, and RLUIPA did serve to energize America's religious communities, however. They are now extremely sensitive, for example, to how RLUIPA can serve as an important bargaining tool in land use disputes. Plus, the statute directed the federal government to intervene in selected suits, giving further impetus to claims under the act. As a result, the Department of Justice issued a report in 2010 cataloging the effects of RLUIPA. Its conclusion was that "RLUIPA has had a dramatic impact in its first ten years on protecting the religious freedom of and preventing religious discrimination against individuals and institutions seeking to exercise their religions through construction, expansion, and use of property."[4] It followed up by giving numerous examples of religious institutions besting local governments in disputes over zoning, auxiliary activities, and construction permits.[5]

When it comes to prison administration, the outcome has been muddier.[6] Despite Justice Ginsburg's admonition in *Cutter*, some analysts believe that RLUIPA presented serious impediments to the operation of the nation's prisons, especially in its early years.[7] Others disagree. However, it seems that in recent years the courts have adopted a more jaundiced approach to prisoner claims and have often used the element of "costs" as a measure of compelling interest to accomplish that. In the Department of Justice report much less was said, for example, about the protection of prisoner rights.

As for federalism, our case represents a rather extreme form of rigid judicial federalism, a position that personified the Rehnquist Court perhaps more than any other. Following along in the steps of the general federalism principles that underlay *Boerne*, the court handed down three cases in June 1999 that increased a state's sovereign immunity under the Eleventh Amendment.[8] In each case, the justices held that Congress had exceeded its power when it sought to abrogate state sovereign immunity by passing the statutes in question. In all three of these cases, Congress had relied on Article I powers. However, the justices left a slight opening when they asserted that statutes passed under section 5 powers were to be given wider latitude than statutes passed under Article I powers when it came to overriding state sovereign immunity. In 2001, they nevertheless dealt a blow to any hopes people might have harbored that they might actually adopt a more flexible approach when it came to section 5. In *Board of Trustees of the University of Alabama v. Garrett*, Chief Justice Rehnquist spoke for a 5–4 majority and held that under the Americans with Disabilities Act (passed under the authority of section 5) Congress could not authorize suits against states to collect monetary damages unless there was an explicit pattern of discrimination.[9] Borrowing *Boerne*'s language, he said that granting a general right to bring such suits was not a "congruent and proportional" response to the problem. According to Paul Clement, former George W. Bush administration solicitor general, this was the high-water mark of Rehnquist Court federalism.[10]

Even before Rehnquist left the court in 2005, though, the justices had begun to soften this view somewhat. In *Nevada Department of Human Resources v. Hibbs*, handed down in 2003, the court ruled 6–3, with Rehnquist joining the majority, that the federal Family Medical Leave Act was a prophylactic measure that did not substantively redefine the rulings of the court.[11] It was, therefore, a valid exercise of section 5 powers and, consequently, the Eleventh Amendment's bar would have to fall in this instance. The next year the court held, in *Tennessee v. Lane*, that a different title of the Americans with Disabilities Act from that at issue in *Garrett* also abrogated the Eleventh Amendment.[12] Here, however, Rehnquist sided with the three dissenting justices from *Hibbs* (Scalia, Thomas, and

Kennedy) in a 5–4 vote. He felt the facts were similar enough to *Garrett* to make it controlling.

The direction the Supreme Court's federalism jurisprudence might take under Chief Justice Roberts is still uncertain. Two cases from 2006 offer mixed clues. In *United States v. Georgia*, the state was violating the terms of the Fourteenth Amendment itself, and the court held unanimously that Congress could enforce the Eighth Amendment via section 5.[13] In *Central Virginia Community College v. Katz*, the court voted 5–4, with Roberts joining the three other conservatives in dissent, that the bankruptcy clause of Article I waives the Eleventh Amendment's immunity.[14] Of some note also, even though it did not deal with Congress's authority to enact legislation, is the decision in *Medellin v. Texas*, a 2008 case.[15] The president had ordered state courts to comply with a treaty signed by the United States, one provision of which involved certain procedures in criminal trials. State courts in Texas had declined to comply, and the Supreme Court upheld their actions in a 6–3 vote. There is also the mixed message of the case upholding the Affordable Care and Patient Protection Act, *National Federation of Independent Businesses v. Sebelius*.[16] On the one hand, an important federal statute was upheld; on the other, serious restrictions on federal control over the Medicaid program were promulgated. At the end of their recent comprehensive study of federalism in the Rehnquist and Roberts courts, Christopher Banks and John Blakeman conclude that, for the most part, we are likely to witness continued restrictions of federal power from the Roberts court.[17]

Of more direct importance for the future of section 5 is the fate of the Voting Rights Act (VRA).[18] As early as 2003 Victor A. Rodriguez argued that *Boerne* was the beginning of the end for the VRA.[19] The court proved his thinking may be pointing in the right direction when in 2009 it hinted, in *Northwest Austin Utility District No. 1 v. Holder*, that the VRA might suffer from constitutional defects.[20] The circumstances that made it valid in the 1960s and 1970s no longer existed, the majority of justices felt. By 2012, Glenn Kunkes was arguing outright that the changed realities of our day rendered the law unconstitutional.[21] Should the VRA eventually fall, *Boerne* will always be seen as an important milestone in the court imposing serious limits on section 5 power.

The role of the Supreme Court in American political life, though, is what is most important about *Boerne*. We glimpse in Justice Kennedy's opinion one of the most extreme statements of unbridled judicial power. Despite his nod of deference to Congress, Kennedy's words in effect make the legislature a subordinate, not a coordinate, branch of government. To the Supreme Court, and to the Supreme Court alone, is to be given the power to make whatever decisions they choose about the allocation of governmental power under the Constitution. By extension, the members of the court may or may not take into account whatever factors they wish. It is the end point in an evolution that began with *Cooper v. Aaron*.[22] Rather curiously, it is a role that partisans of all persuasions seem to endorse, seeking only to have people representing their policy and political views, dressed up as constitutional doctrine, appointed to the court.

The strength of this orientation can be seen in any number of areas. Three brief examples will suffice. One would be Justice O'Connor's opinion in *Grutter v. Bollinger*, the 2003 case involving affirmative action at the University of Michigan's law school.[23] O'Connor upheld the program, which in one sense is deferring to decisions made by other public officials. However, the rationale does not speak of deferring to others at all; instead she wades into a discussion of the merits of the policy and its probable futures (as she sees them). The clear implication is that if she had seen the facts differently, she would have felt perfectly free to rule the other way. Or take, for another, the court's opinions in the gun control cases.[24] There is no credence given to how others might read the Second Amendment. Finally, the oral argument in the health care case focused heavily on purely policy issues. And the vigor of the dissent on those very grounds—as well as the loud conservative criticism of Chief Justice Roberts—exhibits how far we have come to expect political and partisan considerations to control the court.

On the other hand, there are now important intellectual voices making the case for a more restrained judiciary. Mark Tushnet and Larry Kramer have both criticized the court for assuming a more powerful mantle than the Constitution grants it.[25] As noted in Chapter 4, Tushnet would rely on the political leadership of our other institutions to engage the judiciary in a dialogue while Kramer would look beyond the institutions to the public itself. Either way, constitutional ideas, rooted in a constitutional culture that is not entirely driven by partisan passions, would become the subject of debate and interinstitutional dialogue. We may be witnessing the embryo of a new—actually an old—constitutional theory about the proper way separation of powers should work. If so, *Boerne* will surely have played a significant part in the articulation and development of these ideas. Thus its ultimate legacy may be that it undermined rather than advanced judicial power.

St. Peter's Catholic Church, 1993

Model of original expansion plan, 1993

Demolition of the back 20 percent of the 1923 church during construction, June 1998

St. Peter's in 2000

# NOTES

## INTRODUCTION

1. Anna Marie Davison, *A History of St. Peter's Catholic Church, Boerne, Texas* (Boerne, TX: St. Peter's Restoration and Preservation Society, 1987).
2. 521 U.S. 507 (1997).
3. Robert F. Drinan, "Reflections on the Demise of the Religious Freedom Restoration Act," *Georgetown Law Journal* 86 (1997): 101.
4. There were a few exceptions, where special institutions such as prisons and the military were involved. These cases are discussed in Chapter 1.
5. Employment Division of Oregon, Department of Human Resources v. Smith, 494 U.S. 872 (1990).
6. Since this case dealt with a city ordinance passed under the authority of a state statute, the question of whether Congress could adopt a law tying its own hands was not considered. Later, the Supreme Court did uphold the applicability of RFRA to the federal government. Gonzales v. O Centro Espirita Beneficente Uniao do Vetegal, 546 U.S. 418 (2006).
7. This position was confined to conflicts between Congress and the states, however. The Supreme Court began, especially during the Warren years, supervising many more areas of state law: civil rights, criminal procedure, and legislative apportionment, for example.
8. Sotirios A. Barber and James E. Fleming, *Constitutional Interpretation: The Basic Questions* (New York: Oxford University Press, 2007), especially Chapter 3.
9. Stephen Breyer, *Active Liberty: Interpreting Our Democratic Constitution* (New York: Knopf, 2005), 56–65.

## CHAPTER 1

1. 521 U.S. 507 (1997).
2. The background and development of the free exercise clause is discussed in Michael McConnell, "The Origins and Historical Understanding of the Free Exercise of Religion," *Harvard Law Review* 103 (1990): 1421–25, and Thomas Curry, *The First Freedom: Church and State in America to the Passage of the First Amendment* (New York: Oxford University Press, 1987).
3. 494 U.S. 872 (1990).
4. 98 U.S. 145 (1879).

5. The story of the background of this case is ably told in Sarah B. Gordon, *The Mormon Question: Polygamy and Constitutional Conflict in Nineteenth-Century America* (Chapel Hill: University of North Carolina Press, 2002).
6. This term was included in the Republican Party platform of 1856. Its use in public discourse is discussed in Gordon, *Mormon Question*, Chapter 2.
7. Donald Drakeman covers Waite's handling of this case in detail in *Church, State, and Original Intent* (New York: Cambridge University Press, 2010), Chapter 2.
8. This statute and Thomas Jefferson's letter are both quoted in the opinion. Both are discussed at length in McConnell, "Origins and Historical Understanding."
9. 32 U.S. 243 (1833).
10. Permoli v. New Orleans, 44 U.S. 589 (1845).
11. The arguments regarding incorporation are reviewed in Bryan Wildenthal, "Nationalizing the Bill of Rights: Revisiting the Original Understanding of the Fourteenth Amendment in 1866–67," *Ohio State Law Journal* 68 (2007): 1509–626, and George Thomas, "The Riddle of the Fourteenth Amendment: A Response to Professor Wildenthal," *Ohio State Law Journal* 68 (2007): 1627–57.
12. Butchers' Benevolent Association v. Crescent City Livestock Landing and Slaughterhouse Co., 83 U.S. 36 (1873).
13. On this era, see Gerard N. Magliocca, "Why Did the Incorporation of the Bill of Rights Fail in the Late Nineteenth Century?" *Minnesota Law Review* 94 (2009): 102–39.
14. 259 U.S. 530 (1922).
15. Gitlow v. People of the State of New York, 268 U.S. 652 (1925).
16. Near v. State of Minnesota ex. rel. Olson, 283 U.S. 697 (1931).
17. 293 U.S. 245 (1934).
18. 310 U.S. 296 (1940).
19. 366 U.S. 599 (1961).
20. 374 U.S. 398 (1963).
21. 406 U.S. 208 (1972).
22. 475 U.S. 503 (1986).
23. 482 U.S. 342 (1987).
24. 476 U.S. 693 (1986).
25. 485 U.S. 439 (1988).
26. 450 U.S. 707 (1981).
27. 480 U.S. 136 (1987).
28. 489 U.S. 829 (1989).
29. 455 U.S. 252 (1982).
30. 461 U.S. 574 (1983).
31. 490 U.S. 680 (1989).
32. 494 U.S. 872 (1990).
33. There are two excellent book-length studies of this case, Carolyn Long, *Religious Freedom and Indian Rights: The Case of* Oregon v. Smith (Lawrence: University Press of Kansas, 2000), and Garrett Epps, *To an Unknown God: Religious*

*Freedom on Trial* (New York: St. Martins, 2001), on which the following paragraphs draw heavily.

34. Quoted in Long, *Religious Freedom*, 197.
35. 310 U.S. 587 (1940).
36. 319 U.S. 624 (1943).
37. These discussions are reported in Long, *Religious Freedom*, 204–12. The legislative history of the act can be found in Robert F. Drinan and Jennifer I. Huffman, "The Religious Freedom Restoration Act: A Legislative History," *Journal of Law and Religion* 10 (1993): 531–41.
38. House Subcommittee on Civil and Constitutional Rights, *Hearings on Religious Freedom Restoration Act of 1990*, 101st Cong., 2nd sess., September 27, 1990, 13.
39. The first hearing is cited in the previous note. The other is House Subcommittee on Civil and Constitutional Rights, *Hearings on Religious Freedom Restoration Act of 1991*, 102nd Cong., 2nd sess., May 13 and 14, 1992.
40. Senate Committee on the Judiciary, *Hearings on Religious Freedom Restoration Act of 1992*, 102nd Cong., 2nd sess., September 18, 1992.
41. David M. Ackerman, Congressional Research Service Report for Congress, *The Religious Freedom Restoration Act and the Religious Freedom Act: A Legal Analysis*, April 17, 1992.
42. See the written statements of Mark Chopko, counsel for the U.S. Conference of Catholic Bishops, and James Bopp, representing the National Right-to-Life Committee in House, *Hearings*, 1992, 36–47 and 273–301.
43. 500 U.S. 833 (1992).
44. 410 U.S. 113 (1973).
45. Quoted in House, *Hearings*, 1992, 7.
46. See the statement of Robert Dugan of the National Association of Evangelicals, along with those of Douglas Laycock, Stephen Solarz, and other backers of the bill. House, *Hearings*, 1992, 20–138.
47. Ackerman, CRS, *Legal Analysis*, 28.
48. Statement by Representative Solarz to Representative Henry Hyde in House, *Hearings*, 1992, 138.
49. Senate, *Hearings*, 43.
50. House Committee on the Judiciary, *Report to Accompany H.R. 1308, The Religious Freedom Restoration Act of 1993*, Report 103–88, May 11, 1993, 8.
51. Senate Judiciary Committee, *Report to Accompany S. 578, The Religious Freedom Restoration Act of 1993*, Report 103–11, July 27, 1993, Additional Views of Senator Simpson, 20.
52. See Drinan and Huffman, "Legislative History," 538–40 for more detail on Senator Reid's efforts.
53. Laycock's letter is reprinted on pages 330–71 of the House, *Hearings*, 1992 (hereafter cited as Laycock statement). He also provided a letter to the earlier hearing that is reprinted in House, *Hearings*, 1990, 72–79.
54. Lupu's statement is reprinted on pages 375–95 of the House, *Hearings*, 1992 (hereafter cited as Lupu statement). Fein's statement is in the same hearing, 120–28 (hereafter cited as Fein statement).

55. Laycock statement, 354.
56. House, *Hearings*, 1990, Laycock statement, 74.
57. Lupu statement, 375.
58. Ibid., 388.
59. 384 U.S. 641 (1966).
60. Lupu statement, 389.
61. Ibid., 391.
62. 508 U.S. 520 (1993).
63. Lupu statement, 394–95.
64. House, *Hearings*, 1992, 397.
65. Ibid., 1992, 398.
66. Ibid., 398–99.
67. Fein statement, 125.
68. Senate, *Hearings*, 50–58.
69. Ibid., testimony of William Yang, 14–28. The quotation is from Judge Raymond Pettine in Yang v. Sturner, 750 F. Supp. 558 (D.R.I. 1990).

## CHAPTER 2

1. Garland A. Perry, *Historic Images of Boerne, Texas* (Boerne, TX: Perry Enterprises, 1982), vii. The information regarding the history of Boerne and Kendall County that follows is taken from this book and a volume published by the Kendall County Historical Commission, *A History of Kendall County* (Dallas, TX: Taylor Company, 1984). The February 23, 1994, edition of the *Boerne Star* also has a lengthy article detailing the history of Boerne. There were two weekly newspapers published in Boerne during these years, the *Star* and the *Hill Country Recorder*. I will henceforward merely cite them as the *Star* and *Recorder* respectively. They have since merged.
2. A bust of Herr Boerne stands today in the visitors' center.
3. A profile of Kendall was published in the *New Orleans Picayune*, March 12, 1922.
4. The information on Fr. Fleury and the history of St. Peter Church is taken from Anna Marie Davison, *A History of St. Peter's Catholic Church, Boerne, Texas* (Boerne, TX: St. Peter's Restoration and Preservation Society, 1987). The technical name of the church is St. Peter Apostolic Catholic Church. However, members and other locals use "St. Peter" and "St. Peter's" interchangeably. I will simply follow their form.
5. Reproduced in Davison, *History of St. Peter's*, 35–36.
6. "Boerne's New Church Solemnly Dedicated," *The Southern Messenger*, January 3, 1924.
7. *San Antonio Express*, December 23, 1923.
8. Interview with Kit Brenner, September 14, 2010.
9. This quotation and the next one are both from the *Star*, April 22, 1992.
10. The information and conclusions in this section come from interviews conducted with many people in Boerne and the extensive collection of documents

stored at the archives division of the Boerne Public Library (BLA). A smaller set of documents is housed at the Texas Collection at Baylor University (BU). The recordings and transcripts of the recorded interviews are available at the Institute for Oral History at Baylor University. For those that were not recorded (and there were a variety of reasons for this), I have deposited my handwritten notes in the Texas Collection archives. I will cite the public library documents as BLA and folder name if available. The BU documents are not categorized as yet and will simply be cited as BU file. Where a specific document is identified in the text, I will not add a superfluous footnote.

11. An undated typewritten document in BLA, Men's Club Folder discusses the background and conflict.
12. A copy of the bulletin is in the BLA Men's Club Folder.
13. A copy of the survey and the results can be found in the BLA Men's Club Folder.
14. Dub Smothers, a member of St. Peter's, proposed this in several letters and proposals. He put together an extensive work on the various architectural details in a document he called "The Battle for Truth." It is available at the BLA.
15. An original of the petition and the 552 signatures is available in the BU file.
16. *Recorder*, May 6, 1992.
17. A copy of the letter is in the BLA Men's Club Folder and the BU file.
18. Copies of the letters from Mrs. Davison and the Texas Historical Commission are in the BLA Men's Club Folder.
19. BLA Litigation 1989–95 Folder.
20. BLA Men's Club Folder.
21. Mrs. Davison's handwritten notes of these meetings are in the BLA Men's Club Folder.
22. *Recorder*, July 8, 1992.
23. BLA Men's Club Folder.
24. Ibid.
25. A copy of the letter is in the BLA Litigation 1989–95 Folder.
26. A copy of the letter is in the BLA Men's Club Folder.
27. Mrs. Davison's handwritten notes of this meeting are in the BLA Men's Club Folder.
28. A copy of the letter is in the BLA Litigation 1989–95 Folder.
29. See the photograph following Chapter 9. A detailed schematic is in the BLA Men's Club Folder.
30. *San Antonio Express-News*, August 8, 1993.
31. Copies of both these letters are in the BLA Litigation 1989–1995 Folder.
32. These were printed in the *Star*, August 11, 1993; August 11, 1993; August 18, 1993; October 6, 1993; September 1, 1993; and July 28, 1993 respectively.
33. Reprinted in the *Star*, August 25, 1993.
34. A copy of the flyer is in the BU file.

## CHAPTER 3

1. It is also a rather affluent town, which creates a more natural constituency for historic preservation than might be found elsewhere. In 2011, for example, the median household income in Texas was $49,646; in the United States as a whole, $51,914; and in Kendall County, $66,655. U.S. Census Bureau, *2010 American Community Survey 5-Year Estimates.*
2. There are numerous architects' drawings and notes from these meetings in the files at the Boerne Public Library (BLA).
3. Beginning in 2009, the city changed to single member council districts, with a mayor elected at large.
4. Interview with Phillip Bell, May 3, 2010.
5. City of Boerne, Ordinance 91-05.
6. All city documents referred to in this chapter are on file at the City of Boerne archives.
7. In order to avoid a large number of repetitious footnotes, all the formal documents, correspondence, and church bulletins and newsletters referred to in this chapter, unless otherwise indicated, are available in the BLA, either in the Historic Landmark Commission Folder or the Litigation 1989–95 Folder.
8. A description of the meeting can be found in the *Recorder*, February 9, 1994.
9. A copy of this presentation is also in the BLA Litigation 1989–95 Folder.
10. Bell stressed in the 2010 interview the fact that he still felt his public duty trumped any personal feelings he had.
11. Available in Baylor University (BU) archives.
12. *Recorder*, April 20, 1994.
13. *Recorder*, April 20, 1994.
14. P. F. Flores, Archbishop of San Antonio v. The City of Boerne, Texas, Civil Action No. SA94CA0421, May 23, 1994.
15. A copy of the bulletin is in the BLA Litigation 1989–95 Folder.
16. "No human authority ought, in any case whatever, to control or to interfere with the rights of conscience in matters of religion." Texas Constitution, Article 1, Section 6.
17. No elaboration of this point was offered.
18. Bowman's comment is from the *Recorder*, June 1, 1994. Turk's thoughts were recorded in an interview August 7, 2012.
19. Reports of the meeting are in the *Recorder*, November 2, 1994, and the *Star*, November 9, 1994. The quotations are found in the *Recorder*.
20. *Flores v. City of Boerne*, 877 F. Supp. 355 (1995), Western District of Texas.
21. *Star*, March 15, 1995.
22. *Recorder*, March 15, 1995.
23. A copy of the bulletin is in the BU file.
24. *Recorder*, April 5, 1995.
25. *Star*, May 3, 1995.
26. The artist's sketch is available in a binder labeled "The Battle for Truth," in which Mr. Smothers collected many of his letters and papers. It is available at the BLA.

27. A copy of the bulletin is in the BLA Litigation 1989–95 Folder.
28. "Federal District Court Rejects Challenge to Preservation Ordinance under Religious Freedom Restoration Act," *Preservation Law Reporter*, March 1995, 1045–48.
29. "Federal District Court Rejects," 1048.
30. Thaddeus Herrick, "Preservation Law Pits Church vs. State," *Houston Chronicle*, August 27, 1995.

## CHAPTER 4

1. Louis Fisher, *Constitutional Dialogues: Interpretation as a Political Process* (Princeton, NJ: Princeton University Press, 1988), 5. Directly pertinent to our concerns, a few years ago, in fact, he argued that Congress had done as well as if not better than the court when it came to protecting religious liberty. *Religious Liberty in America: Political Safeguards* (Lawrence: University Press of Kansas, 2002).
2. Mark Tushnet, *Taking the Constitution Away from the Courts* (Princeton, NJ: Princeton University Press, 1999); Larry Kramer, *The People Themselves: Popular Constitutionalism and Judicial Review* (New York: Oxford University Press, 2004).
3. From a letter to Spencer Roane, September 6, 1819. Quoted in Kramer, *The People Themselves*, 106.
4. McCulloch v. Maryland 17 U.S. 316 (1819).
5. James D. Richardson, ed., *A Compilation of the Messages and Papers of the Presidents* (Washington: Bureau of National Literature and Art, 1908), 2:581–82.
6. 60 U.S. 393 (1857).
7. Richardson, *Messages and Papers*, vols. 6, 9
8. 5 U.S. 137 (1803).
9. Kramer, *The People Themselves*, 125–26.
10. See Michael Kamen, *A Machine That Would Go of Itself: The Constitution in American Culture* (New York: St. Martin's, 1994), Chapter 7, and Owen M. Fiss, *Troubled Beginnings of the Modern State, 1888–1910* (New York: Cambridge University Press, 2006).
11. This episode is covered in many sources. An especially thorough one is Marcia C. McKenna, *Roosevelt and the Great Constitutional War* (New York: Fordham University Press, 2002).
12. 317 U.S. 111 (1941).
13. 304 U.S. 144 (1938).
14. The origin and development of the jurisprudence surrounding the footnote are discussed in John Hart Ely, *Democracy and Distrust: A Theory of Judicial Review* (Cambridge, MA: Harvard University Press, 1980), 75–77.
15. 347 U.S. 483 (1954).
16. 358 U.S. 1 (1958).
17. Kramer, *The People Themselves*, 221.
18. Alexander Bickel's work remains the starting point. See his *The Least Dangerous Branch: The Supreme Court at the Bar of Politics* (Indianapolis: Bobbs-Merrill,

1962) and *The Supreme Court and the Idea of Progress* (New Haven, CT: Yale University Press, 1978; originally given as the Holmes Lecture in 1969).

19. "The Law of the Constitution," *Tulane Law Review* 61 (1987): 983.
20. Quoted in Kramer, *The People Themselves*, 228. The sentiment continues. More recently, President Obama and Attorney General Eric Holder had to reiterate their conviction that the Supreme Court was the authoritative interpreter of the Constitution. See Jerry Markon, "In Letter to Judge, Holder Defends Obama's Comments Urging Supreme Court to Uphold Health-Care Law," *Washington Post*, April 5, 2012.
21. See, for instance, Richard Esptein, *Takings: Private Property and the Power of Eminent Domain* (Cambridge, MA: Harvard University Press, 1985), and Stephen Macedo, *The New Right versus the Constitution* (Washington, DC: Cato Institute, 1986). Since then that view has become even more dominant in conservative circles. See Randy Barnett, *Restoring the Lost Constitution: The Presumption of Liberty* (Princeton, NJ: Princeton University Press, 2004), and Clint Bollick, *David's Hammer: The Case for an Activist Judiciary* (Washington, DC: Cato Institute, 2007).
22. Kramer, *The People Themselves*, 225.
23. For an in-depth discussion of federalism and the founding, see Edward A. Purcell, *Originalism, Federalism, and the American Constitutional Enterprise* (New Haven, CT: Yale University Press, 2007).
24. Purcell, *Originalism*, 7.
25. This logic is not airtight. It could be maintained that the Supreme Court is best seen as an institution that is to protect national interests. Therefore, while it is legitimate for it to void state enactments that infringe on federal authority it should be left to Congress to decide where to draw the line when it comes to federal authority.
26. The standard statement is Herbert Wechsler, "The Political Safeguards of Federalism: The Role of the States in the Composition and Selection of the National Government," *Columbia Law Review* 54 (1954): 543–60. Wechsler's views have been subjected to a number of criticisms. A good review, with ample citations to both the critiques and rebuttals, can be found in Ernest A. Young, "The Rehnquist Court's Two Federalisms," *Texas Law Review* 83 (2004): 1–165. For an argument for what she calls "balanced federalism," see Erin Ryan's *Federalism and the Tug of War Within* (New York: Oxford University Press, 2011).
27. In *The Federalist No. 45*, James Madison commented that "the State governments may be regarded as constituent and essential parts of the federal government; whilst the latter is nowise essential to the operation or organization of the former."
28. There is a difference, of course, between the political communities that make up states and state governments. Just because the former are represented does not mean that the latter will be. Further, it is debatable whether state populations are really any longer (or whether many of them ever were) meaningful political communities. See Robert A. Schapiro, *Polyphonic Federalism* (Chicago:

University of Chicago Press, 2009) for an argument that federalism should be promoted today as a more effective way to organize a political system rather than as a mechanism for giving voice to (largely nonexistent, in his view) state political communities.

29. Garcia v. San Antonio Metropolitan Transit Authority, 460 U.S. 528 (1985).
30. 312 U.S. 100 (1941).
31. This case was decided at the same time as Wickard v. Filburn, discussed earlier.
32. For example, a statute barring racial discrimination in hotels and restaurants that served interstate travelers or that purchased a significant amount of their merchandise from out-of-state suppliers was upheld. Heart of Atlanta Motel, Inc. v. United States, 379 US 241 (1964) and Katzenbach v. McClung, 379 US 294 (1964). It is interesting that Justice William O. Douglas would have upheld these statutes on section 5 grounds rather than the commerce clause. Had his view prevailed, it might have created a different precedent set when *Boerne* was heard.
33. Schapiro, *Polyphonic Federalism*, 46.
34. William Riker went so far as to say that approving of federalism meant approving of racism: "if in the United States one disapproves of racism, one should disapprove of federalism." William Riker, *Federalism: Origin, Operation, Significance* (Boston: Little, Brown, 1964), 155.
35. 421 U.S. 542 (1975).
36. Erwin Cherminsky, *Enhanced Government: Federalism for the 21st Century* (Palo Alto, CA: Stanford University Press, 2008), 48–54.
37. For a comprehensive analysis of federalism during the Rehnquist Court's years, see Christopher P. Banks and John C. Blakeman, *The U.S. Supreme Court and New Federalism: From the Rehnquist to the Roberts Court* (Lanham, MD: Rowman and Littlefield, 2012).
38. 379 U.S. 241 (1964).
39. 514 U.S. 549 (1995).
40. 505 U.S. 144 (1992).
41. 2 U.S. 419 (1793).
42. 517 U.S. 44 (1996).
43. The commerce clause grants the federal government the power "to regulate Commerce . . . with the Indian tribes."
44. The internal quotation is from Hans v. Louisiana, 134 U.S. 1 (1890).
45. Pennsylvania v. Union Gas Co., 491 U.S. 1 (1989).
46. 501 U.S. 452 (1991).
47. 469 U.S. 528 (1985).
48. It would be extending the equal protection clause of section 1.
49. United States v. Morrison, 529 U.S. 598 (2000) (commerce clause); Printz v. United States, 521 U.S. 898(1997) (noncommandeering of state officers); *Alden v. Maine*, 527 U.S. 706 (1999) (Eleventh Amendment); Solid Waste Agency of Northern Cook County v. United States Army Corps of Engineers, 531 U.S. 159 (2001) (clear statement rule). However, there is some debate whether the Rehnquist court's federalism legacy was a lasting one. See, for example,

Kathleen M. Sullivan, "From States' Rights Blues to Blue States' Rights: Federalism after the Rehnquist Court," *Fordham Law Review* 75 (2006): 799–813.

## CHAPTER 5

1. Transcript of Oral Argument, City of Boerne v. Flores, Case No. 94-2074, 1.
2. Belgard v. Hawaii, No. 93-00961 (D. of Haw., February 3, 1995).
3. 28 U.S.C. Section 2403 (a).
4. Religious Freedom Restoration Act, Public Law No. 103-141; 42 USC 2000.
5. 80 U.S. 128 (1871). It is discussed in J. Richard Doidge, "Is Purely Retroactive Legislation Limited by the Separation of Powers? Rethinking *United States v. Klein*," *Cornell Law Review* 79 (1993): 910–74.
6. 100 U.S. 303 (1879) and 100 U.S. 339 (1879).
7. 109 U.S. 3 (1883).
8. It also rejected an argument that Congress was acting under the Thirteenth Amendment to remove the "badges and incidents" of slavery.
9. 384 U.S. 641 (1966).
10. 360 U.S. 45 (1959).
11. 383 U.S. 301 (1966)
12. 383 U.S. 347 (1966). The internal quotations are from McCulloch v. Maryland,17 U.S. 421 (1819) and Ex Parte Virginia, 100 U.S. 345–46 (1879).
13. This was put in the act in order to keep Southern states from using literacy tests in a discriminatory fashion, as was common practice in many places.
14. 384 U.S. 651 (1966).
15. 384 U.S. 653 (1966).
16. New York made an argument that this provision would discriminate against people educated in languages other than English when that education was obtained outside the United States. This would violate the due process clause of the Fifth Amendment, the state said. The court held, though, that Congress need not enact perfect laws when it enhances rights.
17. For more detail, see Matt Pawa, "When the Supreme Court Restricts Constitutional Rights Can Congress Save Us? An Examination of Section 5 of the Fourteenth Amendment," *University of Pennsylvania Law Review* 141 (1993): 1029–01, esp. 1062–70; and Douglas Laycock, "RFRA, Congress, and the Ratchet," *Montana Law Review* 56 (1995): 145–70.
18. Belgard v. Hawaii, No. 93-00961 (D. of Haw., February 3, 1995).
19. 437 U.S. 678 (1978).
20. 369 U.S. 186 (1962) and 418 U.S. 683 (1974).
21. The internal quotation is from Marci A. Hamilton, "The Religious Freedom Restoration Act: Letting the Fox into the Henhouse under Cover of Section 5 of the Fourteenth Amendment," *Cardozo Law Review* 16 (1994): 366. Note that Hamilton refers only to federal power.
22. Interview with Lowell Denton, September 18, 2012.
23. 73 F.3d 1352 (5th Cir. 1996).
24. 446 U.S. 179 (1980).

25. The quotation is from Morgan, 384 U.S. 651 (1966).
26. This approach had been used in City of Richmond v. J. A. Croson Co., 488 U.S. 469 (1989), a case involving affirmative action.
27. The test is from Lemon v. Kurtzman, 403 U.S. 602 (1971). It will be discussed in more depth in Chapter 7.
28. Corporation of the Presiding Bishop v. Amos, 483 U.S. 337 (1987).

## CHAPTER 6

1. Supporting the archdiocese and the United States were the state of Maryland (joined by the states of Connecticut, Massachusetts, and New York); the Virginia legislature; Senator Orrin Hatch (joined by six other senators and two representatives); Senator Edward Kennedy (joined by nine other senators and twenty representatives); the American Bar Association; the American Center for Law and Justice; the Beckett Fund for Religious Liberty; the Church of Jesus Christ of Latter-Day Saints; the Coalition for the Free Exercise of Religion (joined by eight religious and civil rights groups); Defenders of Property Rights (joined by a number of similarly named organizations); the Minnesota Family Council (joined by other state affiliates); the NAACP Legal Defense and Educational Fund; the National Committee for Amish Religious Freedom; the National Jewish Commission on Law and Public Affairs; the Prison Fellowship Ministries and the Aleph Institute; the United States Catholic Conference (joined by the Evangelical Lutheran Church in America, the Orthodox Church in America, and the Evangelical Covenant Church); the Knights of Columbus; the state of Texas; the American Jewish Congress; the Rutherford Institute; and the Northstar Legal Center. Supporting the city, in addition to Ohio and the other states mentioned, were the state of Virginia; the Clarendon Foundation; the National Right to Work Legal Defense Foundation; the San Antonio Conservation Society (joined by the Municipal Art Society and the National Alliance of Preservation Commissions); the National Trust for Historic Preservation; the Texas Municipal League and the International Municipal Lawyers Association; Children's Healthcare is a Legal Duty, Inc.; the Center for Community Interest; and the American Professional Society on the Abuse of Children. The brief for neither side was from Thurston Greene (who argued that care should be devoted to the terms *religion* and *conscience* whichever side won).

   The decision of the state of Texas to support the archdiocese caused a bit of ill feeling in Boerne.
2. Interview with Patricia Millett, August 17, 2012.
3. Interview with Douglas Laycock, February 24, 2009.
4. Interview with Lowell Denton, September 18, 2012.
5. Brief for Petitioner, Lowell F. Denton, Gordon L. Hollon, and Marci A. Hamilton (Counsel of Record). 1995 US Briefs 2074. November 29, 1996.
6. Thomas v. Review Board of Indiana Employment Security Division, 450 U.S. 707 (1981).

7. A footnote adds another dimension of congressional imperialism. Congress is trying to usurp the peoples' role in amending the constitution, since RFRA is changing an established constitutional doctrine.
8. 508 U.S. 520 (1993). The city of Hialeah had enacted a thinly veiled ordinance aimed at preventing animal sacrifice rituals performed by the church. Thus, in this instance, any reasonable person could see the motive behind the law. The court decision supporting the church was unanimous.
9. The cases and their implications are discussed in Daniel O. Conkle, "The Religious Freedom Restoration Act: The Constitutional Significance of an Unconstitutional Statute," *Montana Law Review* 56 (1995): 39–93.
10. Brief of amici curiae for the states of Ohio, Arizona, Colorado, Delaware, Florida, Hawaii, Idaho, Mississippi, Nevada, New Hampshire, North Carolina, Oklahoma, Pennsylvania and the territories of American Samoa, Guam, and the Virgin Islands. Betty D. Montgomery, Attorney General of Ohio, Jeffrey S. Sutton, State Solicitor of Ohio (Counsel of Record), and Robert C. Maier and Todd Marti, Assistant Attorneys General of Ohio. 1995 US Briefs 2074. November 29, 1996.
11. Of course, there is a logical fallacy here: just because they used the term *regulate* when they gave Congress broad authority does not mean that the framers meant to restrict it when they used another term.
12. Brief for Respondent, Douglas Laycock (Counsel of Record), Thomas Drought, and Patricia Schofield. 1995 US Briefs 2074, January 13, 1997.
13. These cases are listed in footnote 2 of the brief. Further discussion can be found in Douglas Laycock, "Conceptual Gulfs in *City of Boerne v. Flores*," *William and Mary Law Review* 39 (1998): 743–44.
14. Again, I will discuss some of the problems here in more detail later.
15. This ignores the distinction between a legislative body stipulating exemptions for itself (clearly endorsed by *Smith*) and the imposing of standards on another level of government as RFRA was attempting.
16. Brief for the United States. Walter Dellinger, Acting Solicitor General, Frank W. Hunger, Assistant Attorney General, Seth P. Waxman, Deputy Solicitor General, Patricia A. Millett, Assistant to the Solicitor General, Michael Jay Sinder, Matthew Collette, Attorneys, Department of Justice. 1995 Briefs 2074. January 10, 1997.
17. This is parallel to the framework announced in McCulloch v. Maryland to measure Article I powers.
18. See Kurt T. Lash, "The Second Adoption of the Free Exercise Clause: Religious Exemptions under the Fourteenth Amendment," *Northwestern Law Review* 88 (1994): 1106–54 for an extended discussion.
19. 501 U.S. 452 (1991).
20. 460 U.S. 226 (1983).
21. Charles E. Hughes, *The Supreme Court of the United States* (New York: Garden City Publishing, 1936): 58. On oral argument in general see Timothy Johnson, *Oral Arguments and Decision Making on the U.S. Supreme Court* (Albany: State University of New York Press, 2004).

22. This is not an unusual problem. The first semester I taught the case I mispronounced the city's name and was quickly corrected by a student from Texas. At a recent academic conference, a panelist made the same mistake. A transcript of the oral argument is available at the Supreme Court's website.
23. 384 U.S. 436 (1966).
24. 521 U.S. 507 (1997).
25. The internal quotation is from Marbury v. Madison.
26. The internal quotation is from Katzenbach v. Morgan.
27. The internal quotation is from Fitzpatrick v. Bitzer, 427 U.S. 445 (1976).
28. The internal quotation is from Oregon v. Mitchell, 400 U.S. 112 (1970).
29. There are a number of excellent works on the history of the Fourteenth Amendment. Among the most highly regarded are William E. Nelson, *The Fourteenth Amendment: From Political Principle to Judicial Doctrine* (Cambridge, MA: Harvard University Press, 1988); Michael Kent Curtis, *No State Shall Abridge: The Fourteenth Amendment and the Bill of Rights* (Durham, NC: Duke University Press, 1986); Earl Maltz, *Civil Rights, The Constitution, and Congress, 1863–1869* (Lawrence: University Press of Kansas, 1990); Garrett Epps, *Democracy Reborn: The Fourteenth Amendment and the Fight for Equal Rights in Post-Civil War America* (New York: Henry Holt, 2006); and Richard L. Aynes, "On Misreading John Bingham and the Fourteenth Amendment," *Yale Law Journal* 103 (1993): 57–104. With the exception of Epps's book, all would have been available to Kennedy. However, he chose to rely solely on a much older work, Horace E. Flack, *The Adoption of the Fourteenth Amendment* (Baltimore, MD: Johns Hopkins University Press, 1908).
30. Schurz's report was printed as *Senate Executive Document No. 2*, 39th Cong., 1st sess. (December 19, 1865).
31. There were three possible ways to circumvent this. First, all people, especially public officials, who had participated in the rebellion could be deprived of the vote. Second, state representation could be based on the number of registered voters, which would reduce Southern power in the House since the three-fifths clause would no longer apply. Third, blacks could be given the right to vote. Sections 2 and 3 of the Fourteenth Amendment were a compromise attempt to address this problem. Ultimately, of course, the Fifteenth Amendment was adopted to guarantee the right of African Americans to vote.
32. Epps, *Democracy Reborn*, 166.
33. Curtis, *No State Shall Abridge*, and Aynes, "Misreading John Bingham" cover this topic thoroughly.
34. Some of them even thought that the Bill of Rights applied to the states before the Civil War and that *Barron v. Baltimore* had been wrongly decided. Further, some contended that the due process clause of the Fifth Amendment and the "guaranty clause" (Article IV, Section 4) gave Congress power to enact legislation to carry out this objective.
35. Epps, *Democracy Reborn*, Chapter 8 has the most extended discussion of Owen's role. He visited many of the Radical Republicans in Washington in March of 1866 and presented his five-section amendment. The first section barred state

and federal governments from any discrimination against "the civil rights of persons, because of race, color, or previous condition of servitude." The second gave blacks the right to vote after a ten-year period. His thinking was that would allow time for education to take hold. The third allowed Southern states to restrict voting to whites during that time if they chose, but if they did so the former slaves could not be counted for representation in the House or the Electoral College. The fourth prohibited the payment of the Confederate debt or any "loss of involuntary service or labor." The fifth, as all proposals, gave Congress power to enforce the amendment "by appropriate legislation."

36. Epps, *Democracy Reborn*, 71.
37. Nelson, *The Fourteenth Amendment*, 55.
38. Maltz, *Civil Rights*, 56.
39. 383 U.S. 745 (1966).
40. On Kennedy's jurisprudence, see Frank Colucci, *Justice Kennedy's Jurisprudence: The Full and Necessary Meaning of Liberty* (Lawrence: University Press of Kansas, 2009), and Helen J. Knowles, *The Tie Goes to Freedom* (Lanham, MD: Rowman and Littlefield, 2009).

## CHAPTER 7

1. *New York Times*, June 26, 1997.
2. *Christian Science Monitor*, June 26, 1997.
3. *Washington Times*, June 26, 1997.
4. *Jerusalem Post*, June 26, 1997.
5. *Washington Post*, June 26, 1997.
6. *Washington Times*, June 26, 1997.
7. Available at www.aclu.org.
8. Editorial, *New York Times*, June 27, 1997. Not all major papers' editorial opinions were critical. See "Editorial," *Washington Post*, June 26, 1997. It offered only lukewarm endorsement, saying merely that the court's opinion was "not unreasonable."
9. On state RFRAs see David Claborn, "Effects of Judicial and Legislative Attempts to Increase Religious Freedom in U.S. State Courts," *Journal of Church and State* 53 (2011): 615–34. For an analysis of the factors leading states to adopt RFRAs, see David Bridge, "Religious Freedom or Libertarianism: What Explains State Enactment of RFRA Laws?" *Journal of Church and State*, forthcoming.
10. Christopher Lund, "Religious Liberty after *Gonzales*: A Look at State RFRAs," *South Dakota Law Review* 55 (2010): 466–97.
11. Tony Mauro and Lori Sharn, "Court Ruling Bodes Ill for All Faiths, Critics Claim," *USA Today*, June 26, 1997.
12. House Subcommittee on the Constitution, *Hearings on Protecting Religious Freedom after* Boerne v. Flores, 105th Cong., 1st sess., July 14, 1997, 2. We will discuss the first matter Rep. Canady raised at the end of this chapter.
13. House, *Hearings*, July 14, 1997, 21.

14. House Subcommittee on the Constitution, *Hearings Regarding the Need for Federal Protection of Religious Freedom after* Boerne v. Flores,105th Cong., 2nd sess., February 26, 1998; *Hearings Regarding the Need for Federal Protection of Religious Freedom after* Boerne v. Flores II, 105th Cong., 2nd sess., March 26, 1998; *Hearings on the Religious Liberty Protection Act of 1998 (H.R. 4019)*, 105th Cong., 2d sess., June 16, 1998; *Hearings on the Religious Liberty Protection Act of 1998 (H.R. 4019)*, July 14, 1998; *Hearings on the Religious Liberty Protection Act of 1999 (H.R. 1691)*, 106th Cong., 1st sess., May 12, 1999; Senate Committee on the Judiciary, *Hearings on the Religious Liberty Protection Act of 1998 (S. 1248)*, 105th Cong., 2nd sess., June 23, 1998; *Hearings on Issues Relating to Religious Liberty Protection, and Focusing on the Constitutionality of a Religious Protection Measure*, 106th Cong., 1st sess., September 9, 1999. Hearings cited hereafter by body and date.
15. I have analyzed the passage of this statute in more detail elsewhere. Jerold Waltman, *Religious Free Exercise and Contemporary American Politics: The Saga of the Religious Land Use and Institutionalized Persons Act of 2000* (New York: Continuum, 2011).
16. House, *Hearings*, July 14, 1997, 54.
17. 252 U.S. 416 (1920).
18. The details of the covenant and how it could be applied in the United States can be found in Gerald L. Newman, "The Global Dimension of RFRA," *Constitutional Commentary* 14 (1997): 33–54.
19. House, *Hearings*, July 14, 1997, 105. Emphasis in original.
20. Justice Kennedy, for example, was roundly criticized for citing foreign sources in his opinion in Lawrence v. Texas, 539 U.S. 558 (2003).
21. E. C. Knight Co. v. United States, 156 U.S. 1 (1895).
22. Hammer v. Dagenhart, 247 U.S. 251 (1918).
23. The two important cases are National Labor Relations Board v. Jones and Laughlin Steel Corporation, 301 U.S. 1 (1937) and United States v. Darby Lumber Company, 312 U.S. 100 (1941).
24. 317 U.S. 111 (1942).
25. Heart of Atlanta Motel v. United States, 379 U.S. 241 (1964); Katzenbach v. McClung, 379 U.S. 294 (1964). In a concurring opinion, Justice William O. Douglas said that he would have preferred to uphold the act on section 5 grounds.
26. 514 U.S. 549 (1995).
27. See especially the testimony of Marc Stern in House, *Hearings*, June 16, 1998, 125–41.
28. 483 U.S. 203 (1987).
29. The internal quotation is from Massachusetts v. United States, 435 U.S. 461 (1978).
30. House, *Hearings*, July 14, 1998, 405.
31. The study is reprinted in House, *Hearings*, June 16, 1998, 234–60. The study was inspired by a paper written by Rebecca Benyon for a seminar at the University of Texas.

32. House, *Hearings*, July 14, 1997, 124.
33. Senate, *Hearings*, September 9, 1999, 177.
34. Ibid., 67.
35. Quoted in Senate, *Hearings*, June 23, 1998, 17–18.
36. Cited in House, *Hearings*, March 26, 1998, 86.
37. Daniel J. Solove, "The Religious Freedom Restoration Act and Religion in the Prisons," *Yale Law Journal* 106 (1996): 459–91.
38. The organization's head also railed against federal use of the commerce power to enact a variety of regulatory statutes. It was, he felt, a menace to liberty.
39. Hamilton's testimony can be found in House, *Hearings*, June 16, 1998, 94–99, and Senate, *Hearings*, September 9, 1999, 188–92.
40. House, *Hearings*, June 16, 1998, 164.
41. Ibid., 80–91. A more complete elaboration of their views can be found in their article "Unthinking Religious Freedom," *Texas Law Review* 61 (1994): 1245–315.
42. Smith v. Fair Employment and Housing Commission, 12 Cal. 4th 1143 (1996).
43. Thomas v. Municipality of Anchorage, 165 F. 3d 692 (9th Cir. 1999).
44. Senate, *Hearings*, June 23, 1999, 21.
45. ACLU Press Release, May 5, 1999.
46. House Judiciary Committee, *Religious Liberty Protection Act of 1999*, House Report 106–219 to Accompany H.R. 1691, 106th Cong., 1st sess., July 1, 1999, 13.
47. The debate and vote can be found in *Congressional Record*, July 15, 1999.
48. Details can be found in Louis Jacobson, "A Coalition with a Liberal-Leave Policy," *National Journal*, October 30, 1999, 3154.
49. Both quotes are from *Congressional Record*, July 27, 2000, H7191.
50. Ibid., S7774.
51. 544 U.S. 709 (2005). Prior to this decision, several district courts and courts of appeals had reached varying conclusions regarding RLUIPA's constitutionality. Charles v. Verhagen, 314 F. 3d (7th Cir. 2003); Mayweathers v. Newland, 314 F. 3d 1062 (9th Cir. 2002); Johnson v. Martin, 223 F. Supp. 2d 820 (W.D. Mich. 2002); Madison v. Riter, 240 F. Supp. 2d 566 (W.D. Va. 2003); and Kilaab Al Ghashiyah (Khan) v. Department of Corrections, 250 F. Supp. 2d 1016 (E.D. Wis. 2003).
52. Memorandum of Terrence P. Kemp, magistrate judge for the Southern District of Ohio, Eastern Division, 221 F. Supp. 2d 827, 834.
53. For a discussion of the court's Eleventh Amendment jurisprudence, see John T. Noonan, *Narrowing the Nation's Power: The Supreme Court Sides with the States* (Berkeley: University of California Press, 2002).
54. Lemon v. Kurtzman, 403 U.S. 602 (1971).
55. 483 U.S. 327 (1987).
56. Cutter v. Wilkinson, 349 F. 3d 257 (6th Cir. 2003).
57. 397 U.S. 664 (1970).
58. 544 U.S. 719.

59. 544 U.S. 726.
60. Midrash Sephardic, Inc. v. Town of Surfside, 366 F.3d 1214 (11th Cir. 2004); Saints Constantine and Helen Greek Orthodox Church v. City of New Berlin, 396 F. 3d 895 (7th Cir. 2005); and Guru Nanak Sikh Society of Yuba City v. County of Sutter, 456 F. 3d 978 (9th Cir. 2006).
61. See, for example, Tyson Tamashiro, "RLUIPA and the Individualized Assessment: Special Use Permits and Variances under Congressional Strict Scrutiny," *University of Hawai'i Law Review* 31 (2008): 257–90; Susan C. Galvan, "Beyond Worship: The Religious Land Use and Institutionalized Persons Act of 2000 and Religious Institutions Auxiliary Uses," *Tulane Environmental Law Journal* 21 (2008): 207–39; and Alan C. Weinstein, "The Effect of RLUIPA's Land Use Provisions on Local Governments," *Fordham Urban Law Journal* 39 (2012): 1221–47.
62. 546 U.S. 418 (2006).

## CHAPTER 8

1. *San Antonio Express-News*, January 25, 1996.
2. *Star*, January 31, 1996.
3. *Recorder*, January 31, 1996.
4. *San Antonio Express-News*, February 7, 1996.
5. *San Antonio Express-News*, February 7, 1996.
6. *Star*, February 7, 1996.
7. The minutes of all city council and Historic Landmark Commission meetings are available from the archives of the City of Boerne. Unless there is some specific reason for a footnote, I will allow the date in the text to suffice for a reference.
8. *Star*, February 14, 1996.
9. The parish bulletins and newsletters are available at the Boerne Public Library archives (BLA), in litigation folders for the specific years. Many of these were gifted by Dub Smothers. Again, unless there is some reason to give a detailed reference, I will not provide repetitious footnotes.
10. *Star*, September 6, 1996.
11. *Star*, September 27, 1996.
12. *Star*, September 27, 1996.
13. *Star*, October 9, 1996.
14. BLA Litigation 1996 Folder.
15. *Star*, October 25, 1996.
16. See the *RichmondTimes-Dispatch*, June 15, 1997, for a survey of local sentiment. Richmond had a similar dispute pending with a local church and sent a reporter to Boerne.
17. *Austin American-Statesman*, February 16, 1997.
18. *Star*, February 21, 1997.
19. *New York Times*, April 20, 1997.
20. Interview with Patrick Heath, August 16, 2010.

21. BLA Litigation 1997 Folder.
22. *San Antonio Express-News*, June 26, 1997.
23. *Dallas Morning News*, June 26, 1997.
24. *San Antonio Express-News*, June 26, 1997.
25. *Houston Chronicle*, June 26, 1997.
26. Reprinted in an "Update on Status of Church Building" from Fr. Cummins to members of St. Peters. BLA Litigation 1997 Folder.
27. *San Antonio Express-News*, June 29, 1997.
28. BLA Litigation 1997 Folder.
29. *Recorder*, July 2, 1997.
30. Both this press release and the one from the church are in the BLA 1997 Litigation Folder.
31. Bell took serious exception to this characterization of his remarks, quoted in the article cited in note 23. He sent a note to the city council with copies of this press release and the newspaper article with his comment circled, pointing out the inaccuracy. BLA Litigation 1997 Folder. He also spoke out on this matter at the July 22 city council meeting.
32. *San Antonio Express-News*, July 12, 1997.
33. Both the Memorandum of Understanding and the subsequent Memorandum of Agreement are in the BLA Litigation 1997 Folder.
34. *San Antonio Express-News*, August 13, 1997.
35. *Recorder*, August 20, 1997.
36. *Recorder*, August 20, 1997.
37. Interview with Phillip Bell, May 3, 2010.
38. BLA Litigation 1997 Folder.
39. BLA Litigation 1997 Folder.
40. BLA Litigation 1997 Folder.
41. *San Antonio Express-News*, December 17, 1997.
42. BLA Litigation 1997 Folder.
43. *Recorder*, December 25, 1997.
44. *Star*, October 15, 1999.
45. BLA Dub Smothers papers.
46. *San Antonio Express-News*, October 18, 1999. The following quotations from Fr. Cummins and David Boerner are from the same article.
47. *San Antonio Express-News*, September 26, 2000.

## CHAPTER 9

1. Interview with Kit Brenner, September 14, 2010.
2. *Star*, June 8, 1994.
3. *San Antonio Express-News*, January 30, 1996.
4. Department of Justice, *Report on the Tenth Anniversary of the Religious Land Use and Institutionalized Persons Act*, September 22, 2010.

5. Although it focuses on only one aspect of land use, Kelli Stout, "Tent Cities and RLUIPA: How a New Religious Land Use Issue Aggravates RLUIPA," *Seton Hall Law Review* 41 (2011): 465–99, contains a good summary of the case law.
6. A good source on prisoner rights cases is the site maintained by Professor Howard Friedman: http://religionclauseblogspot.com/2012/11/recent-prisoner-free-exercise-cases.html.
7. See Taylor G. Stout, "The Costs of Religious Accommodation in Prisons," *Virginia Law Review* 96 (2010), 1201–39.
8. *Florida Prepaid Postsecondary Education Expense Board v. College Savings Bank*, 527 U.S. 627 (1999); *College Savings Bank v. Florida Prepaid Postsecondary Education Expense Board*, 527 U.S. 666 (1999); *Alden v. Maine*, 527 U.S. 706 (1999).
9. 531 U.S. 356 (2001).
10. "Minutes from a Convention of the Federalist Society: The Roberts Court and Federalism," *New York University Journal of Law and Liberty* 4 (2009): 347.
11. 538 U.S. 721 (2003).
12. 541 U.S. 509 (2004).
13. 546 U.S. 151 (2006).
14. 546 U.S. 356 (2006).
15. 552. U.S. 491 (2008).
16. 567 U.S. ___ (2012).
17. Christopher P. Banks and John Blakeman, *The U.S. Supreme Court and New Federalism: From the Rehnquist to the Roberts Court* (Lanham, MD: Rowman and Littlefield, 2012), Chapter 6.
18. A comprehensive discussion can be found in Franita Tolson, "Reinventing Sovereignty? Federalism as a Constraint on the Voting Rights Act," *Vanderbilt Law Review* 65 (2012): 1195–259.
19. Victor Andres Rodriquez, "Section 5 of the Voting Rights Act after *Boerne*: The Beginning of the End of Preclearance," *California Law Review* 91 (2003): 769–826.
20. 557 U.S. 193 (2009).
21. Glenn Kunkes, "The Times, They are Changing: The VRA is No Longer Constitutional," *Journal of Law and Politics* 27 (2012): 357–85.
22. 358 U.S. 1 (1958).
23. 539 U.S. 306 (2003).
24. District of Columbia v. Heller, 554 U.S. 570 (2008) and McDonald v. Chicago, 561 U.S. 3025 (2010).
25. Mark Tushnet, *Taking the Constitution Away from the Courts* (Princeton, NJ: Princeton University Press, 1999); Larry Kramer, *The People Themselves: Popular Constitutionalism and Judicial Review* (New York: Oxford University Press, 2004).

# Bibliography

## Archival Sources

### Boerne Public Library

The Boerne Public Library has an extensive collection of documents; personal papers; local, regional, and national press clippings; correspondence; and so forth. It has been ably arranged into folders, which are cited by name in the notes. In addition, Mr. Dub Smothers donated thirty additional boxes of papers to the library as I neared completion of the manuscript for this book. I have gone through this material, but it is not yet been sorted into thematic or chronological folders.

### *Boerne Star*

During the time of the case, Boerne had two weekly newspapers, the *Boerne Star* and the *Hill Country Recorder*. They have since merged and now publish under the name of the *Star*. Back issues of both papers are available in the *Star* archives. They are open to the public with an appointment.

### Texas Collection, Baylor University Archives

The Texas Collection at Baylor University has a more limited cache of material that has been donated.

### City of Boerne

The city of Boerne has retained minutes of official meetings along with related correspondence. The Texas Public Information Act provides all citizens with access to public documents with adequate notice.

## Interviews

I conducted personal interviews with many of the participants in the case. A good number of these were recorded for the Institute of Oral History at Baylor University and are on file there. For the others, I have deposited my handwritten notes at the Texas Collection at Baylor University

## Government Documents

Ackerman, David. Congressional Research Service. *The Religious Freedom Restoration Act and the Religious Freedom Act: A Legal Analysis.* April 17, 1992.

US Congress. *Congressional Record.*106th Congress. 2nd sess. July 27, 2000.

US Congress. House. Committee on the Judiciary. *The Religious Freedom Restoration Act of 1993.* 103rd Cong., 1st sess., 1993. H. Rep. 103–88.

US Congress. House. Subcommittee on Civil and Constitutional Rights. *Religious Freedom Restoration Act of 1990: Hearing before the Subcommittee on Civil and Constitutional Rights.*101st Cong., 2nd sess., September 27, 1990.

US Congress. House. Subcommittee on Civil and Constitutional Rights. *Religious Freedom Restoration Act of 1991: Hearing before the Subcommittee on Civil and Constitutional Rights.*102nd Cong., 2nd sess., May 13 and 14, 1992.

US Congress. House. Subcommittee on the Constitution. *The Need for Federal Protection of Religious of Religious Freedom after* Boerne. v. Flores: *Hearings before the Subcommittee on the Constitution.*105th Cong., 2nd sess., February 26, 1998.

US Congress. House. Subcommittee on the Constitution. *The Need for Federal Protection of Religious Freedom after* Boerne v. Flores II: *Hearings before the Subcommittee on the Constitution.*105th Cong., 2nd sess., March 26, 1998.

US Congress. House. Subcommittee on the Constitution. *Protecting Religious Freedom after* Boerne v. Flores: *Hearings before the Subcommittee on the Constitution.* 105th Cong., 1st sess. July 14, 1997.

US Congress. House. Subcommittee on the Constitution. *The Religious Liberty Protection Act of 1998: Hearings before the Subcommittee on the Constitution.*105th Cong., 2nd sess., June 16 and July 14, 1998.

US Congress. House. Subcommittee on the Constitution. *The Religious Liberty Protection Act of 1999: Hearings before the Subcommittee on the Constitution.* 106th Cong., 1st sess., May 12, 1999.

US Congress. Senate. Committee on the Judiciary. *Issues Relating to Religious Liberty Protection, and Focusing on the Constitutionality of a Religious Protection Measure: Hearings before the Senate Committee on the Judiciary.* 106th Cong., 1st sess., September 9, 1999.

US Congress. Senate. Committee on the Judiciary. *Religious Freedom Restoration Act of 1992: Hearing before the Committee on the Judiciary.*102nd Cong., 2nd sess., September 18, 1992.

US Congress. Senate. Committee on the Judiciary. *The Religious Liberty Protection Act of 1998: Hearings before the Senate Judiciary Committee.* 105th Cong., 2nd sess., June 23, 1998.

US Congress. Senate. Committee on the Judiciary. *The Religious Freedom Restoration Act of 1993.* 103rd Cong., 1st sess., 1993. S. Rep. 103–11.

## FEDERAL COURT DOCUMENTS

Briefs for Supreme Court cases are available at the Supreme Court's website. Briefs for the Court of Appeals level must be obtained from the National Archives and Records Administration (NARA). These were located in the Fort Worth office of the NARA.

Brief amicus curiae for the State of Ohio. United States Supreme Court.

Brief amicus curiae for the United States Government. United States Court of Appeals for the Fifth Circuit.

Brief amicus curiae for the United States Government. Supreme Court of the United States.

Brief for Petitioner Archbishop A. J. Flores. United States Court of Appeals for the Fifth Circuit.

Brief for Respondent City of Boerne. United States Court of Appeals for the Fifth Circuit.

Brief for Petitioner City of Boerne. United States Supreme Court.

Brief for Respondent Archbishop A. J. Flores. United States Supreme Court.

Briefs amici curiae for all amici submitted to United States Supreme Court.

Filings by all parties in the Federal District Court for the Western District of Texas regarding *Flores v. City of Boerne.*

Transcript of oral argument before the US Supreme Court, *City of Boerne v. Flores.* February 19, 1997. Available at the Supreme Court's website.

## BOOKS AND ARTICLES

Aynes, Richard L. "On Misreading John Bingham and the Fourteenth Amendment." *Yale Law Journal* 103 (1993): 57–104.

Baker, Ross. *Strangers on a Hill: Congress and the Courts.* New York: Norton, 2006.

Banks, Christopher P., and John C. Blakeman. *The U.S. Supreme Court and the New Federalism: From the Rehnquist to the Roberts Court.* Lanham, MD: Rowman and Littlefield, 2012.

Barber, Sotirios A., and James E. Fleming. *Constitutional Interpretation: The Basic Questions.* New York: Oxford University Press, 2007.

Barnett, Randy. *Restoring the Lost Constitution: The Presumption of Liberty.* Princeton, NJ: Princeton University Press, 2004.

Berg, Thomas C. "The Constitutional Future of Religious Freedom." *University of Arkansas at Little Rock Law Review* 20 (1998): 715–65.

Bickel, Alexander. *The Least Dangerous Branch: The Supreme Court at the Bar of Politics.* Indianapolis: Bobbs-Merrill, 1962.

———. *The Supreme Court and the Idea of Progress.* New Haven, CT: Yale University Press, 1978.

Bollick, Clint. *David's Hammer: The Case for an Activist Judiciary.* Washington, DC: Cato Institute, 2007.

Breyer, Stephen. *Active Liberty: Interpreting Our Democratic Constitution*. New York: Knopf, 2005.

Bridge, David. "Religious Freedom or Libertarianism: What Explains State Enactment of RFRA Laws?" *Journal of Church and State* (forthcoming).

Bybee, Jay S. "Taking Liberties with the First Amendment: Congress, Section 5, and the Religious Freedom Restoration Act." *Vanderbilt Law Review* 48 (1995): 1539–633.

Cherminsky, Erwin. *Enhanced Government: Federalism for the 21st Century*. Palo Alto, CA: Stanford University Press, 2008.

———. "The Religious Freedom Restoration Act is a Constitutional Expansion of Rights." *William and Mary Law Review* 39 (1998): 601–36.

Claborn, David. "Effects of Judicial and Legislative Attempts to Increase Religious Freedom in U.S. State Courts." *Journal of Church and State* 53 (2011): 615–34.

Colucci, Frank. *Justice Kennedy's Jurisprudence: The Full and Necessary Meaning of Liberty*. Lawrence: University Press of Kansas, 2009.

Conkle, Daniel O. "The Religious Freedom Restoration Act: The Constitutional Significance of an Unconstitutional Statute." *Montana Law Review* 56 (1995): 39–93.

Curry, Thomas. *The First Freedom: Church and State in America to the Passage of the First Amendment*. New York: Oxford University Press, 1987.

Curtis, Michael Kent. *No State Shall Abridge: The Fourteenth Amendment and the Bill of Rights*. Durham, NC: Duke University Press, 1986.

Davison, Anna Marie. *A History of St. Peter's Catholic Church, Boerne, Texas*. Boerne, TX: St. Peter's Restoration and Preservation Society, 1987.

Doidge, J. Richard. "Is Purely Retroactive Legislation Limited by the Separation of Powers? Rethinking *United States v. Klein*." *Cornell Law Review* 79 (1993): 910–74.

Drakeman, Donald. *Church, State, and Original Intent*. New York: Cambridge University Press, 2010.

Drinan, Robert F. "Reflections on the Demise of the Religious Freedom Restoration Act." *Georgetown Law Journal* 86 (1997): 101–21.

———, and Jennifer I. Huffman. "The Religious Freedom Restoration Act: A Legislative History." *Journal of Law and Religion* 10 (1993): 531–41.

Eisgruber, Christopher L., and Lawrence G. Sager. "Why the Religious Freedom Restoration Act is Unconstitutional." *New York University Law Review* 69 (1994): 437–76.

———. "Unthinking Religious Freedom." *Texas Law Review* 61 (1994): 1245–315.

Ely, John Hart. *Democracy and Distrust: A Theory of Judicial Review*. Cambridge, MA: Harvard University Press, 1980.

Epps, Garrett. *Democracy Reborn: The Fourteenth Amendment and the Fight for Equal Rights in Post-Civil War America*. New York: Henry Holt, 2006.

———. *To an Unknown God: Religious Freedom on Trial*. New York: St. Martins, 2001.

Epstein, Richard. *Takings: Private Property and the Power of Eminent Domain*. Cambridge, MA: Harvard University Press, 1985.

Federalist Society. "Minutes from a Convention of the Federalist Society: The Roberts Court and Federalism." *New York University Journal of Law and Liberty* 4 (2009): 330–71.

Fisher, Louis. *Constitutional Dialogues: Interpretation as a Political Process*. Princeton, NJ: Princeton University Press, 1988.

———. *Religious Liberty in America: Political Safeguards*. Lawrence: University Press of Kansas, 2002.

Fiss, Owen M. *Troubled Beginnings of the Modern State, 1888–1910*.New York: Cambridge University Press, 2006.

Flack, Horace E. *The Adoption of the Fourteenth Amendment*. Baltimore, MD: Johns Hopkins University Press, 1908.

Galvin, Susan C. "Beyond Worship: The Religious Land Use and Institutionalized Persons Act of 2000 and Religious Institutions Auxiliary Uses." *Tulane Environmental Law Journal* 21 (2008): 207–39.

Gardbaum, Stephen. "The Federalism Implications of *Flores*." *William and Mary Law Review* 39 (1998): 665–98.

Gordon, Sarah B. *The Mormon Question: Polygamy and Constitutional Conflict in Nineteenth-Century America*. Chapel Hill: University of North Carolina Press, 2002.

Grossman, Eugene, and Angela C. Cormella. "The RFRA Revision of the Free Exercise Clause." *Ohio State Law Journal* 57 (1996): 65–143.

Hamilton, Marci. "The Religious Freedom Restoration Act: Letting the Fox into the Henhouse under Cover of Section 5 of the Fourteenth Amendment." *Cardozo Law Review* 16 (1994): 357–98.

———. "The Religious Freedom Restoration Act is Unconstitutional, Period." *University of Pennsylvania Journal of Constitutional Law* 1 (1998): 1–19.

Hoff, Robert. "Losing Our Religion: The Constitutionality of the Religious Freedom Restoration Act Pursuant to Section 5 of the Fourteenth Amendment." *Brooklyn Law Review* 64 (1998): 377–421.

Hughes, Charles E. *The Supreme Court of the United States*. New York: Garden City Publishing, 1936.

Johnson, Timothy. *Oral Arguments and Decision Making on the U.S. Supreme Court*. Albany: State University of New York Press, 2004.

Kamen, Michael. *A Machine That Would Go of Itself: The Constitution in American Culture*. New York: St. Martin's, 1994.

Kendall County Historical Commission. *A History of Kendall County*. Dallas, TX: Taylor Company, 1984.

Knowles, Helen J. *The Tie Goes to Freedom*. Lanham, MD: Rowman and Littlefield, 2009.

Kramer, Larry. *The People Themselves: Popular Constitutionalism and Judicial Review*. New York: Oxford University Press, 2004.

Krent, Harold J. "Turning Congress into an Agency: The Propriety of Requiring Legislative Findings." *Case Western Reserve Law Review* 46 (1996): 731–56.

Kunkes, Glenn. "The Times, They Are Changing: The VRA Is No Longer Constitutional." *Journal of Law and Politics* 27 (2012): 357–85.

Lash, Kurt T. "The Second Adoption of the Free Exercise Clause: Religious Exemptions under the Fourteenth Amendment." *Northwestern Law Review* 88 (1994): 1106–54.

Laycock, Douglas. "Conceptual Gulfs in *City of Boerne v. Flores*." *William and Mary Law Review* 39 (1998): 743–92.

———. "RFRA, Congress, and the Ratchet." *Montana Law Review* 56 (1995): 145–70.

———, and Oliver S. Thomas. "Interpreting the Religious Freedom Restoration Act." *Texas Law Review* 73 (1994): 209–45.

Lee, Rex E. "The Religious Freedom Restoration Act: Legislative Choice and Judicial Review." *Brigham Young University Law Review* 1993 (1993): 73–96.

Long, Carolyn. *Religious Freedom and Indian Rights: The Case of* Oregon v. Smith. Lawrence: University Press of Kansas, 2000.

Lund, Christopher. "Religious Liberty after *Gonzales:* A Look at State RFRAs." *South Dakota Law Review* 55 (2010): 466–97.

Lupu, Ira C. "The Failure of RFRA." *University of Arkansas at Little Rock Law Review* 20 (1998): 575–617.

———. "Why the Congress Was Wrong and the Court Was Right—Reflections on *City of Boerne v. Flores*." *William and Mary Law Review* 39 (1998): 793–817.

Macedo, Stephen. *The New Right versus the Constitution*. Washington, DC: Cato Institute, 1986.

Magliocca, Gerard N. "Why Did the Incorporation of the Bill of Rights Fail in the Late Nineteenth Century?" *Minnesota Law Review* 94 (2009): 102–39.

Mallamud, Jonathan. "Religion, Federalism and Congressional Power: A Comment on *City of Boerne v. Flores*." *Capital Law Review* 26 (1997): 45–63.

Maltz, Earl. *Civil Rights, the Constitution, and Congress, 1863–1869*. Lawrence: University Press of Kansas, 1990.

McConnell, Michael. "Freedom from Persecution or Protection of the Rights of Conscience? A Critique of Justice Scalia's Historical Arguments in *City of Boerne v. Flores*." *William and Mary Law Review* 39 (1998): 819–47.

———. "Institutions and Interpretations: A Critique of *City of Boerne v. Flores*." *Harvard Law Review* 111 (1997): 153–95.

———. "The Origins and Historical Understanding of the Free Exercise of Religion." *Harvard Law Review* 103 (1990): 1421–25.

McKenna, Marcia C. *Roosevelt and the Great Constitutional War*. New York: Fordham University Press, 2002.

Meese, Edwin. "The Law of the Constitution." *Tulane Law Review* 61 (1987): 979–87.

Nelson, William E. *The Fourteenth Amendment: From Political Principle to Judicial Doctrine*. Cambridge, MA: Harvard University Press, 1988.

Newman, Gerald L. "The Global Dimension of RFRA." *Constitutional Commentary* 14 (1997): 33–54.

Noonan, John T. *Narrowing the Nation's Power: The Supreme Court Sides with the States*. Berkeley: University of California Press, 2002.

Paulsen, Michael Stokes. "A RFRA Runs through It: Religious Freedom and the US Code." *Montana Law Review* 56 (1995): 249–94.

Pawa, Matt. "When the Supreme Court Restricts Constitutional Rights Can Congress Save Us? An Examination of Section 5 of the Fourteenth Amendment." *University of Pennsylvania Law Review* 141 (1993): 1029–101.

Perry, Garland A. *Historic Images of Boerne, Texas*. Boerne, TX: Perry Enterprises, 1982.

Purcell, Edward A. *Originalism, Federalism, and the American Constitutional Enterprise*. New Haven, CT: Yale University Press, 2007.

Richardson, James D, ed. *A Compilation of the Messages and Papers of the Presidents*. Vols. 2 and 6.Washington, DC: Bureau of National Literature and Art, 1908.

Riker, William. *Federalism: Origin, Operation, Significance*. Boston: Little, Brown, 1964.

Rodriquez, Victor Andres. "Section 5 of the Voting Rights Act after *Boerne:* The Beginning of the End of Preclearance." *California Law Review* 91 (2003): 769–826.

Ryan, Erin. *Federalism and the Tug of War Within*. New York: Oxford University Press, 2011.

Schapiro, Robert A. *Polyphonic Federalism*. Chicago: University of Chicago Press, 2009.

Solove, Daniel J. "The Religious Freedom Restoration Act and Religion in the Prisons." *Yale Law Journal* 106 (1996): 459–91.

Stout, Kelli. "Tent Cities and RLUIPA: How a New Religious Land Use Issue Aggravates RLUIPA." *Seton Hall Law Review* 41 (2011): 465–99.

Stout, Taylor G. "The Costs of Religious Accommodation in Prisons." *Virginia Law Review* 96 (2010): 1201–39.

Sullivan, Kathleen M. "From States' Rights Blues to Blue States' Rights: Federalism after the Rehnquist Court." *Fordham Law Review* 75 (2006): 799–813.

Tamashiro, Tyson. "RLUIPA and the Individual Assessment: Special Use Permits and Variances under Congressional Scrutiny." *University of Hawai'i Law Review* 31 (2008): 257–90.

Thomas, George. "The Riddle of the Fourteenth Amendment: A Response to Professor Wildenthal." *Ohio State Law Journal* 68 (2007): 1627–57.

Tolson, Franita. "Reinventing Sovereignty? Federalism as a Constraint on the Voting Rights Act." *Vanderbilt Law Review* 65 (2012): 1195–259.

Tushnet, Mark. "The Story of *City of Boerne v. Flores:* Federalism, Rights, and Judicial Supremacy." In *Constitutional Law Stories* ed. Michael C. Dorf, 505–31. New York: Foundation Press, 2004.

———. *Taking the Constitution Away from the Courts*. Princeton, NJ: Princeton University Press, 1999.

Waltman, Jerold. *Religious Free Exercise and Contemporary American Politics: The Saga of the Religious Land Use and Institutionalized Persons Act of 2000*.New York: Continuum, 2011.

Wechsler, Herbert. "The Political Safeguards of Federalism: The Role of the States in the Composition and Selection of the National Government." *Columbia Law Review* 54 (1954): 543–60.

Weinstein, Alan C. "The Effect of RLUIPA's Land Use Provisions on Local Governments." *Fordham Urban Law Journal* 39 (2012): 1221–47.

Wildenthal, Bryan. "Nationalizing the Bill of Rights: Revisiting the Original Understanding of the Fourteenth Amendment in 1866–67." *Ohio State Law Journal* 68 (2007): 1509–626.

Young, Ernest A. "The Rehnquist Court's Two Federalisms." *Texas Law Review* 83 (2004): 1–165.

## Magazine Articles

"Boerne's New Church Solemnly Dedicated." *The Southern Messenger*, January 3, 1924.

"Federal District Court Rejects Challenge to Preservation Ordinance Under Religious Freedom Restoration Act." *Preservation Law Reporter*, March 1995.

Jacobson, Louis. "A Coalition with a Liberal Leave Policy." *National Journal*, October 30, 1999.

# Index

CPSIA information can be obtained at www.ICGtesting.com
Printed in the USA
LVOW04*1725300115

425057LV00008B/177/P

9 781137 300638